Islamic identity and development

Islamic identity and development

Studies of the Islamic Periphery

Ozay Mehmet

London and New York

First published 1990 by Routledge
11 New Fetter Lane, London EC4P 4EE

Simultaneously published in the USA and Canada
by Routledge
a division of Routledge, Chapman and Hall, Inc.
29 West 35th Street, New York, NY 10001

© 1990 Ozay Mehmet

Typeset by Pat and Anne Murphy, Highcliffe-on-Sea, Dorset

Printed and bound in Great Britain by
Billings & Sons Limited, Worcester

British Library Cataloguing in Publication Data

Mehmet, Ozay
  Islamic identity and development: studies of the Islamic
  Periphery.
  1. Islamic countries. Economic development. Influences
  of Islam
  I. Title
  330.917671

  ISBN 0-415-04386-7

Library of Congress Cataloging in Publication Data

Mehmet, Ozay.
  Islamic identity and development: studies of the Islamic
  Periphery / Ozay Mehmet.
     p.   cm.
  Includes bibliographical references.
  ISBN 0-415-04386-7
  1. Islam – Turkey.   2. Islam – Malaysia.   3. Islam and
state – Turkey.   4. Islam and state – Malaysia.
  5. Islam – Economic aspects – Turkey.   6. Islam – Economic
aspects – Malaysia.   7. Turkey – Economic policy.
  8. Malaysia – Economic policy.   9. Economics – Religious
aspects – Islam.   I. Title.
  BP63.T8M44   1990
  297′.1978′09561 – dc20   90-8353
                                                            CIP

Contents

Contents

Figures

A note on terminology

Of necessity this study contains several Turkish, Malay and Arabic terms. These have been defined in the text as they occur, and in addition there is a Glossary at the end of the book.

For those readers unfamiliar with Malay and Turkish history, the following clarifications may be useful. Malaysia is a country which gained its independence in 1957. Formerly it was known as Malaya. Its population is multi-ethnic (Malays, Chinese, Indians and other smaller groups). Malays, who are Muslim, constitute the majority and are known as the Bumiputera (sons of the soil). The terms 'Malay world' or 'Malay Archipelago' refer to Malay-speaking peoples in Malaysia, Indonesia, Singapore, Thailand, the Philippines and elsewhere in South-east Asia.

The Republic of Turkey was established in 1923 out of the ruins of the Ottoman Empire which was destroyed by the First World War. It is populated by Western Turks who share linguistic and ethno-cultural affinities with the Eastern Turks who consist of Turkic ethnic groups in the Caucasus, Central Asia, Northern Iran, Afghanistan and China. Turkish, the language of all Turks, belongs to the Ural-Altaic group of languages.

Introduction

The world of Islam, torn between forces of traditionalism and modernity, is facing a profound dilemma: how can the universalism of Islam be reconciled with the reality of the nation-state, the embodiment of modernity. The Islamic world-view, shaped by the oneness of God and the indivisibility of the *Umma* (community of believers), is confronted by nationalism, the ideology of the nation-state. Nationalism is a reductionist view of a world rebuilt on ethnicity and territoriality, ideas incompatible with Islamic universality.

There is more: the nation-state shifts allegiance from God to state. In return, it promises its citizens the benefits of socio-economic development in this life. Here too the nation-state conflicts with Islam. For it is precisely in the area of development that Islam has generally failed to evolve an ethos, to mobilize the masses for improving the quality of life in this life on the road to the next. The central challenge in the Muslim world remains under-development: how to liberate the masses from poverty, illiteracy and oppression. How should this challenge be conducted, who should lead it, and should it rest on secular or Islamic rules? It is over these questions that the forces of traditionalism and modernity are so fundamentally divided.

Islamic culture is rich and compares favourably with others in man's story of civilization. Islamic scholarship has made major contributions to human knowledge. 'During the better part of the Middle Ages Muslim scientific and material superiority was undeniably and widely acknowledged' (von Grunebaum 1953: 337). As a religion Islam can claim perfection, and as a culture the current inequality of the Islamic world is 'the product of specific adverse historical circumstances' (von Sivers in Tibi 1986: vii) which are by no means beyond repair. But what exactly are these 'adverse historical circumstances'? How did they come about? These questions require careful analysis and clear answers. This study is a modest contribution towards this end.

Introduction

The central argument of the study is that Islamic societies need to be modernized on the basis of an instrumentalist theory of state. This is essential to improve the quality of life in these societies. An instrumentalist state — i.e. one that formulates and implements a public policy responsive to human needs, both material and spiritual — acquires legitimacy on the basis of its capacity to overcome economic inequality and social injustice, and to sustain accountability to the people.

Islam is a religion of social justice. This derives from doctrine as well as actual practice originating with the Prophet's own Constitution of Medina. Yet, the Islamic social contract ceased to flourish when a new age of darkness, *jahiliyya*, descended upon the Muslim world starting midway through the Abbasid dynasty (AD 750–1258). The Islamic scholars, *ulama*, declared the Gate of *Ijtihad* (independent analysis) closed and opted for increasingly dysfunctional theological teachings at the expense of rational and empirical study. While Islamic scholarship stagnated, Europe emerged out of its Dark Ages; the Renaissance led to the Age of Enlightenment, great scientific and geographic discoveries followed culminating in the Industrial Revolution. By then, the centre of economic gravity had shifted westwards away from the land of Islam. New prosperity paralleled the growth of human rights, especially in the nineteenth century following the age of liberty ushered in by the French Revolution. While colonialism and imperialism contributed to western prosperity and power at the expense of other parts of the globe, the economic rise of the west resulted fundamentally from the emergence of the nation-state designing and implementing public policy to promote national well-being. The rise of Japan in the more recent period underscores the importance of the same basic point: nurturing by the nation-state, under conditions of efficiency, is an essential pre-condition of sustained socio-economic development.

The Gate of *Ijtihad* finally began to open in the nineteenth century and, in the process, some Islamic countries began slowly to come to terms with modernity, nationalism, and secular public policy. Kemalist Turkey was the pioneering case. Ataturk substituted a new nationalist ideology in place of the Ottoman–Islamic past. After 1923, the new Turkish Republic abolished the Sultanate, disestablished Islam and adopted secularism as its motto. For the next quarter of a century, the Turks seemed to abandon both their Islamic and Ottoman heritage in pursuit of a new Turkish identity based on westernization.

The Turkish experiment, while impressing the more modern-minded in the Islamic world, nevertheless remained a peripheral case. But it seemed to gain confirmation in the post-Second World War period. During the wave of de-colonization, such western concepts as development planning became highly fashionable. Development planning strengthened budding nation-states of the Third World. Thus, newly independent Muslim societies such as Pakistan, Indonesia and Malaysia, found themselves on the road to planned development and national reconstruction. More by colonial accidents than popular design, nationalism and nation-building began to enter the rest of the Islamic world. In an *ad hoc* fashion, the state assumed the vanguard role of developing and transforming Islamic societies.

Developmentalism has proved to be an illusion: it promised the masses more than it could deliver. As a result, the credibility of the nation-state, and its secular ideology, have come under increasing attack from Islam. The alienated victims of maldevelopment are everywhere turning to Islam.

Turkey and Malaysia, after decades of secular, top-down development, find themselves caught in this Islamic resurgence. This resurgence gives expression to new identity crises. The Turks, passionately patriotic, wish to integrate with Europe, but where do they really belong: the Islamic Middle East or the Christian west? The Malays, residing in a multiracial country, need Islam as an identity tag to differentiate themselves from other races, but they also have a strong sense of nationalism, which raises the delicate question of where their ultimate loyalties lie: Islam, race or state? But, these identity crises are not insurmountable; they are on-going problems of coming to terms with modernity, of having to face complex issues of public policy.

These problems make a comparison of Turkey and Malaysia interesting, especially since comparative studies in the Islamic world are so rare. But there is a further reason for selecting this particular pair of countries for study: Turkey and Malaysia have travelled a long way on the road of secularist development and their joint experience places them very much in the forefront of Islamic modernization. They have the potential for reconciling Islam with modernity via public policy, as this study hopes to illustrate.

The study is organized in five parts consisting of eleven chapters. Chapter 1 examines the Turkish and Malay identity crisis in the Islamic Periphery. The Islamic Periphery is differentiated from the Islamic (Arab and Middle East) Core. This underscores the fact that Islam is not homogeneous; cultural relativity abounds as much in the lands of Islam as in other religions. It is therefore important to realize at the outset that the coverage of the study is limited: it excludes the Islamic Core, except in the sense that the identity crisis in the Periphery is part and parcel of the larger Islamic dilemma.

The Islamic dilemma – how to reconcile Islam with modernity – is the subject of Part II. What are the roots of this phenomenon? In contemporary terms they are poverty, alienation, and inequality. These are consequences of the global strategy of uneven, top-down developmentalism introduced during the post-war period. In Chapter 2 Islamic revival is seen as a social protest movement, concentrated among urban migrants victimized by uneven post-war growth.

Poverty and alienation also raise the further Islamic challenge of how to explain Islamic underdevelopment. This is the task of accounting for the lower quality of life, inferior level of economic achievement, and the lowly status of women generally found in Islamic societies. Searching for answers to this question takes us back into history. In Chapter 3 Islamic underdevelopment is attributed primarily to endogenous factors, principally to the fact that Islamic societies failed to institutionalize a public policy tradition – an instrumentalist theory of state responsible for delivering public goods and services to its citizens. This failure is quite surprising in view of two outstanding facts about Islam: its strong egalitarian and social-justice ideals; and the existence of an Islamic social contract. This contract governs not only the ruled– ruler relations, but also determines the expectations and hopes of the Islamic masses.

But, perhaps, the roots of Islamic underdevelopment are scriptural. Accordingly, Chapter 4 is focused on the question of compatibility of Islam with economic development, taken as an index of modernity. The historical and analytical evidence presented show that while Islam is quite compatible with modernity – the central assumption of which is rational behaviour – Islamic scholarship suddenly stopped flourishing in the medieval period; and with it Islamic public policy traditions disintegrated. The major responsibility for this astonishing stoppage and disintegration can be attributed to the social and political role of the *ulama*, the traditional moral voice of Islam and the custodians of Islamic knowledge.

The modernization debate in the Islamic Periphery has gone through two major phases: the nationalist phase, when Islam, equated with traditionalism, was subordinated to the ideology of nationalism, and the privatization phase dominated by the ideology of market forces. These two phases of the modernization debate constitute the focus of Parts III and IV. Nationalism, a western innovation, confronted Islam first in the Islamic Periphery.

Kemalism in republican Turkey suffered from one basic deficiency: it was an imposed, top-down, cultural restructuring; it did not emerge bottom-up. It was not an example of organic growth reflecting a symbiotic relationship between leaders and followers. For example, the abolition of the Caliphate in 1924 was not the result of a popular demand; it created a spiritual vacuum, destroying the essential element of unity in the Islamic world. It set the stage for a full-scale confrontation between Islam and the secular ideology of national modernization.

Chapter 5 gives a brief historical overview of this heated, and at times violent, confrontation in Malaysia and Turkey. What is remarkable in this comparative perspective is that, despite differences in geography and structure, the modernization debate in these two countries reveals a number of major commonalities, such as the ascendancy of western secularism over Islamic values, the vanguard role of the state in development planning, the selection of state capitalism as the key instrument of economic transformation, and the failure of national development ideology largely attributable, in both countries, to the rent-seeking behaviour of ruling elites. Yet, notwithstanding these negative outcomes, the crucial fact is that within the Islamic world the Islamic Periphery has pioneered in creating a public policy, secularist in content and orientation, that provides a hope for the ultimate resolution of the Islamic dilemma. These issues are elaborated in Chapters 6 (on Turkey) and 7 (on Malaysia).

Part IV is a study of alternative public policy options in the context of the new privatization challenge now facing public policy in the Islamic Periphery. This challenge raises new risks. Higher costs of living (due to deregulated prices, new user fees and inflation) as well as greater foreign control and more wealth concentration at the top, can be expected to add to the number of converts to militant Islam. The remedy lies not in *laissez-faire* market forces, but in more responsible government regulation in the public interest: more health and safety regulations; new anti-trust and unfair trade practice rules with teeth to prevent collusion and business fraud; and more socio-economic pluralism (e.g. consumer and social-action groups) to operate as countervailing powers and deliver voluntary services to the disadvantaged.

Islamic injunctions on monopolies and imperfect competition are seriously inadequate. Anything unlawful – and opinions on what constitutes 'unlawful' vary greatly – is banned outright. What is required urgently is an Islamic theory of imperfect competition to guide responsible regulation. Accordingly, Chapter 8 is concerned with this and related issues, as a prelude to a brief discussion of privatization strategy in Malaysia (Chapter 9) and Turkey (Chapter 10).

The study concludes with a call for a more open society in the Islamic Periphery and a more accountable, responsive public policy. This requires a more organic relationship between the leaders and followers; it means coming to terms with Islamic values since Islam is at the very core of personal and collective identity. Input from expert witnesses, including Islamists, into public-policy formulation, encouragement of Islamic voluntary organizations under state law, and restoration of a modernized version of the Caliphate, under a joint Turkish-Malaysian project, are seen as some of the ways and means of reconciling Islam with modernity.

Many people and institutions have contributed, in numerous ways, to make this study possible. To all of them I say a collective, but sincere 'thank you'. I acknowledge with much appreciation a research grant from the Social Sciences and Humanities Research Council of Canada which funded work in Malaysia, Turkey and North America. In Malaysia several friends contributed to the study, but in particular I owe special thanks to Ungku Aziz who first introduced me to the 'Turkish–Malay' connection, Hussein Alatas, Naquib Al-Attas, K.S. Jomo, A.B. Shamsul, H.M. Dahlan, Syed Husin Ali and Mavis and James Puthucheary. In Turkey, I gratefully acknowledge the encouragement and co-operation of Mumtaz Soysal, Metin Heper, Erol Manisali, Selim Ilkin, Kaya Toperi and Gencay Saylan. In Canada, Tozun Bahceli, Marc Beaudoin, Ahmed Mohiddeen, Martin Rudner, Leonard Librande and M.A. Choudhury were extremely helpful with advice and comment on earlier drafts as were Vamik Volkan and Kemal Karpat in the USA. I would also like to express my thanks to the editors at Routledge. Last, but not least, I owe my wife and children a huge debt of gratitude for their patience and understanding during the many months of research and writing.

Ozay Mehmet,
Ottawa

Part one

The Islamic identity crisis

The typical manifestation of the Islamic dilemma is a deceptively simple question: Am I a Muslim first or a citizen of my country? This question discloses an identity crisis even in the relatively homogeneous Islamic (Arab) Core where the objective of Arab unity remains an elusive ideal. But, it reflects an even more profound identity crisis in such countries in the Islamic Periphery as Turkey and Malaysia. The Turks, living at the border where Europe meets Asia, seem unsure whether they belong in the Islamic Middle East or in Christian Europe. The Malays, living in a multiracial country at the other end of the Islamic world, are uncertain whether they are first Malays, Malaysians or Muslims. Additionally, both the Turks and Malays, as with inhabitants of other parts of the Islamic world, are caught in an Islamic revival, despite decades of secular development modelled after western blueprints. To what extent is Islam an essential ingredient of being Turk or Malay, and of prescriptions aimed at solving Turkish and Malay problems in the modern world? This introductory Part deals with these questions.

Crises in the periphery are often more crucial than those in the core, for they may be harbingers of fundamental change, as has been observed by historians such as Toynbee (Somervell 1960: especially Chapter VII). This is what makes the Turkish and Malaysian experiences examined in the following pages far more appealing than just a pair of case studies.

Chapter one

Identity crisis in the Islamic Periphery
Turkey and Malaysia

This is an age of identity crisis. Who am I? What are my roots? Where do I belong? These are the central questions of our age. The search for identity is mixed with a wave of scepticism about development, technology and environment. This is a universal phenomenon. Questions about one's roots and about ecological, technological and demographic limits of growth and development (Olson and Landsberg 1973, Schumacher 1973) are being asked in the mass consumption societies of the developed world (Scitovsky 1976, Hirschman 1977). They are also being asked in the post-colonial societies of the developing world.

The timing of the global identity crisis is paradoxical. In the developed world economic affluence was expected to liberate man for leisure and creativity. In the search for materialism, western man has lost his soul to 'technomania' (Grant 1969: 39) and, as a reaction, Christian fundamentalism and born-again Christianity are on a rising curve.

But the clearest expression of the paradox of identity is found in the developing world. Often western colonialism is held as the destroyer of indigenous cultures and identity. Thus, decolonization in the post-war period should have provided the opportunity for regaining loss of culture due to external domination. Fanon (1965), the father of *negritude*, even justified violence in the cause of decolonization since this was the path for the wretched of the earth to regain their lost identity. Yet, in Africa as elsewhere in the Third World, the central question at the dawn of a new century is still: Who am I? Is my identity national or religious?

In an age of collective and self doubt, established authority suffers; institutions and rules of legitimacy are questioned on grounds of adequacy, efficiency and equity. These doubts generally display two diametrically opposed currents of social forces: a search backwards in history for indigenous roots, and a leap forward towards a future world ethics. Significantly, both visions lead to the same promise of some new Utopian social order based on some concept of peace, justice and harmony.

The Muslim dilemma

The search for Utopia, lost in some historical past, is at the heart of contemporary revival of religious fundamentalism. This is especially true in the Islamic world where the rule of the Four Righteous Caliphs, AD 632–661 (Esposito 1984: 8) is held as an ideal model awaiting restoration.

The central issue facing the Muslim world is how to reconcile the concept of universality and homogeneity, most clearly embodied in the ideas of the *Umma* (community of the faithful), and *Tawhid* (unity of God), with the reality of the nation-state. The concept of nation-state and the doctrine of nationalism, from which it is derived, are European inventions of the nineteenth century (Kedourie 1971). The contemporary Islamic dilemma is, most simply stated, how to modernize Islam so that the Muslim world can come to terms with nationalism and its manifestation, the nation-state.

A major theme of this book is that socio-economic development is a necessary condition for regaining an Islamic sense of identity in the modern world. What is socio-economic development in this case? It is a systematic, problem-solving public policy, initiated and regulated by the state, which generates growth, but is also responsive to Islamic ethics and social justice.

The core of Islamic identity

At the core of Muslim identity is the idea of time as an ethical (not just economic) value: life in this world is but a True Path leading to God in the next. The faithful, like a pilgrim, must travel along this Path in this life, ultimately facing God on the Final Day of Judgement for his eternal reward calculated in proportion to merit earned in *ibadah* (prayer) and *muamalat* (inter-personal relations). Islam (which means submission to God) encourages individuality; each individual submits to God in his or her own way, which is why Islam manifests such a bewildering range of variation. One's identity in this life is tentative; one fulfils one's real identity on the Final Day. In this tentative life, however, the faithful are commanded to utilize God-given resources for material well-being and enhancement of the human condition. The Qur'an states explicitly that God has provided all the necessary resources for man's material well-being: 'He it is Who has created for you everything on earth' (2: 29) and 'has made subservient to you whatever is in the heavens and the earth and granted you His bounties, manifest and hidden' (31: 20; 16: 12–14; 22: 65 and 45: 12).

The Muslim True Path has more than doctrinal value; it has historical and political validity as well. Using the conventional calendar, its origin can be fixed in the seventh century AD (CE), i.e. point A in Figure 1.1. But the difficulty is to determine its slope: whether it is a positively-sloped line such as AZ, implying a rising level of development, or, as Islamic fundamentalists seem to argue, a constant line such as AT. At any rate, the Islamic golden age, A-A', a period of about thirty years, was followed, in the next three centuries, by a wave of Islamic expansion and growth both militarily and intellectually. Islamic scholars, *ulama*, pushed the frontiers of ancient Greek rationalism to new heights. Then, in the tenth century, quite mysteriously, the *ulama* declared the 'Gate of Knowledge' closed, believing that all possible human problems had been answered, and decreed that henceforth only education by imitation would be permissible. Theology replaced rationalism and Islamic scholarship and creativity entered a long period of decline. Its current general position is probably somewhere at point C and the Islamic challenge is to identify the prescription for restoring its past glory.

Figure 1.1   The Muslim True Path

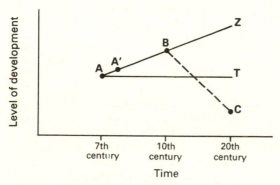

Key

A-A' : The Islamic Golden Age
        (the Rule of the Four Righteous Caliphs)
    B : Closing the 'Gate of Knowledge'
    C : Current level of Islamic Development
A-T : The Fundamentalists' conception of
        the 'True Path'
A-Z : The Progressives conception of
        the 'True Path'

11

The fundamentalists dream of the restoration of the Islamic golden age when a just and wise king ruled over the faithful in perfect social and political order. They see the lost Islamic identity as a deviation from the True Path, AT, caused by internal corruption and degeneracy which, subsequently, attracted external domination such as European colonialism and imperialism. Their prescription for regaining the Islamic identity is in terms of theocracy along the path AT in Figure 1.1. But whether this theocracy is to be a Caliphate with universal jurisdiction over the *Umma*, as was the case with the Four Righteous Caliphs, or theocracy on a reduced scale, as within an Islamic republic however defined, is ambiguous.

In contrast, secularists and progressives approach the identity crisis from a rational and modern perspective. Here personal identity derives from national identity, and is a legal derivation from man-made, state-law. Thus a man's identity is defined on the basis of his citizenship as prescribed in the relevant state-law. The path of development is a positively-sloped, progressive line, such as AZ, in Figure 1.1, whereby the socio-economic condition of each cohort of citizens is better than that of the preceding generation. The state, which assumes direct responsibility for this betterment, also confers the identity of its citizens.

The problem of legitimacy and rule-making

But state authority to define identity conflicts with the Islamic norm of divine-sanctioned identity and thereby creates a problem of legitimacy. Progressives attempt to overcome this difficulty with an appeal to a second anti-Islamic formula. They rely on a national ideology representing the pure, in contrast to Islamic, sources of identity. The roots of such an ideological identity search are typically traced to pre-Islamic traditions and beliefs, and are utilized as legitimizing tools by the nation-state.

Thus nationalism, as a secular ideology, represents an alternative source of legitimacy to Islam and offers a second path to identity definition. A Muslim, who in an earlier age identified himself solely as a traveller along the True Path, can now acquire a second sense of identity from his membership in a nation with a distinct territory and culture of its own, and symbolized by a sovereign state legitimately enacting man-made laws in the national interest. The source of this legitimacy is national will, freely expressed, not divine authority. While nationalism mobilizes the national will to secure legitimacy of the state, it is state-law which gives meaning and content to the identity of the modern individual, and, in the aggregate, it is the same man-made law which limits and safeguards the national interest. Economic and social development in the national interest is the clearest example of the instrumentality of the nation-state; for development liberates both the individual and the nation and insures survival of both.

Kemalist ideology

Kemalist ideology is the pioneering example of nationalist ideologies in the Islamic world (Feyzioglu 1987, Giritli 1988). It shaped the Turkish nationalist revolution aimed at redefining the Turkish identity in a new, secular mould imposed from above (Chapter 5). Although Kemal Ataturk was its architect, the major intellectual ideologue of Turkish nationalism was the sociologist, Ziya Gokalp (Berkes 1959). Gokalp differed from other Young Turk intellectuals who sought to unify the multinational Ottoman state around the idea of Ottomanism dedicated to the ideal of one people, the Ottomans, with equal political and civil rights. Gokalp was more realistic. His intellectual roots were the new sociological theories of Weber, Durkheim and Comte. He sought Turkish identity in pre-Islamic customs and traditions. Writing in simple and clear Turkish, he was the major force in the awakening of the modern Turkish nationalist movement. His journal *Turk Yurdu* (the Turkish Homeland), and his extensive writings influenced a new generation of Turkish nationalists, such as the feminist leader Halide Edib, who were exposed, for the first time, to new sociological classifications and modern concepts such as 'nation' and 'state' in the final phase of the Empire.

> In order to define the word 'nation', it is necessary to distinguish it from other seemingly kindered concepts – race, ethnic community (*kavm*), Church (*ummet*), people, and state . . . *Kavm* means a group of individuals who have a common language and usage, i.e. Arab, Turkish, German, and Serbian *Kavms*. . . . The term *ummet* or religious community corresponds in use to the term *eglise* (Church), and therefore we can use it in this sense. . . . The term *halk* (people) is sometimes used [in Turkish] for *kavm* and sometimes for the citizens of a state, and at other times for the nation.
>
> (Gokalp quoted in Berkes 1959: 126–7)

Gokalp was particularly keen on making a sharp distinction between the Islamic and the pre-Islamic Turkic roots of Turkish identity:

The Turkish *kavm* existed before the Islamic *ummet* and the Seljuk and Ottoman Empires. It had its own ethnic civilization before it entered into a common Iranian civilization. The Iranian civilization and the [Islamic] *ummet* and [Ottoman] imperial organizations in which the Turks participated destroyed many of their ethnic institutions.

(Gokalp quoted in Berkes 1959: 133)

Gokalp was a populist. He believed that the soul of Turkish nationalism lay in the social structure of Anatolia. The spring source of Turkish nationalism was the egalitarian, democratic, social solidarity which prevailed in the Anatolian peasant villages and communities.

When we look at Anatolia from the point of view of social structure, we find that neither a tribal nor a feudal organization exists there now. There are only village communities and peasantry who own their lands. Peasants are not dependent upon lords. They are under one [political] rule. That means that there is an entirely democratic social structure . . . which is also homogeneous from the point of view of ethnic composition. Each community administers its mosque and school. There exists, not a tribal solidarity, but a unity within a state. The whole nation is like a family. That means that a national solidarity exists in Turkey.

(Gokalp quoted in Berkes 1959: 143)

Gokalp's populist, secularist and nationalist ideas set the Kemalist ideological agenda. Although several other Islamic reformers, such as Afghani and Abduh, had written on Islam and modernity, Kemalism was the clearest and most decisive confrontation between nationalism and Islam. Kemalism saw Islam and nationalism as incompatible world-views; religion must be subordinated to nationalism.

The spring-head of Kemalism is its deep commitment to secularism, a rejection of Islamic theocracy as the way to define and assert identity. As such it provides the Islamic antithesis. Kemalists saw long before other Muslim leaders that religion can have no special priority in a modern nation-state. Thus Islam and Kemalism could not be bedfellows; one of them had to go. In Turkey Islam was let go, too abruptly it seems, judging by the recent Islamic revival in the country (Albayrak 1984). For collective identity, Kemalism substitutes nationalism and secularism centred on the idea of a reforming state spearheading the search for group identity in the modern world. Thus a Turk may be Muslim by private faith, worshipping God according to his own *vicdan* (Islamic conscious-ness), but derives group identity from citizenship in the Turkish nation and not from membership in the universal Islamic com-munity (*ummet*). Membership in the *ummet*, paralleling member-ship in the Roman Catholic church for example, is of a different order from his citizenship; the former is spiritual, the latter is legal and political. In a world of nation-states (Piscatori 1986), citizen-ship, rather than religion, is the most pragmatic, but not necessarily the most meaningful, assertion of identity.

Yet, in view of the Islamic resurgence in Turkey (Toprak 1981, Mardin in Caldarola 1982, Albayrak 1984, Mumcu 1987), it is evident that the Kemalist view of religion as a purely private consciousness is an inadequate prescription. The choice is not simply between state religion or private religion. It is a rather more complex question of how to balance competing, and often con-flicting material and spiritual human needs, through a political process commanding sufficient social consensus.

Kemalism is not free from internal contradictions. In fact, the contradictions that have bedevilled the Turkish identity search pre-date Kemalism (Lewis 1968). After some two hundred years of debate and experimentation about whether they belonged to the east or west, the Turks seem to have decided in favour of Euro-peanization while also seeking a more balanced reconciliation with their Islamic past. If Turkey, with its Islamic heritage, could successfully integrate within a Christian European community, it would not only be the culmination of the long westernization move-ment, but, even more fundamentally, it could signal the end of the historic 'confrontation' between Islam and Christianity (Vatikiotis 1987). The Turkish westernization movement is older than Japan's modernization (Rustow and Ward 1964), but unlike the Japanese, the Turks have yet to achieve a synthesis of culture, modernity and identity.

Who is a Turk?

This is not an easy question. It is tempting to define a Turk as one who speaks Turkish, professes Islam and has Turkish citizenship. However, serious inadequacies arise when this definition is analysed against the common criteria of group identity: language, religion, territory and citizenship.

Language

Turks, i.e. people speaking Turkish, are subdivided into two main groups: Eastern and Western Turks (Czaplika 1918). The Eastern Turks consist of Turks and Turkic groups in China, Soviet Central Asia, Iran and Caucasian Russia. Western Turks, on the other hand, are resident in Turkey proper, in the Balkans and smaller communities in such places as Cyprus. All these groups have a common pre-Islamic origin, located in Central Asia, and speak a variation of the Turkish language which belongs to the Ural-Altaic group. These linguistic and ethno-cultural commonalities add up, however, to a fundamental problem of cultural insecurity. Everywhere, with the sole exception of Turkey, Turkish-speaking people are ethnic minorities subject to political and cultural oppression (Caroe 1967; Simsir 1989).

Religion

The Islamic faith, which enables the Turks to identify themselves within the trans-national *Umma* introduces further complications. The Turks can find comfort in the spirituality of Islam, but what is the cultural price of this spirituality? Must they also submerge their own language and culture to become good Muslims? Should Arabic be substituted for the Turkish language in prayer, in literature and in politics? Historically, the Turks submerged their ethnic identity, subordinated their language and literature, for the greater glory of Islam, building an empire not for Turkification but for Islam. Cultural insecurity aside, Islam remains as the spiritual core of Turkish identity. This spirituality is especially significant for Turks living in a minority status outside the boundaries of the Turkish homeland, Turkey.

Territory

A territory, a homeland, is an essential condition of cultural distinctiveness. But such a territory is more than a piece of real estate, it must go hand in hand with sovereignty to guarantee national existence and survival. For the widely scattered Turkish-speaking people, these conditions exist fully only within the boundaries of the Republic of Turkey. But the Republic of Turkey is an inadequate Turkish homeland since it houses only a minority of the Turkish-speaking people of the world. In the USSR alone, the number of Turkish and Turkic groups are no less than the population of Turkey and in China there is a large Turkish-speaking ethnic minority. By religion and language, as well as culture, these Turkish-speaking people would qualify as Turks, but their Turkish identity may nevertheless be suppressed by lack of sovereign legal authority to give meaning to it.

Citizenship

The legal criterion of national identity, certified by citizenship, is the most common contemporary symbol of identity. In the case of Turks, it is, as with the other three criteria, only a partial identification. It is both too restrictive and too broad. While it excludes Turkish-speaking people outside Turkey, it qualifies non-Turkish ethnic groups (e.g. Kurds, Armenians and Greeks) in Turkey who are qualified as Turkish citizens. Pan-Turanism, which emerged as a strong ideology in the last days of the Ottoman Empire was driven by an idealistic, yet totally impractical, goal of uniting all Turks. While Pan-Turanist ideologues in Istanbul were pursuing wishful dreams of uniting Eastern and Western Turkish-speaking peoples within a new Asian empire, there was hardly any response or encouragement from the Turkish-speaking people in the Caucasus or the Central Asian regions.

The Turkish cultural insecurity

Contemporary Turkish identity suffers from cultural insecurity unmatched in other empire-building people. Turks are conspicuous among such people by the fact that, despite almost seven hundred years of empire, they did not evolve a distinct cultural identity, for example through Turkification, but instead submerged their own identity to Islamic requirements. At the end of the Ottoman Empire, the cultural insecurity of the Turks was at its greatest. They were abandoned by the Ottoman ruling class, for whom the term 'Turk' was an offensive label, and their homeland was about to be partitioned away by the European powers. Turkish identity was saved, not by Ottomanism, Turanism or Pan-Islam, but by the nationalism of the Kemalist Revolution.

Yet in the Turkish psyche there is still a split personality. Deep down in the minds of the citizens of Turkey there is an indecision whether they belong to the Islamic Middle East or the Christian west. By religion and geography they have more in common with the Arabs than with the Europeans. Yet, ever since the appearance of the Turks in the Islamic Core during the Caliphate of Al-Mu'tasim (833–42), relations with the Arabs have been uneasy at best; the Arabs commonly regard the Turkish entry into the Arab world as a devastating incursion which effectively checked an otherwise brilliant Islamic/Arab culture (Farouki 1987: 146–8; Tibi 1988: 49).

This is more myth than history. The origin of the myth can be traced to Ibn Sa'ad, a contemporary of Al-Mu'tasim, who 'put a prophecy in the mouth of one of the Prophet's associates, 'to the effect that one day the Turks would drive the Arabs back to their deserts' (quoted in Brockelmann 1948: 130). Far from being a negative force, the Turks actually rejuvenated Islam. Both the Umayyad (AD 661–750) and the Abbasid (AD 750–1258) dynasties were military in nature dedicated to militarism and torn by palace *coup d'états*, and their achievements did not extend much beyond military conquest (Crone 1980). Although Islamic scholarship flourished, particularly during the reign of Harun Al-Rashid (786–809) and Al-Mamun (813–33), this was scholarship by co-optation for the greater glorification of the ruler. Thus, under Al-Rashid, when Arab literature flowered, vast sums of public revenues were wasted on flattery and conspicuous consumption on a lavish scale (Fisher 1979: 78–83). While Al-Mamun was a champion of rational sciences and encouraged great scholarship in such fields as astronomy, medicine and algebra, it was nevertheless during his reign that Islamic scholarship became increasingly dogmatic and degenerated into an instrument of schism amongst various schools of religious fanaticism dominated by such controversies as the legitimacy of Ali's Caliphate or whether the Quran was man-made or created for eternity (Brockelmann 1948: 127–9).

The establishment of government and public administration was achieved by the Turks (Hourani 1981: 4–5) who at first came as mercenary soldiers (Hodgson 1974: I, 482). Unlike the Arabs, the Turks had a tradition of man-made law, *kanun* and *yasa*, which they utilized to the greater glory of Islam. These Turks fell in love with the inner logic of Islam, which appealed to their search for simplicity and individualism; and they willingly became the sword of Islam, bringing law and order to the decaying world of the Abbasid Caliphate of Baghdad, and carrying Islamic conquest into the Balkans and central Europe. The Turks built and ruled an empire for some seven hundred years by fighting for Islam to the bitter end, even at the expense of their own identity. Yet this generated for them the hostility of a Christian Europe, and the mistrust of the Arabs. The final paradox was the Arab Revolt in 1914–18 while the Ottoman Sultan-Caliph, in his last gasp, was involved in a *jihad* in the name of Islam. The Revolt was the decisive act of breaking up the universality of the modern *Umma*;

it got the Arabs broken promises, and it turned the Turks towards secular nationalism.

Thus, in the end, the strongest measure of modern Turkish identity is its national basis. Turkish nationalism emerged late at the end of the Ottoman Empire. Its chief architect was a progressive military leadership which employed a top-down policy of cultural restructuring, partly by imitating European civilization, but partly by rediscovering pre-Islamic Turkish identity. The name Turk, so much scorned by the Ottomans, was chosen as a new symbol of national pride, and education and language were utilized as tools of cultural restructuring to promote a new self-image for the Turks. Those already in Anatolia were significantly increased by waves of immigration of both Western and Eastern Turks from lands previously controlled by the Ottomans: the Balkans, Crimea and Caucasia. These Turks became the first generation citizens of the new Turkish Republic. Given security, status and a stake in the new republic, it is understandable that this generation would make nationalism an obsession. They willingly and eagerly blended in the republican melting-pot, submerged their Islamic values and sustained economic sacrifice for the sake of Kemalist nation-building. Subsequent generations, however, especially those growing up in *gecekondus* (shanty towns), were less inclined to tolerate sacrifice and more amenable to substitute Islam for nationalism in a new manifestation of Turkish identity.

The new Turkish identity in modern Turkey is a blend of Kemalist nationalist ideology and 'the rich historical heritage of the Turkish nation' (Feyzioglu 1987: 99). Recognition of the 'historical heritage' is the new factor. As a nation-builder, Ataturk was ahistorical (similar to Mao); he wished to disconnect his work from the Ottoman–Islamic past. Thus, in his *Great Speech* in 1927, he declared: 'It was by violence that the sons of Osman acquired the power to rule over the Turkish nation and to maintain their rule for more than six centuries' (quoted in Volkan and Itzkowitz 1984: 212). Ataturk's unique achievement was that he created the nation-state, not that he started Turkish history.

The Islamic Core

The Turkish quest for national identity via the nation-state stands in sharp contrast to the Middle East Islamic Core. Although Mehmed Ali had given Egypt a head start in modernization, it did not spawn Arab awakening. This was influenced more by Europeans from Napoleon to Lawrence, promoting hidden agendas than the *ulama*. As a result, the Islamic Core has suffered fragmentation, violence and oppression. There is still much confusion about public policy, not only about its means, but over its ends as well. Such key concepts as 'Arabism' or 'Arab unity' remain ambiguous. How can Pan-Arabism be reconciled with Islam and nationalism, such as, for example, 'Magrabi unity' (Faris ed. 1987)?

In the Arab Core there is still a dominant exclusionist view that Islam is an 'Arab religion for the Arabs' and that 'the assimilation of Islam by non-Arab cultures has to be interpreted as de-Arabization of Islam' (Tibi 1988: 66). Realistic social science research among Arab intellectuals, supporting a secular public policy based on science and technology, began to emerge only after the crushing defeat of the June 1967 War. Only then did Arabs begin to 'face realities as they are' and 'to move from self-congratulatory attitudes and even more from self-glorification to self-criticism' (Tibi 1988: xi).

The Islamic revolution in Iran presents additional difficulties. For example, what is the nature of an Islamic state? What should be its first objective, domestic development or export of revolutionary Islam? Is there room in such a state for political or civilian authority? What are its agenda and programme to better the human condition? When one looks at the writings of Ali Shari'ati, regarded as one of the key intellectual figures of the revolution, one finds only generalities about corruption, Islamic history and spiritual cleansing (Shari'ati 1986). Public policy in revolutionary Iran has not been a shining model of efficiency or equity. Traditionalists who yearn for an Islamic theocracy may see a model in Khomeini, but the realities of Iran since 1978 are hardly encouraging. Diplomatic isolation based on anti-western xenophobia (Al-i Ahmad 1984) provide no substitute for realistic, problem-solving public policy responding to human problems. This can only generate cultural inferiority by putting Islam on the defensive in the age of science and technology. Islam, as religion and civilization, is too rich to be bottled up for its own good! In the end, there is no escape from the 'global village' and the reality of 'the state'. Islam, as a *social reality* (Tibi 1988), must be modernized and reconciled with the nation-state.

Identity crisis in the Islamic Periphery

The concept of 'Islamic Periphery', a central concept in this study, requires elaboration. In Islam there is no differentiation or division between centre and periphery. There is equality of all before one God. Nevertheless, there is merit in the concept of 'peripheral Islam' in relation to Turkey, partly in a geographic and partly in an ethnographic sense. Geographically, Turkey is removed from the Islamic heartland of the Arab Middle East. Ethnographically, the Turkish world-view is shaped as much by the long history of Ottoman multiculturalism as by Islam (Haddad and Ochsenwald 1977).

Some may dismiss the Turkish Kemalist secularism as a 'special case'. Thus, the Islamists might argue that, under the weight of Kemalist secularism, Turkey has chosen to define its identity in an anti-Islamic mould. Extreme fundamentalists would argue that this is not success, it is 'betrayal' (Algar in Ahmad and Ansari 1979). Extremism aside, however, the Turks have achieved considerable progress in mobilizing nationalism, without abandoning Islam, for a secular public policy tradition, an achievement which, while still incomplete, deserves more sympathetic attention.

Turkey is not the only peripheral Islamic society. Both geographically and ethnographically, Malaysia and Indonesia, for example, are in the Islamic Periphery. But this is true only in a territorial sense. In demographic terms, Turks, including all the Eastern and Western Turkish-speaking groups, number somewhere between 100 and 150 million. This would make them, along with the Indonesian-Malay group, one of the largest ethnic groups in the Muslim world. Combined, these two groups are anything but peripheral in the Islamic world; they represent over one-third of the total Muslim population of 1 billion.

While Turkey is officially a secular state, Malaysia is officially a Muslim state. There are historical, structural and demographic differences between Malaysia and Turkey, but there are also remarkable similarities, with ancient and modern links existing between the Turks and the Malays, as we shall see presently. In particular their respective searches for identity reveal many similarities, including the confrontation between nationalism and religion. Accordingly, the Malays' search for identity, their attempt to come to terms with Islam and nationalism, provides the basis of a useful study in contrast to the Turkish Kemalist experience.

The search for Malay identity

Who is a Malay? This is a complex question (Syed H. Ali 1984). In a relative sense he is a *Bumiputera* (literally, son of the soil), but this is merely a historical dimension of identity differentiating a group for setting prior claim to a territory relative to more recent arrivals such as the Chinese and Indians. It is an unsatisfactory 'identity tag' because Malays are ethnically different from other older indigenous people, such as Dayaks and Kadazans and they are also pre-dated by the *Orang Asli*. Nor are the Malays homogeneous. Language may be a common factor, but linguistic heritage is a complicating factor. On the one hand it links Malays with Indonesians as in the notion of *Nusantara* or Greater Indonesia (Dahlan 1986), but this raises the problem of secularism and puts the Malays at risk in a multiracial Malaysia while reducing them to an insignificant minority within Indonesia. On the other hand language reveals significant regionalism. Malays in Perak are significantly different in *adat* (custom) and language than those in Negeri Sembilan, and regional differences clearly separate Malays of Kelantan from Malays of the west coast or those in Johore. In northern Malaysia, in states bordering Thailand, the Malays, by custom and history, are closer to the Thais than to Malays in the southern parts of the country.

In the end, Islam, not nationalism as in the case of the Turks (or Indonesians), emerges as the strongest source of identification for Malays (Chandra 1987). Islam clearly sets them apart from other ethnic groups. It reinforces Malay ethnicity in a rapidly changing multiracial country, and gives meaning to 'Malayness', i.e. the traditions of speaking *Bahasa Malaysia*, following Malay customs and professing Islam. Islamic resurgence among the Malays, then, is a reflection of their identity search in a rapidly modernizing plural society. But there are many complicating factors: the underlying motives behind this identity search can be Islamic spirituality or social protest (Nagata in Gale 1987) or even contradictions within the Malay community itself (Shamsul 1986).

Islam may reinforce the Malays' sense of ethnicity, but it does not resolve their identity crisis. In fact, it gives rise to a new set of challenges of reconciling Islam with nationalism and modernity. Thus, how can a Malay, sharing the same faith as a Muslim Thai and a Javanese, differentiate himself from these neighbours except in terms of nationalism? How can he aspire to catch up with the Chinese, for example, unless he can reconcile his faith with modernity? These are issues in which the Turks have achieved some success, although serious challenges still remain. The Malays, too, have achieved considerable progress in economic development, but they have yet to confront nationalism with Islam and Islam with modernity.

This is the *real* Malay dilemma (Mahathir 1970). The old debate between traditionalists representing the Old Order or *Kaum Tua* and modernists representing the New Order or *Kaum Muda* (Roff 1967), continue, in a new form and setting, to divide and confuse the Malay visions of their future destiny. In addition, the multiracial population of Malaysia remains a fundamental stumbling-block. Is Malaysia for Malaysians (i.e. Malays, Chinese, Indians, etc.)? Or, as implied in the term *Bumiputera*, are the Malays the real citizens while the non-Malays are somehow less so, with a weaker sense of loyalty or attachment to Malaysia? If so, then how can a Malaysian 'melting pot' be achieved? These questions demonstrate two characteristics shared by the Turks and Malays: they both suffer from a deep sense of cultural insecurity, yet Islam, while providing an essential spirituality, is quite unable to resolve either the Turkish or the Malay identity crisis. This is what makes them both peripheral in the Islamic world.

The concept of Islamic Periphery is not the only link between Turkey and Malaysia. There are also significant historical links between the Turkish and Malay–Indonesian worlds, both old and modern. These historical links have largely gone unnoticed and unresearched by historians. Some of them will be sketched below, primarily in order to stimulate further research and study in this potentially important, yet relatively unexplored, field.

Turkish–Malay links: old and modern

It seems that the Turks had a role in the spread of Islam in the Malay Archipelago beginning in the thirteenth century, and in more recent history the Kemalist Revolution has had a major impact on the evolution of Malay nationalism. These links are sketched out in three main periods.

The early period

One of the largest concentrations of Muslims in the world is in the Malay Archipelago, comprising Indonesia, Malaysia, the Philippines and Thailand. How exactly Islam came and conquered South-east Asia, and when and by whom it was brought to and spread in this region, are still some of the most unexplored questions of history. One of the theories postulated is the 'Arab traders theory', that Islam was brought to South-east Asia by Arab traders from Arabia, Persia and the Middle East. It gained a foothold in the coastal towns like Malacca where Arab missionaries followed the path of traders.

This theory may explain the *arrival* of Islam in the Malay world, but it does not explain how Islam *stayed on*, i.e. how it spread beyond the coastal towns, and how it flourished and remained intact, especially after the Portuguese conquest of Malacca in 1511. Why did Christianity fail where Islam succeeded among the ordinary masses? If, in fact, religion (any religion) follows trade, then the opening of colonial trade with the Christian west should have led to massive conversion in the region, especially when it is recalled that 'the Path of Salvation', i.e. the spread of Christianity, was a major objective of the Portuguese and the Dutch (Fatimi 1963: 80–90).

According to more recent research, Christianity failed because the Europeans used force, whereas Islam won the hearts and minds of the indigenous people with persuasion and social intercourse. The great period of Islamization of South-east Asia began in the thirteenth century (Fatami 1963: chap. 4) and Islam quickly gained political power. In this period, the source of Islamic influence in the Malay world was India, which was then under Moghul–Turkish rule. It was under this rule of *Pax Turcica* that Sunni Islam spread in the Indian sub-continent, especially in present-day Pakistan and Bangladesh. From this source, and from towns like Gujerat and Cambay, a new breed of Muslim missionaries went out to the Malay world: *sufis*, *sheyks* and eclectic teachers to set up *tarikats*, to live among the ordinary masses, to mix and intermarry, and to spread Islam. These Sunni missionaries popularized a moderate, tolerant and speculative version of Islam, a view which coincided with the Malays' own concept of the cosmos as a mysterious place dominated by spirits. But there was a sociological explanation for the success of these Sunni eclectics. Their version of Islam was quite adaptable and progressive, acting as a new and powerful force in ending debt slavery and human bondage which was at that time quite endemic among the Malays. Thus, Islam gave the small man a sense of his individual worth. Politically, too, Islam gave the local ruler legitimacy in exchange for his promise of social justice. It added divine sanction to his authority and made him and his subjects members of the *Umma*, the world-wide Islamic community.

Who were these *sufis*, *sheyks* and Muslim missionaries? There is evidence of a significant Turkish connection and role. An eighteenth-century French historian of the region writes:

Thus this religion [i.e. Islam] which has nothing very disgustful in it, establishing itself by degrees in sundry places, and because yet more powerful when some Moors or Arabians, who were raised to the first employments in the courts of Cambaya and Guzerat, drew thither a great number of the Asian Turks, called *Rumis*, some of whom made themselves masters of some ports, as Melique Az, who made a considerable settlement at Diu, where he was a long time troublesome to the Portuguese. From the continent they passed to the Molucca island, where they converted their kinds of Tidor and Ternate to their religion.

(Quoted in Fatimi 1963: 81)

These *Rumis* were, in fact, the Ottoman Turks. Likewise, the Ottoman Sultan was traditionally known in South-east Asia as Raja Rum (Snouck Hurgronje 1906: I, 208).

In 1511 Malacca fell to the Portuguese. On several occasions in the sixteenth and seventeenth centuries, the Ottoman Sultan sent naval and military aid to the Malays in their futile efforts to recapture Malacca. After the fall of Malacca, the centre of Islam in the Malay world shifted to Atjeh on the northern part of Sumatra. In fact, Atjeh has long maintained a reputation as the 'Verandah of Islam' in the Malay world. This reputation rested, to some degree, on the fact that Atjeh was under the Ottoman protection from the sixteenth century until its destruction by the Dutch in 1904 (Reid 1969b).

How did this Ottoman connection, so little known in history books, come about? As the Portuguese power began to increase in the Malay world after 1511, the Sultan of Atjeh sent an embassy to the Ottoman Sultan, then regarded as the most powerful man on earth, for protection and military aid. The embassy resulted in a formal declaration of Ottoman protection, confirmed by *ferman* (edict) and symbolized by the Ottoman flag, cannons and other forms of aid given to Atjeh. Since the Ottoman state was at its apex of power, there was no need to register its protection of Atjeh with European powers. The Atjehenese offered an annual tribute as a token of protection, but the Ottoman Sultan refused, on account of distance (Snouck Hurgronje 1906: I, 208–10).

These ancient links between the Ottomans and Atjeh helped preserve Atjehene independence against European penetration for over three hundred years. Every time European colonialists threatened Atjeh, the Ottoman connection was revived. Thus, in mid-1850, ancient Turkish protection was reconfirmed in two *fermans* issued by Sultan Abdul Mejid, although they were not publicized in the usual diplomatic manner for the benefit of European powers.

In 1868 the Dutch made a final attempt to conquer Atjeh. The Sultan of Atjeh sent a brilliant strategist, Abd ar-Rahman, to Istanbul for help. During the period from 1869 to 1873, the fate of Atjeh became a major factor in Ottoman foreign policy. Midhad Pasha, the great reformer, became a great spokesman for the cause of Atjeh, and the *Basiret*, the leading daily in Istanbul at the time, called for the dispatch of the Ottoman fleet to Sumatra (Reid 1969a: 121). The Dutch were alarmed and 'the cabinet at The Hague was in consternation' (Reid 1969b: 122). In the end, despite intense diplomatic efforts, the Ottoman Empire was too weak to save the Atjehenese as it had done in its earlier days of power and glory. The sultanate of Atjeh was, in 1904, destroyed by the Dutch colonial power. The Atjehene question was, nevertheless, a contributing factor in the Ottoman policy of Pan-Islamism.

The pre-First World War period: Pan-Islam in the Malay world

In the last period of the Ottoman Empire, Pan-Islam was a major force. In western accounts the Pan-Islamic movement is presented as a desperate act of the Sick Man of Europe. In fact, however, in some cases at least it was an Ottoman response to requests for assistance to the Sultan-Caliph from weak Muslim rulers threatened by European colonialism. This clearly was the case with Atjeh.

The Atjehene question opened a new relationship between the Turkish and Malay world. It contributed to the Pan-Islamic policy of Sultan Hamid (Reid 1967) which, in turn, had a tremendous influence on the emergence of Malay and Indonesian nationalism and decolonization. It also led to the Singapore Mutiny in 1915, discussed below.

The Ottoman Pan-Islamic policy in South-east Asia was a constant source of worry for the Dutch and English colonial powers in South-east Asia before the First World War. At that time the Ottoman Sultan, as the Caliph of all Muslims, was revered widely among the Malays and Indonesians as 'God's Shadow on Earth', and, quite mistakenly, as 'the most powerful ruler in the world bound to come to the succour of his oppressed cobelievers if they could prove worthy of him' (Reid 1967: 267). The first, and last, Ottoman Ambassador to Batavia, Muhammed Kamil Bey, 1897–9, was expelled by the Dutch for his Pan-Islamic activities in the cause of Malay and Indonesian nationalism, and his attempts to become the official Turkish representative in Singapore, then a British colony, were vetoed by the British (Reid 1967: 280–2).

Kamil's activities in South-east Asia had important consequences for the emergence of Indonesian and Malay nationalism and anti-colonialism. It is largely to his credit that Turkish public opinion became aware of the injustices of colonialism in South-east Asia, while, on the other hand, the Malays became sensitized, through Pan-Islamic connections and the role of men such as Kamil, to the new trends of reform and nationalism in the Middle East. From 1897, the Istanbul press, especially *Idkam* and *Al-Malumat*, the *Thamarat al-Funun* of Beirut and several Egyptian papers, had correspondents in Batavia or Singapore, printing regular stories against colonial injustices and oppression of local Muslim populations (Reid 1967: 281). These reformist influences from Turkey and Egypt before the First World War were the principal sources of Malay nationalism known as *Kaum Muda*, the New Order, as opposed to *Kaum Tua*, the Old Order (Roff 1967: chap. 3).

One of the major consequences of Sultan Hamid's Pan-Islamic policy in South-east Asia was the Singapore Mutiny of 1915 – an event that was virtually unknown until a few years ago, owing to the British policy of keeping it under a tight colonial lid. The Mutiny started mainly as a result of the refusal of Indian and Malay Muslim soldiers to be sent off to the Middle East to fight the Muslim Turks (Harper and Miller 1984). One of the central figures behind the Mutiny was an Indian Muslim, Kassim Ali Mansoor, who was convicted and hanged for possession of a copy of a letter sent to his son for personal delivery to the honorary Turkish consul in Rangoon. The letter 'asked for a Turkish warship to be dispatched to Singapore to take the Malay States Guides to any place where they would come "into conflict with British troops"' (Harper and Miller 1984: 205). The British were so worried about the potential consequences of the Mutiny that they never explained its real causes.

The modern period: the end of the Caliphate and Kemalism

The chief attraction of Turkey in the Malay world derived from the Caliphate. The Ottoman Sultan was popularly perceived as the symbol of unity among the *Umma*. In terms of *realpolitik*, the power and influence of the Ottoman Empire was greatly exaggerated. Turkish power and diplomacy in the late nineteenth and early twentieth centuries could in no way match the strength of European colonial powers in South-east Asia. Yet, among the Indian Muslims, Indonesians and Malays living under colonial rule, the visions of Ottoman greatness and the omnipotent Caliph survived. The leaders of the Malay world, as well as the *rakyat* (masses), looked to the Ottoman Middle East for inspiration and leadership – for Islamic traditionalism and faith, as well as for reform and modernization. Prior to 1924 when Ataturk abolished the Caliphate, the Malay world sympathized with Turkish causes in the Turkish–Russian war of 1877, the war with Greece in 1897, the Balkan wars, the Italian campaign in Libya, the First World War and the Turkish War of National Independence. In the vernacular press, books and articles about the Turkish War of National Independence and about Ataturk were published and read widely (Za'ba 1939: 151–62).

In February 1924, Ataturk abolished the Caliphate. This created a shock effect in the Malay world, especially among the *Kaum Tua* traditionalists, some of whom have continued to brand Ataturk as a betrayer of Islam to this day. But, on the other hand, Ataturk's Revolution has had a great positive impact in the Malay world. Many progressive and reformist Malay and Indonesian leaders, including Sukarno, have studied Ataturk's nationalist and secularist policies of reform, and have based their policies on Ataturk's model (Milner 1986: 118). In the 1920s and 1930s several books in Malay were published detailing the Kemalist Revolution. One, *Turki dan Mustapha Kemal Ataturk*, covered the history of the reform movement, and another one, *Turki dan Tamadunnya* (Turkey and Its Civilization) examined the Ataturk reforms in depth. There was also a biography of Ataturk, *Kitab Mustafa Kemal*. Newspapers and periodicals, such as *Idaran Zaman* and *Saudara*, gave extensive coverage to the Turkish Revolution. These books and news media raised the nationalistic sentiments of the Malays and contributed to the formation in 1946 of a Turkish-style party (i.e. secular and progressive), United Malays National Organization (UMNO), under the leadership of Dato Onn, himself of Turkish descent (Milner 1986: 124–7).

Dato Onn's leadership role in Malay nationalism opens another important window on the Turkish–Malay connection. This relates to the historic connection between the House of Johore and the Ottoman Empire.

The Sultan of Johore, as with other Malay Sultans, had close relations with the Caliph-Sultan in Istanbul. In the mid-1860s, the Sultan of Johore, Abu Bakar, visited the Ottoman Sultan in Istanbul as part of his European tour. As a gift he was given a lady-in-waiting, a certain Rugayyah Hanum, of Circassian origin. After their arrival in Johore, Rugayyah Hanum married Ungku Abdul Majid. Three sons were born to them, one of whom, Ungku Abdul Hamid, was the father of Ungku Abdul Aziz, the former Vice-Chancellor of the University of Malaya. When Ungku Abdul Majid died, Rugayyah Hanum remarried, this time to Dato Jaafar, a commoner, and this marriage resulted in seven children, one of whom, Dato Onn, was the founder of UMNO and his son, Tun Hussein, was the third Prime Minister of Malaysia. The remarkable fecundity of Rugayyah Hanum was manifested further when she married a third time, upon Dato Jaafar's death, this time to an Arab trader from Yemen, Abdullah al-Attas. This marriage resulted in only one son, Ali. Ali Al-Attas had three sons; one of them, the prominent Malay sociologist Hussein Alatas (1977a, 1977b, 1980) is the current Vice-Chancellor of the University of Malaya, and his younger brother Naquib Al-Attas (1978), a leading Malay Sufi scholar, is the source of this information on the family tree communicated to the author.

Thus, the Turkish—Malay links are both old and significant. These two peoples, so distantly situated at the polar ends of the Islamic Periphery, are nevertheless united together by Islam. While Islam has been a source of spiritual identity in both cases of nation-building, it has also given rise to two regional manifestations of the contemporary global Muslim dilemma of reconciling Islam with modernity. In short, a Turkish or a Malay search for identity is not an isolated case; nor is the development experience of any one nation-state unique. These are merely regional variations around a global theme. Part II will detail these regional variations within the broad framework of the Islamic dilemma: how to explain and remedy Islamic underdevelopment.

Part two

The Islamic dilemma

The Turkish and Malay identity crises, discussed in the previous chapter, are manifestations of the age-old problem of reconciling Islam with modernity. While 'modernization' has been variously defined as the passing of traditional society (Lerner 1958), emergence of pluralism (Weiker 1981), competitive drive (Geertz 1963), westernization (Eisenstadt 1973, 1987) or in some other manner, there is wide consensus that improving the quality of life is the central dimension. Higher income per capita is necessary, but not sufficient. It is necessary to finance basic human needs and to sustain further growth, but income alone cannot attain higher goals such as fundamental human rights. Higher quality of life, comprising both income and fundamental human rights, is the challenge of development policy, the most vital component of modern public policy.

Accordingly, in the contemporary world the Islamic dilemma can be expressed as a series of questions. How can we explain the fact that Muslim societies are everywhere underdeveloped relative to western (Christian) countries? Why are large segments of these societies, especially in rural areas and urban ghettos, subsisting in conditions of abject poverty? Why are the education and status of women so deficient? Why are fundamental human rights so restricted? The traditional reply to these sorts of questions (Tibi 1988: 137) is based on the Qur'anic verse: 'God does not change people's lot unless they (first) change what is in their hearts' (XIII: 11). This, of course, is an unsatisfactory reply since, for one thing, it implies the moral superiority of the west, notwithstanding its high incidence of crime, drugs, prostitution, pornography, etc., which the traditional *ulama* so readily condemn as western degeneracy! The argument is also evasive since it merely postpones Islamic development indefinitely.

The historical fact is that the comparative underdevelopment of *dar-ul Islam* (the realm of Islam) is of relatively recent origin. Until the Middle Ages, Muslims were competitive in world trade, leaders in knowledge and highly advanced in civilization. 'Islam carried to the West superior knowledge' in such fields as astronomy, mathematics and philosophy during its great expansion, and it was the new knowledge from ancient Greece preserved and enhanced by Muslim thinkers and scientists which triggered the European Renaissance (Al-Attas 1978: 97). Islamic scholars such as Averroes, Avicenna, Farabi and Ibn Khaldun were masters of science and philosophy derived from ancient Greek rationalism; for this reason they were suppressed by the *ulama*. Yet, they are among the intellectual fathers of the European Reformation and Enlightenment. By rejecting rationalism in favour of dogmatic theology, the *ulama* set in motion a long, gradual decline from which the world of Islam is yet to recover. The Muslim quest for a place, purpose and identity in the modern world continues.

Chapter two

Islamic underdevelopment
Cause and response

The overall purpose of this chapter is to demonstrate that Islamic underdevelopment stems, fundamentally, from a lack of positive public policy tradition. The institution of a nation-state as a tool of public policy maximizing public good is a western innovation. No comparable evolution occurred in Muslim lands except, in the present century, in a few countries in the Islamic Periphery. Turkey and Malaysia, at the opposite ends of the Muslim world, are two notable cases where national and secular development policies have been relied upon. Unfortunately, these policies have, to date, failed to achieve development with Islamic social justice. This chapter will attempt to provide an explanation for this fact within the wider context of the contemporary Islamic dilemma.

Endogenous or exogenous underdevelopment?

It will be argued here that, while exogenous factors (such as colonialism and imperialism) did contribute to Islamic under-development, the main causes are endogenous: Islamic societies have not been development oriented. Islam has not been mobilized for economic and social development. The idea of state as the instrument of public administration enhancing the quality of human condition simply did not evolve in Islamic societies. Instead what evolved amounted to a tradition of unaccountable leadership, bureaucratic inertia and dysfunctional intellectual elitism.

The role of Muslim scholars and jurists, the *ulama*, is of special importance in the explanation of Islamic underdevelopment. In the tenth century, at the height of Islamic civilization, they declared that the Gate of *Ijtihad* (independent analysis) was closed, i.e. that all possible questions had been answered and henceforth only learning by imitation would be permissible. Especially after the fourteenth century, the *ulama* emphasized theological and specu-lative education at the expense of secular and empirical knowledge

(Rahman 1982). While the Age of Enlightenment led Europe to scientific and geographic discoveries, and while European countries developed new trade routes to replace the old Silk Road, the *ulama* resisted new ideas and technologies. Unable to understand such new ideas as nationalism and market competition, they simply resisted anything western as 'un-Islamic' or declared it *haram* (prohibited).

But superior knowledge recognizes no boundaries. In an earlier age superior Islamic knowledge had invaded Europe, but after the Age of Enlightenment, superior western knowledge penetrated the lands of Islam. This penetration occurred as a result of three factors: superior technology, more efficient public administration, and economic competition. Technology facilitated conquest, public administration provided essential services, and economic competition supplied modern goods at affordable prices. In all three, the Muslims could provide no competition. The root cause was the declining quality of Islamic scholarship in science, public administration and economics.

But there is also an alternative paradigm which seeks to attribute Islamic underdevelopment to exogenous factors. This is the *dependency theory* associated with Frank (1966), Wallerstein (1974), Amin (1977) and others who, arguing within a world-systems framework, divide the international economy into a centre of wealth and power, and a dependent periphery of poor and exploited countries. Centre–periphery relations are based on an 'unequal exchange' whereby the former penetrates the latter to underdevelop it for the centre's permanent supremacy and enrichment. In this centre–periphery world-view, all important decisions are made in the centre, which also controls capital and technology and uses them for neo-mercantilistic ends. The poverty and underdevelopment of the peoples of the periphery are determined by decisions in the centre.

Islamic countries belong in the periphery. Dependency theorists would, therefore, attribute the blame for Islamic decline and underdevelopment to the actions of such decision-makers as the imperialists, colonialists, financiers, multinational corporations and so on. Historically, these theorists see a causal relationship between the rise of western imperialism and Islamic decline.

It is true, of course, that in the age of western imperialism, Muslim lands, as other regions of the periphery, fell victim to monopoly capitalism in search of global profits. Thus it could be argued that British Malaya was administered first and foremost for the benefit of British imperialist interests (Emerson 1964, Mehmet 1978: chap. 5). Likewise, a case can be made that the Ottoman

Empire was de-industrialized as a result of secret free trade treaties it concluded with European powers in 1839–41 (Pamuk 1987; Kasaba 1988).

But the dependency theory is no more than half the story because it is, in reality, a Eurocentric abstraction. Historically, it misses the point that at its zenith, the 'centre' of world trade and civilization was the Islamic Core itself: the fabled Silk Road and spice trading linked the peripheral sources from China, South-east Asia, India and Africa to the great centres of Islamic wealth in Baghdad, Damascus and Cairo (Figure 2.1). Trade-based Islamic prosperity financed high culture and civilization in such (now forgotten) places as Samarkand, Timbuctu and Qum. It is no historical accident that Arabia was known as Arabia Felix, that Marco Polo journeyed to China searching for wealth, that the standard of living in the Indonesian archipelago before the advent of Europeans surpassed the standard of living in Europe at the time.

Figure 2.1   The westward shift in economic centre of gravity

A. Before the Age of Enlightenment

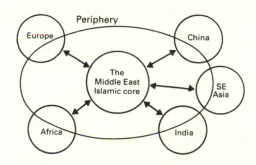

B. After the Age of Enlightenment

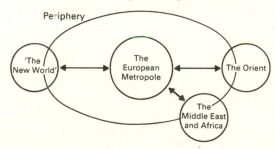

The origin of Islamic decline pre-dates European colonialist penetration in Islamic lands. This secular decline had begun long before, when the *ulama* opted in favour of theology at the expense of rational knowledge and decided to concentrate on 'other-world' concerns. By so doing the *ulama* effectively turned their backs on Islamic public policy. As a result, the quality of Islamic public administration, as well as education and knowledge, began to deteriorate. Science and mathematics stopped flourishing. Geographic discovery became a European monopoly. Trade and commerce, long in Muslim hands, passed to Christian Europe.

The Islamic state began to rot from within. The *ulama* failed to notice the fundamental shift of the economic centre of gravity westwards from the Islamic Core. The *ulama*, who elected to pursue spiritual education at the expense of problem-solving, socially relevant knowledge, failed to grasp the crucial connection between prosperity and civilization; as custodians of Islamic civilization they abdicated their responsibility as a 'functioning intellectual group' (Alatas 1977b) to guide Islamic public policy. Thus, no remedial action was defined, designed or implemented. In the ensuing course of long-term Islamic economic decline (Issawi 1966, 1982), the emerging nation-states of Europe, each pursuing its national public policy, moved in aggressively, with new technology, military power and comparative advantage, all derived from rational knowledge, to fill the vacuum in the Islamic Core.

Incorporation of the Islamic world within the capitalist system and its peripheralization in the age of imperialism occurred primarily by default of the Muslim ruling elites. Thus, the origins of the economic collapse of the Ottoman Empire can be traced back to the *capitulations* (extra-territorial trade privileges) granted to European merchants by Sultans Beyazit, Mehmet Fatih and Suleyman the Magnificent at the height of Ottoman power. In the last phase of the Empire, fiscal mismanagement had become endemic. Foreign loans were contracted to finance military campaigns or royal weddings, and banks and tax revenues were placed in the hands of foreign interests. By the mid-nineteenth century the Ottoman war spending and territorial losses had so greatly reduced the revenue capacity of the Empire that the default of 1876 and the resulting direct European financial control of the Ottoman state were, sooner or later, quite inevitable (Blaisdell 1966).

As regards the British penetration into Malaya, this came about in the first place because the Malay sultans were eager to trade with the East India Company *on its terms*. The Sultan of Kedah eagerly signed the Treaty of Pangkor and the other sultans, one by one, accepted the Residency system of indirect British rule in order to cash in on the tin and rubber revenues. West-coast states such as Perak and Selangor, where tin mines and rubber plantations were located, enriched the British, while the east-coast states, such as Pahang and Trengganu, the traditional home of the Malays, stagnated. The Malay sultans, in theory protectors of the Malays, allowed the British a free hand. It has also been argued that 'the ease with which the British took over the Malay states, ruling them as protected states in form, but in substance treating them as colonies' (Mahathir 1970: 158) is best explained by such internal factors as succession feuds, fatalism and feudalism (Syed Husin Ali 1975). As in the case of the Ottomans, the Malay sultans were unable to deliver to their faithful followers the good government and social justice promised by Islam.

Dependency theorists underrate indigenous culture and leadership in the periphery. For example in Samir Amin's *The Arab Nation* (1978), culture is treated as the lifestyle of a ruling class that has been too westernized to have any claim to authenticity. Thus there is little indigenous Arab culture as a unique historical heritage of customs and beliefs capable of being harnessed for social cohesion and organic growth. Orthodox dependency theorists reject the view that, even after decolonization, peripheral countries have the capacity to promote autonomous development (Alavi 1982). They concentrate attention on such issues as terms of trade and debt crisis. Their agenda remains Eurocentric. Implicitly, dependency theorists would dismiss Islamic rulers and the *ulama* as trivial actors in the periphery with no causal role in the Islamic decline or any capacity to reverse it.

The promise of social justice

One of the major themes of this study is that the primary source of Islamic decline is to be found in the failure of Muslim societies to sustain the original promise of social justice. The next chapter describes how Islam began with a highly advanced form of social contract, exemplified in the Constitution of Medina written under the guidance of the Prophet himself. In the beginning, trade, extending to China and South-east Asia, was an important source of Islamic prosperity, and social justice was maintained, to varying degrees of efficiency, by implementing charitable and welfare schemes based on *zakat* (personal wealth tax), *waqfs* (trusts and endowments), and *bayt al-mal* (public welfare fund). The concept of Islamic social justice has been beautifully articulated in Ibn Khaldun's Circle of Equity (see p. 64). This concept gave meaning and content to the idea of an organic relationship between the rulers and the ruled, built upon a cohesive and well-integrated body politic. At the core of Khaldun's organic relationship is a biological metaphor: that society is like a body in an integrated, ordered balance with its various organs; without such an organic balance, society inevitably becomes a sick body, weakened by disease, unable to withstand external threats and domination.

By Ibn Khaldun's time the Islamic body politic was already showing signs of disintegration. Trade and prosperity were shifting westward. The *ulama*, who had abandoned rational inquiry, were unable to notice this secular shift. No longer able to conduct original and independent thinking, the *ulama* legitimized tyranny by choosing order over justice, and by preaching fatalistic acceptance of the status quo however unjust it might be, while they themselves indulged in corruption (Alatas 1980). At a time when Europe was emerging from its Dark Ages, the land of Islam was entering a new era of *jahiliyya* (mass ignorance).

Islamic resurgence

The contemporary wave of Islamic resurgence is more an expression of social demand for equitable development than spiritual fundamentalism. This will be evident in Part III where it is demonstrated that in the national phase of development there was a general consensus for progress and modernization. A realistic reading of history shows that the Islamic masses have always opted for progressive development.

Historically, Islam was revealed in the deserts of the Middle East as a remedy to tribal disunity, cultural decay and material corruption characterized by usury and profiteering. Islam replaced tribalism with the universality of a transnational community united in submission to God. It provided a unity of purpose and inspired Muslims to build an empire stretching from the Middle East across Northern Africa to Spain (Esposito 1984: 10).

Islam, like Christianity, is universalistic and, hence, competitive. Competitive spirit provided the original dynamism of Islam. Competition was manifest in two dimensions: market competition, comprising local and international trade, and competition on the battlefield. Military conquest through *jihad* (holy war) was the earliest tool of Islamic expansion and, as a result, militarism and militancy have been integral to Islam (Crone 1980). Trade and search for markets were also important means of Islamic expansion. It was through trade links that Islam originally reached the Malay world (Fatimi 1963). In Indonesia and Malaysia it was especially appealing to the oppressed peasantry suffering under feudalism and human bondage. Islam has not lost its grass-roots appeal as is demonstrated by the fact that it is now expanding in sub-Saharan Africa where, with decolonization, Christianity is receding (Mazrui 1988). What Islam did lose, however, was its competitive drive, especially in trade and commerce, particularly after the European Age of Enlightenment.

Islam is now experiencing a general revival for both positive and negative reasons. In positive terms, Islamic revival is an assertion of identity and pride in past Islamic achievements in scholarship and political power that have long been threatened by the west, first by colonialism and more recently by cultural invasion. In the Middle East, Islamic revival is primarily a response to the Palestinian–Israeli conflict. Having tried various imported ideologies and having flirted with east and west, the Middle East Islamic Core, feeling weak and vulnerable, is now seeking self-identity in spiritual liberation. In Iran, Islamic revival is a process of purification, both spiritual and cultural, a mixture of patriotism, fundamentalism and xenophobia (Shari'ati 1986, Al-i Ahmad 1984).

But there is also a negative aspect of the Islamic revival. It represents broken promises, unfulfilled expectations and increasing disenchantment with the top-down development strategy in the post-war period.

The rise and fall of top-down developmentalism

Post-war development strategies concentrated power in the hands of ruling elites. Elite control of investment choices and resource allocation became institutionalized under a highly centralized system of development administration. These modernizers and their foreign advisors at the centre grossly exaggerated the forces of traditionalism and irrational behaviour amongst the peasantry. Those in charge of decision-making became architects of a high-cost, uncompetitive system of state capitalism or socialism. No political or social checks and balances were deemed necessary to ensure efficiency because the masses were simply expected to follow and adjust to this top-down strategy.

The elitist top-down model, of course, could not work for it had too many systemic faults. The ruling elites disregarded not only the rules of economic efficiency; they also underestimated the complexity of cultural restructuring. Consequently, top-down development upset traditional life-styles and support systems without replacing them with something better. It resulted in a socio-economic disequilibrium. *Ibadah* and *muamalat*, which traditionally had embodied spiritual and interpersonal relations for Muslims, simply disintegrated under the cumulative weight of state-sponsored urbanization and industrialization. Under the top-down strategy, development was equated with economic growth (i.e. GNP maximization), and modernization with urbanization which in turn, meant capital-intensive industrialization. The architects of the top-down strategy, domestic ruling elites and their expatriate advisers, had exaggerated confidence in the 'trickle-down' theory of growth, i.e. the rationalization that in due course industrialization and urbanization would automatically promote social justice (Mehmet 1978).

In the end, for the masses, top-down strategy turned out to be mal-development: it seemed to destroy whatever remained of the old Islamic socio-economic order without any compensations. It concentrated wealth in a few hands, while causing mass poverty; it turned peasants, long accustomed to a tradition of egalitarian culture based on a strong sense of community, into marginalized proletarians victimized by the capital-intensive technology. Now, among the second generation – the children of the poor migrants – growing up in the urban ghetto, there is even less hope. Neither education nor wage-employment offers opportunities for upward mobility. In this setting, Islamic militants, with promises of charity and sponsorship, find fertile ground for winning converts to their cause.

Therefore, in this study Islamic resurgence is regarded as primarily a response of the masses to unfulfilled expectations. These expectations were stimulated, in particular, in the two decades after the Second World War, when top-down development models imported from the west and implemented with foreign technical and financial assistance were supposed to lead to growth with equity. Such an outcome would surely have met the popular demand for progressive development as well as the Islamic goal of social justice. The masses willingly accepted sacrifices in terms of current consumption for promises of future benefits stemming from development.

State-led development in Turkey and Malaysia

The central argument of the last section – that Islamic resurgence is the response of the masses towards mismanaged state-led development strategy – will be documented with reference to Turkey and Malaysia. These two countries on the Islamic Periphery share a pair of remarkable similarities in their development experience: they both utilized a 'leader–follower' model of development administration (Weiker 1981, Esman 1972); and they both chose state capitalism and secularist policy instruments. Etatism in Turkey and trusteeship in Malaysia, discussed in detail in subsequent chapters, were highly interventionist strategies of state capitalism which enriched and empowered the ruling elites at the centre but failed to bring social justice to the masses. In Turkey, secularism has been the corner-stone of Kemalist ideology that has guided Turkish development. In Malaysia, where Islam is the official religion, secularist development at the federal level has been a colonial legacy reinforced by the multi-racial character of the country. At the present time, both of these countries are vigorously attempting to shift from state capitalism to privatization against a backdrop of Islamic resurgence.

Yet, in macro-economic terms development strategies in Turkey and post-independence Malaysia have been quite successful. In the post-1960 period alone, the Turkish and Malaysian GNP per capita increased by more than five times over in real terms and after discounting for significant exchange rate corrections. According to the latest World Bank data (1988), the Turkish GNP per capita in 1986 was $1,160 compared with $1,830 for Malaysia. But these averages hide significant inequality of income distribution. In 1973 in both Malaysia and Turkey the poorest 40 per cent of the population had an income share of only about 11 per cent; whereas, the richest 10 per cent enjoyed about 40 per cent. Since then disparities between the rich and the poor in both countries have grown.

Of central importance here is the failure of the leader–follower model of development strategy in both of these countries to promote social justice for the mass of inhabitants. This is contrary to the objectives of Islamic social justice (see Chapter 3). The failure of a top-down development strategy is also a failure of secularist development policies adopted and implemented in Turkey and Malaysia. Significantly, this should not be interpreted as implying that secularist public policy, *per se*, should be replaced by Islamic theocracy. It merely means that the specific public policies that have been employed, principally state capitalism managed in a non-competitive and highly centralized manner, have been inappropriate. The secularist elites at the centre, possessing monopoly power over decision-making, attempted to impose an elitist vision of development on the masses, ostensibly in order to create a new middle class, but, in fact, manipulating the development process in an authoritarian, self-enriching manner.

In both Turkey and Malaysia the development process went through two discernible phases: a nationalist phase, which lasted until about 1980, and a privatization phase. The former is the subject of Part III while the latter will be taken up in Part IV. In the nationalist phase, the centrist elites relied on a top-heavy, interventionist strategy of development. These modernizing elites utilized development to urbanize a rural Islamic population. Secular tools such as economic planning, forced savings and heavy public investment were chosen to build state enterprises, promote infant industries and expand physical and social infrastructure. The paramount objective was socio-economic restructuring from top to bottom. Spatially it was anti-rural, politically it was elitist, and sociologically it aimed at the creation of a state-sponsored middle class dependent upon subsidies and protection. But this state-nurturing, unlike Japan and the Gang of Four (i.e. South Korea, Taiwan, Hong Kong and Singapore) experience, failed to rely on the rules of economic efficiency (Mehmet 1989). Instead of rewarding productivity and performance, state subsidies were allocated preferentially to sustain loss-making enterprises.

Structurally, the Turkish and Malay socio-economic transformation has had a great impact. The agrarian character of these two economies rapidly changed in the last quarter-century. During the 1965–84 period the contribution of manufacturing to GDP surpassed that of agriculture. While the agricultural share of GDP declined from about a third to a fifth during 1965–84, the share of manufacturing in Turkey jumped in the same period from 16 per cent to 24 per cent and in the case of Malaysia it almost doubled from 10 per cent to 19 per cent.

The socio-economic symptoms of mismanaged development in Turkey and in Malaysia, can best be seen by focusing on urbanization, capital-intensive industrialization, over-investment in higher education, and rent-seeking elite behaviour.

Urbanization: the evolution of urban poverty

The urban bias (Lipton 1977) of industrial development brought about a sharp geographical redistribution in the demographic landscape of Turkey and Malaysia. The urban bias reflected an anti-rural development bias. In 1965, both countries were predominantly rural: 74 per cent of the Malaysians, and 68 per cent of the Turks, lived in rural areas. By 1985, an unprecedented rural–urban migration had urbanized both of these countries. Thus, almost half of the Turkish population and virtually 40 per cent of the Malaysians resided in urban centres.

Far from promoting development, urban-based industrialization seemed to transfer rural poverty into urban poverty centred in rapidly mushrooming urban shanty towns. In Turkey the *gecekondus* (Karpat 1976, Abadan-Unat 1985), in Malaysia the urban *kampongs* (Kamal Salih *et al.* 1978; S. Lee and J. Ariffin in Aziz and Hoong 1984) came into being. At first these were intended as transitory settlements, but now there is a second generation – children of the working poor – growing up in these shanty towns with no other roots than these substandard settlements. The second generation migrants are politically and ideologically far more active than their parents. They see political action as the route for gaining squatter rights and more broadly for controlling their destiny. The urban squatters, along with the university campuses (see below), emerged as the breeding grounds of new ideologies and religious movements.

Alienation in the urban ghetto was a major contributing factor for Islamic resurgence in both Turkey and Malaysia. These ghettos were not only reserves of cheap labour for industrialization, but they also quickly became the breeding grounds for revolutionary movements, including Islamic fundamentalism. Substandard housing, constant danger of eviction by authorities, lack of water, electricity and sewers, and a filthy environment – these factors together with persistent poverty made the exploding ghetto population willing targets of charismatic movements which offered aid and escape from poverty.

Capital-intensive growth: profits and technology

Post-war development in Turkey and Malaysia relied on capital-intensive technology. Tariffs, investment incentives and pricing policies were deliberately aimed at channelling profits and surpluses for the acquisition of imported technologies. Workers were subordinated to machines and assembly lines. Forced savings depressed consumption; cheap labour policies impoverished workers; low interest rates subsidized capital imports. Consequently profits and surpluses realized by economic growth were directed into further capitalist growth at the expense of job creation and wages.

During the period from 1960 to 1980, domestic-oriented manufacturing was the centre-piece of the Turkish and Malaysian development strategies. Manufacturing industries grew very rapidly, often in excess of the GDP. State protection ensured high and rising rates of return. What happened to these returns? They accrued to capitalists, resident and non-resident, and to rent-seeking networks of political, bureaucratic and military elites at the top. Rent-seeking behaviour was institutionalized, especially in the favourable environment of import-substitution industrialization. The rate of job-creation was inadequate, and most of the jobs created paid wages too low to afford a decent standard of living. Urban rents were too high and housing pitifully inadequate. Rapid growth of the GNP failed to filter down to the wage-earners while the profit share accruing to resident and non-resident capitalists rose. The economic distance between the 'haves' and the 'have-nots' widened. Education seemed to offer the only escape route for poverty groups.

Over-investment in higher education

The pursuit of education is of crucial importance in any process of modernization. It is especially so in Muslim societies as it is intricately linked to the Islamic command that to seek knowledge (*ilm*) is to do God's will. Thus, education is seen as the birthright of every individual, both for religious traditions as well as for secular reasons, it being a path – typically the only one – for upward social mobility.

In the post-war modernization drive both the Turkish and Malaysian leadership opted for elitist rather than pragmatic education. They failed to vocationalize education. They did not invest in agricultural education to raise farmers' productivity, and they under-invested in primary and middle-level schooling to train technical and technological manpower. Instead they placed top priority on the expansion of classical-type higher education.

This has been dysfunctional and costly. In part it was due to a heavy 'social demand' for university education seen popularly as the only means of upward social mobility. The centrist elites in charge of the top-down strategy did not see the need for reforming the structure of higher education. Therefore, expansion occurred linearly within the classical format of a liberal arts education intended to produce graduates for public service employment (Mehmet 1986; Krueger 1972). In the end this led to a corresponding acceleration of phoney job creation in the public and parastatal sector to accommodate the new graduates. The growth of higher education to feed an already top-heavy bureaucracy represented a huge over-investment of scarce development resources. It lead to rising deficits and by 1980 to a total freeze on further public sector hirings. As a result, both countries have since been experiencing a sharp increase in graduate unemployment.

During the 1960s and early 1970s both Malaysia and Turkey witnessed a fourfold increase in university enrolments without commensurate investments in educational quality. Overcrowding and declining standards fuelled protest and campus violence. In both Malaysia and Turkey, the mid-1970s were marked by intense campus political and ideological activity resulting in autocratic clamp-downs restricting academic freedoms. Islamic resurgence among university students stems, in part, from these autocratic interventions which had the effect of driving student protest movements from the campus to the relative safety of the mosque, or, worse still, into underground revolutionary factions linked to such sources of support as Iran or Saudi Arabia.

Rent-seeking behaviour

In both Malaysia and Turkey, state capitalism institutionalized a system of rent-seeking behaviour among the centrist elites. As has been demonstrated by the literature on public choice and special interest networks (Olson 1982; Buchanan *et al.* 1980), state subsidies and protective measures augment the power of influential cartel-like groups with privileged access to information about contracts, prices and projects. Those with influence can realize large personal gains through collusion and influence-peddling. These gains, typically bonuses for corruption, bribery or favouritism, are considered as transaction costs or middlemen's margins and, as such, are included in the cost of production. They are ultimately passed on to the consumer in the form of higher retail prices.

The etatist strategy in Turkey, especially in the hectic days of import-substitution-industrialization after 1960 and the New Economic Policy trusteeship in Malaysia after 1970, provided ideal conditions for rent-seeking behaviour to the Turkish and Malay elites. New 'distributional coalitions' (Olson 1982) were formed to enrich the military, political, aristocratic networks in partnership with local and foreign capitalists and businessmen. In 1961 the Turkish military established OYAK, the Army Mutual Assistance Organization, with funding from a compulsory 10 per cent payroll deduction levied on the rank and file (Vaner in Schick and Tonak 1987). In Malaysia, the top military controlled LTAT, the Armed Forces Provident Fund and the Armed Forces Co-operative (Mehmet 1986: 136–8). Both were able to emerge as one of the top holding companies in the two countries as a result of stock acquisitions, joint-ventureships and interlocking company directorships awarded to senior officers. Likewise, influential bureaucrats and politicians in charge of state licensing, import quota regulations or subsidy programmes, were able to enter into personally profitable business arrangements with corporate interests earning quasi-rents while doing so. These quasi-rents, like the proverbial free lunch, had to be paid by the rest of the society either in terms of higher taxes or subsidies. These social costs were the inevitable burdens of building a non-competitive economy, and they contributed significantly to the financial crises at the end of the 1970s, necessitating in both countries the dramatic shift towards austerity budgeting and economic liberalization.

Thus, all of the four major initiatives undertaken by secularist leaders in Turkey and Malaysia appeared, from the standpoint of the masses, to have fallen short of the social justice expectations of the masses. The leaders' nationalist ideology, initially highly successful in mobilizing popular support for state capitalism, in the end found itself facing an increasing challenge from Islamists. The secularist leaders' appeal for support in the name of national ideology proved increasingly inadequate in view of persistent poverty and systemic maldistribution of income, while, by contrast, the services available through Islamic movements became more appealing.

The rise of Islamic voluntarism

It is hardly surprising, therefore, that recent years have witnessed a global resurgence of Islamic voluntarism providing welfare and social assistance to the poor and alienated groups marginalized and impoverished by post-war development efforts. Islamic charity and voluntarism are as old as Islam itself. Altruism is one of the five basic pillars of the faith. *Zakat* (voluntary charitable contributions to the poor equalling 2.5 per cent of one's annual wealth) is only one such instrument of Islamic altruism. *Waqfs*, charitable trusts and bequests willed by the devout, have provided for hospitals, schools and welfare and social service institutions in all ages of Islam. In the current Islamic resurgence, traditional Islamic altruism and voluntarism loom very large. In part it is due to increased flow of Islamic aid from such oil-surplus countries as Saudi Arabia, Kuwait and Libya. But, principally, it is an attempt to fill the vacuum created by the failure of the post-war top-down development planning and policy. Hidden behind Islamic voluntarism, however, are often deeper motives, sometimes fundamentalist, ideological or even subversive.

The remainder of this chapter focuses on Islamic voluntary organizations in Malaysia and Turkey. The aim is to highlight the role of these organizations as voluntary service agencies, utilizing an old Islamic formula of charity with a divine cause.

The Malay Dakwah movement

Literally 'call to Islam', the Malay Dakwah is far from a monolithic movement with a clear programme of aims and strategies.

In fact it is a multiplicity of organizations with differing philosophies and aims, usually centred on a charismatic leader (Nagata in Gale 1987). Nevertheless, two broad aims can be identified. First there is the missionary aim of 'making Muslims better Muslims' and converting non-believers primarily through *muballighs* (missionaries). An example of this is the Jemaat Tabligh which came to Malaysia in the 1950s from India and which is part of a world-wide network. It is active among rural communities as well as in urban centres and university campuses, running discussion groups, retreats and other means that emphasize ritualistic and more formal aspects of Islam. Members wear Arab clothing, eat Arab-style food and stress Arabic prayers (Mehden 1986: 90–2).

The other important aim is Islamic voluntarism through the provision of educational, health and economic activities. For example, Darul Arqan is an Islamic organization which tends to be service oriented and pragmatic (Chandra 1987: chap. 4). On an even larger scale there is PERKIM, the Islamic Welfare and Missionary Association (Mehden 1986: 95–6). These types of organization provide schools and adult education along Islamic lines, operate clinics using western medicine, and manage small-scale businesses and food-processing concerns producing *halal* products. Thus they are able to offer employment and income opportunities to prospective members.

The Malaysia Islamic Youth Movement (ABIM), with 35,000 members, is the largest and most active organization within the Dakwah movement. ABIM was formed in 1972 and was soon involved in campus politics. The consequence was an official clamp-down on university protest movements and political action. When the Malaysian authorities banned campus political societies, this did not damage ABIM. Anwar Ibrahim, leader of the student association at the University of Malaya, emerged as ABIM's leader, adopting an Islamic banner to protect and legitimize the student movement since no Malaysian government could ban or punish an Islamic organization. In 1982, Anwar Ibrahim was co-opted by the ruling party, United Malays National Organization (UMNO), joining the cabinet first as the Minister of Youth, Culture and Sport, and more recently moving to the sensitive and powerful Education portfolio. Under Anwar Ibrahim's influence, the government of Dr Mahathir adopted an Islamization policy and established an Islamic Bank, an Islamic University and an Islamic bureaucracy. In 1987, elements of the *shari'ah* were introduced into the federal jurisdiction.

In the meantime, ABIM has undergone a number of important changes. In the first place, it has moderated its agenda significantly.

Both Anwar Ibrahim and ABIM seem to have come to terms with the multiracial nature of Malaysia and are no longer committed to turning Malaysia into an Islamic state. Some also argue that ABIM's dynamism ended with Anwar Ibrahim's co-optation. This, however, is most likely an overstatement. In fact, ABIM continues to attract new recruits among the university students, so that its popularity seems to be undiminished. Among these students, the headwear movement has continued to flourish, a significant and visible sign of Islamic revival among the youth. But ABIM is not a militant Islamic fundamentalist movement. It has become an Islamic charitable organization, the largest of many other such voluntary organizations. It runs a wide range of social services and aid programmes. For university students it provides financial aid; for graduates facing unemployment it provides employment opportunities staffing ABIM's charitable and welfare programmes. These include adult education, housing, medicare and welfare projects in aid of the poor and anti-drug programmes aimed at combating the huge drug problem among Malaysian youth. ABIM also offers loans and grants to help its members to go into self-employment.

The return of religious sects in Turkey

Although Turkey is a secular republic, there is little doubt that recent years have witnessed a significant Islamic revival. While there are many reasons for this, including the influence of the Iranian revolution, a major explanation lies in militant secularism pursued by the centrist leadership in the name of Kemalism. The failure of secularist development to promote social justice has shaken the confidence of the masses for whom Islam, notwithstanding official disestablishment in the 1920s, never ceased to function as a source of self-identity and as a code of conduct (Mardin 1982, Margulies and Yildizoglu 1988).

As in Malaysia and elsewhere, Islamic resurgence in Turkey manifests a remarkable degree of differentiation in terms of goals, ideologies and organizational strategies. Broadly speaking, three general categories of Islamic groups can be identified. First there are groups with pro-state political aims. These are religious organizations, allied to some political party such as the Motherland Party or the National Salvation Party or the True Path Party, seeking to achieve their aims through the democratic political process. Second, there are the extremist and militant organizations (both on the ideological left and the right, including Khomeini-style fundamentalists), which are typically underground with outside connections and funding. Third, there is a large, heterogeneous group of religious sects, i.e. *tarikats* (religious orders), some dating back to the fourteenth century. Typically, these religious orders have been organized along the standard Anatolian patron— client basis (Kiray 1982) providing charity in return for total obedience to the leader (*sheyk*). These have experienced the fastest growth in the recent past, as a sort of underground Islam, since they are officially banned (Saylan 1987, Dumont 1987, Middle East Report 1988).

What is the explanation for their reappearance and rapid growth? The answer is provided from history. In ancient times, *tarikats* were voluntary organizations, organized around *tekkes* (convents), created by *waqfs* and other Islamic charities in the name of an almsgiver or benefactor doing God's will. Thus *tarikats* were identified with a rich donor or a charismatic *sheyk* serving a particular community or social order such as the Bektasi, Naksebendi or Nurcu. Service included provision of welfare in aid of the poor, education in a *medrese* (religious school), as well as ritual prayers and moral guidance in the *tekke* under the leadership of the *sheyk*.

The secular Kemalist ideology banned all the *tarikats* as part of the wholesale disestablishment of Islam, promising instead the benefits of state-led development. Ritualist feudal allegiance to the *sheyk* was to be replaced by nationalism, and the welfare services of the *tarikats* were to be taken over by the secular state. Education and modernization via industrialization were the instruments of secularist development. Profit-driven urban-centred capitalist growth, however, frustrated these expected promises.

The sects have now re-emerged to fill the vacuum. Some like the Naksebendi, Bektasi and Nurcu now even provide the services of employment agencies for their followers, finding jobs not only in urban centres in Turkey, but sponsoring Turkish guest-workers to West Berlin and other European cities. In return, these workers remit part of their earnings as contributions to the *tarikats*, which then use these funds to run religious institutions, to produce Islamic publications and offer welfare services in Turkey and Western Europe (Mumcu 1987, Saylan 1987, Abadan-Unat 1985).

Conclusion

In the final analysis, Islamic resurgence in both Turkey and Malaysia appears as a response to uneven and badly managed secularist growth. While post-war growth achieved impressive results in terms of macro-economic performance, it also upset the traditional socio-economic order. Despite the initial promises of the centrist elites, the selected growth strategies failed to narrow the gap between the leaders and followers. At first, the followers tolerated short-term sacrifice in terms of consumption and living standards for the sake of nationalist reconstruction. They even submerged their faith and shifted allegiance from traditional Islam to a new ideology of secular modernization.

But the post-war growth process has been mismanaged by the Turkish and Malaysian elites. Pursued in a top-down manner, with little accountability of the leaders to the masses, it violated the Islamic ideal of social justice. The secularist leaders in charge of post-war modernization promised the followers tangible benefits. When, after several decades of patience and sacrifice, the mass of followers only saw poverty and injustice, they joined the Islamic resurgence.

What emerges is the fact that the modernizing role of the national leadership matched neither the expectations of the followers, nor, for that matter, the leadership's own initial promises. In particular, the leadership failed to promote growth with equity because it relied excessively on non-competitive state capitalism at the expense of Islamic social justice. As a result, the distance between the leaders and followers widened and the organic relationship in the body politic weakened, becoming increasingly more vulnerable to Islamic reaction and extremism. The next two chapters will illustrate the historical and cultural roots of this organic relationship. Chapter 3 will briefly survey the age-old quest for Islamic social justice, while Chapter 4 will discuss the related question of whether or not Islamic values are compatible with economic development and modernization.

Chapter three

The Islamic social contract
The quest for social justice and the problem of legislation

A major conclusion of the previous chapter is that, while countries like Malaysia and Turkey have pioneered in adopting a modern public policy in the Islamic world, they have yet to achieve an *organic balance* between development policy and Islamic values that bind these societies together. Organic balance does not mean conformity or regimentation, but responsiveness between the ruler and the ruled. It requires that there should be adequate communication from the grass roots to the top and accountability in the reverse direction. When this two-way relationship exists in a functioning and institutionalized manner, the parts of the body politic are in an organic balance. A strong body politic exists when the political and economic system are synchronized with an indigenous culture so that public policy outcomes reflect societal preferences.

In Islam, the ruler–ruled relations are governed by the Islamic social contract. The purpose of this chapter is to sketch out the evolution of this contract from the time of the Prophet in order to find out why Muslim societies were unable to sustain a secular (i.e. this-worldly) problem-solving public policy tradition through man-made legislation.

The Constitution of Medina was Islam's first social contract (Serjeant 1964). It was the first man-made legislation for social justice enacted in the golden age of Islam. Its intent was to regulate the economic and social affairs of the city by establishing rules and procedures for conflict resolution including dispute settlement arising from war, e.g. blood money. It was a written document concluded soon after Muhammad's arrival in Medina. It was contracted between the various communities of Medina, including the Jews, under the leadership of the Prophet. It was based on the principles of private property and a competitive profit-oriented economy.

The Constitution is significant from several points of view, but in particular in terms of the fact that it was incomplete in its coverage, secular in nature, and relative in time and location. It was incomplete because it covered only *temporal* matters; it excluded scripture. It was concerned with secular (i.e. this-worldly) affairs. This is especially important because it demonstrates the significance which the Prophet himself attached to material and temporal pursuits. The Constitution was a brilliant model of man-made conflict resolution. It was relative in time and location because it dealt with current social and economic needs and problems relevant to the people of Medina at that time. Since the city contained traders and Jews, and since this was a time of war and conflict, many of the clauses of the Constitution naturally related to the regulation of trade, to the conduct of war and blood money, and to the Jews. The Jews received so much attention in the document, not because they were a *chosen people*, deserving special attention, but rather because Islam showed tolerance towards the 'People of the Book', i.e. Jews and Christians.

The Constitution signified a great social, economic and political reform in conformity with the Islamic ideal of social justice. It set a secular model and precedent, giving high priority to the orderly regulation of earthly pursuits. If this model and precedent had been observed in later periods, Islam would have evolved as a religion closer to Protestant ethics rather than one of military conquest.

The tradition of militarism and *coup d'états* evolved during the Umayyad (AD 661–750) and the Abbasid (AD 750–1258) dynasties at the expense of orderly government and administration (Crone 1980). The first major reforms in public administration in Islam were the contributions of the Turkish tribesmen at the time of the Abbasid Caliphate. Initially arriving as mercenary soldiers, the Turks soon emerged to provide effective government and man-made rules to consolidate Islam as an urbanized, sedentary civilization (Hourani 1981).

In spite of the fact that the Constitution of Medina 'is one of the most remarkable documents in the history of early Islam' (Gil 1974: 44), it has remained a virtually unknown document. There are only a few references to it, first in the *Sirah* of Ibn Ishaq and later in the *Bidayah* of Ibn Kathir (Sarjeant 1964: 4). Some scholars dismiss the Medina precedent as an insignificant document concerned with inter-clan obligations (Hodgson 1974: I, 173). But it could have become Islam's Magna Carta. Unfortunately, subsequent generations of the *ulama* failed to design problem-solving theories. Instead they encouraged a tradition of esoteric theological commentary (Rahman 1982) and they discouraged works concerned with secular human affairs. Thus, the works of Ibn

Khaldun, whose *Muqaddimah* contains economic theories parallel-ing Adam Smith (Boulakia 1971), were systematically banned by the *ulama* of Al-Ahzar, the oldest Islamic university, which resisted modernizing its curriculum until the 1970s (Rahman 1982: 67–8).

Islam and social justice

Islam is a universalistic, egalitarian religion of social justice with a special appeal to the poor. It proclaims the equality of all, irre-spective of wealth and status, in submission to one God. Not only are they promised equality before God, it is declared that all resources are God's gift to man, meant for *adl*, just distribution. 'The basic elan of the Qur'an' states Fazlur Rahman (1982: 19), one of the major Islamic modernists, is 'the stress on socio-economic justice and essential human egalitarianism'. This stress is the ideal or the guiding principle. 'All that follows by way of Qur'anic legislation in the field of private and public life . . . has social justice and the building of an egalitarian community as its end'.

But Islam is more than egalitarianism; it is revolutionary in attributing poverty to maldistribution caused by unfairness, oppression and exploitation. This occurs not only in legal or political contexts, but also in all markets through unfair trade practices such as profiteering, monopolistic prices, usury, bribery or cheating with weights. The Prophet himself a successful trader, sought to regulate these unfair trade practices as demonstrated in the Constitution of Medina.

Islam's universality derives from the principle of unity, *tawhid*, and the solidarity of its community of believers, the *Umma*. Islam proclaims a just socio-economic order transcending national, political or racial boundaries. This solidarity is not only ethical and religious but is also economic, being based on domestic and inter-national trade conducted on fair terms of trade. That is why Islamic economics is a synthesis of ethics and economics (Naqvi 1981, Choudhury 1986).

The promise of social justice in this life requires man-made legislation to regulate current socio-economic affairs. This is the fundamental importance of the Constitution of Medina which set an excellent precedent. Although the precedent of Medina was lost by the Islamic scholars, the ideal of Islamic social justice never lost its appeal among the grass roots. Unfortunately, the state, as the instrument for the fulfilment of Islamic social justice, evolved in a dysfunctional way. This was due, primarily, to the failure of Islamic scholars to sustain the precedent of Medina.

State, nation and Islam

The Islamic tradition of state, as it evolved after the death of Muhammad, differs radically from the western secularist state. The idea of a secular state is the by-product of European positivism. In the positivist tradition, the *raison d'être* of the state is the collective good, meaning national progress or development. The nation is a culturally and geographically distinct entity and these attributes sustain social cohesion and political consensus on most public issues. The strength and survival of the nation is secured through legislation which articulates political consensus, implementing it via public policy intended to promote social and economic development for the sake of improving the human condition. This human condition, at any given point in time, is perceived to be sub-optimal; there is always room for improvement.

The implementing arm of the state, i.e. the government, is the instrument for effecting such improvement. Governments are judged by results. A good government is one which succeeds in actually improving the living standards by means of public policy in education, housing, employment and social services, and in establishing appropriate economic, legal, cultural and national institutions. The genius of western political theory is that, by the trial and error method of parliamentary democracy, it has evolved a system of getting rid of 'bad' rulers or governments in a peaceful and orderly manner. This intellectual tradition, built around the abstract theory of state and dating back to Plato, is the cumulative contribution of numerous philosophers and thinkers among whom Machiavelli, Locke, Burke, Jefferson, Rousseau, Mill and Weber are only some of the more notable names. This secular tradition continues today with exciting new contributions by Buchanan, North, Olson and other public-choice theorists (see Chapter 8).

The secular idea of a nation-state as an instrument in the service of citizens is the corollary of the positive theory of state: public servants in the *public service* are servants of the public, providing public goods for the good of all without exclusion. These officials are not masters, but servants of the citizens to whom, of course, they are accountable. This accountability is indirect, extending through political leaders who can be replaced peacefully through periodic elections in which a popular judgement on leadership performance and competence is made.

The western idea of a serving state via public servants and accountable rulers has important religious roots. One of the fundamental differences between Islam and Christianity concerns the idea of *original sin*. For Christians, Christ died to liberate man from sin. Thus, in contemporary terms, some theologists, such as Gustavo Gutierrez (1973), who regard sin as the root of poverty, oppression and injustice, have formulated action-oriented Liberation Theology based on the idea of development through liberation.

Islam, on the other hand, recognizes no original sin (Siddiqi 1981). Man is the Viceroy of God upon earth (Qur'an II: 30). Therefore, man is not regarded, as in Christianity, as inherently sinful, bound to seek divine grace for redemption. Before Luther, the church was in the business of selling indulgences for redemption, but afterwards the idea of temporal prosperity as demonstration of divine grace became a causal force behind the rise of capitalism and Protestant ethics. This is the thesis of Weber and Tawney, among others. In the age of reason and rationalism, history was delinked from transcendent form; the ball of history was taken from the heavens and thrown into the hands of man. Descartes' words, 'I think, therefore, I am', became the new gospel of science and discovery. In the nineteenth century under the influence of utilitarianism, and later under Fabianism, the instrumentalist theory of a secular state, designing and administering public policy, began to take roots, with a cumulative process of democratization via enfranchisement, public education and, finally, the welfare state. In other words, the fall of man cumulatively and progressively led to the secular quest for his perfectibility and, finally, promoted the idea of the nation-state as the instrument of this perfectibility.

In Islamic scholarship, no such progressive evolution of public policy occurred. For one thing, *nass* (clear religious text) was interpreted by the *ulama* as dogma that left no room for the evolution of nation-state (Piscatori 1986). National sovereignty was attributed exlusively to God and scientific knowledge actively discouraged. Likewise, a state not based on piety, however symbolic or superficial, was denounced as un-Islamic. Therefore, secularism, i.e. policies based on science and man-made rules rather than divine criteria, has been rejected as anti-Islamic (Al-Attas 1978). Traditionally, a Muslim is not a nationalist, or citizen of a nation-state; he has no political identity, only a religious membership in the *Umma* (see Figure 5.1, p. 100). For a traditional Muslim, Islam is the sole and sufficient identification tag and nationalism and nation-states are 'obstacles' (Ghayasuddin 1987).

In a doctrinal sense these political deficiencies stem from the Islamic world-view based on *tawhid*, i.e. that the cosmos is a unified, harmonious whole, centred around God omnipotent and omnipresent. In this ordered world-view, there is no room for such reductionist ideas as 'nation' or 'state'.

In Islam, time is an ethical value intended for service to God. Time as an economic resource (for example time devoted to income generation) is meant merely for sustenance, i.e. as a means, not as an end in itself. A believer is inherently good, though initially devoid of knowledge, both scientific and divine. But man is endowed with ability to acquire knowledge; for he is the bearer of God's trust. He seeks God because his vocation is total submission (Qur'an XXXIII: 21). Accordingly in the Islamic tradition, man, by his nature, does not need, and will not submit to, secular authority. His mission is simply to perform *ibadah*, to submit to God in prayer. With spiritual resignation, he may dismiss his current condition, his poverty or wealth, as transitory and tentative; he may seek solace and contentment in the hope that his real rewards are in the real other-world to follow the Day of Judgement. Thus in Islamic tradition the idea of a secular state, with a government administering public policy and having responsibility for the betterment of the socio-economic human condition, has been generally dismissed as diverting the attention of the pious to trivial worldly pursuits at the expense of the real mission of preparation for the life hereafter.

Spiritually, Islam recognizes only one, divine authority; no dualism exists as between civilian and religious authority. The dualism which is recognized is mystical: between the 'real' other-world and this transitory temporal one. In the temporal world, where man's mission is submission, and development implies human development to reach God, there is no convention to give to Caesar his due and to God his. In practice, of course, there is always an Islamic Caesar, a political system and bureaucracy. But legitimacy remains a puzzling problem, for the Islamic tradition fails to explain by what means an Islamic Caesar should take hold of power and how legitimate succession (i.e. transfer of power) should occur. It does, however, explain how a just ruler should conduct himself: in accordance with the Islamic social contract.

The Islamic social contract

What is the Islamic tradition of the ruler—ruled relationship? It is a feudal relationship which evolved from the idealized Islamic social contract dating back to the golden age of the Prophet and the Four Righteous Caliphs. Like a train stopped in its tracks, the ruler—ruled theory never passed beyond the age of feudalism.

In the ideal Islamic state, sovereignty belongs to God who is the source of legitimate authority. The ruler holds office in divine trusteeship (the Caliphate) and he is entrusted to rule wisely and justly. In return, the subjects are expected to show loyalty, obedience and respect. The saying attributed to the Prophet is:

> I charge the Caliph after me to fear God, and I commend the community of the Muslims to him, to respect the great among them and have pity on the small, to honor the learned among them, not to strike them and humiliate them, not to oppress them and drive them to unbelief, not to close his doors to them and allow the strong to devour the weak.
>
> (Lewis 1987: I, 150)

Early and medieval Islamic scholars wrote great and learned volumes on the rules of government and statecraft, including the obligations and eligibility of rulers. An example is the work of Al-Mawardi in the eleventh century entitled *The Contract of the Imamate*, which states:

> The office of Imam was set up in order to replace the office of Prophet in the defense of the faith and the government of the world. By general consensus (*ijma'*), from which only Al-Assam dissents, the investiture of whichsoever member of the community exercises the functions of Imam is obligatory.
>
> (Lewis 1987: I, 171–9)

Al-Mawardi then lists the duties and obligations of the Imam, the eligibility conditions, and the qualifications of electors charged with the responsibility of choosing the Imam.

Why did the Islamic social contract fail to flourish?

The Islamic statecraft, based on the divine-legislated social contract, failed to grow and flourish past the age of feudalism. It became frozen, fossilized in time. Why? What is the explanation? A good part of the answer must lie in the slow death of intellectual creativity which had distinguished the earlier *ulama*. As a result of such creativity, these great *ulama* enjoyed tremendous prestige and independence, able to withstand even the most tyrannical or powerful rulers. By the fourteenth century, however, the quality of Islamic scholarship began a slow and long process of decline and decay. For example, an anonymous contemporary commentator of the Ottoman Sultan Murad I (1360–89) was lamenting the end of 'The good old days' when the

> '. . . rulers were not greedy. Whatever came into their hands they gave away again, and they did not know what a treasury was. But

when Hayreddin Pasha came to the Gate [of the government] greedy scholars became companions of the rulers. They began by displaying piety and then went on to issue rulings [*fetva*]. "He who is a ruler must have a treasury" they said. At that time they won over the rulers and influenced them. Greed and oppression appeared. Indeed where there is greed there must be oppression. In our time it has increased. Whatever oppression and corruption there is in this country is due to scholars.'

(Lewis 1987: I, 135–6)

Thus, gradually, the independence of the *ulama*, which had originally ensured a system of Islamic checks and balances in the state, was destroyed. Corruption and bribery became systemic. Intellectual creativity gave way to expediency and greed. Blind submission to the dictates of tyrannical rulers became standard, justified on the authority of the great eighth century jurist, Ghazali, who had ruled that the necessity of public order supersedes the need for justice. Principle, i.e. the rule of law, was sacrificed for expediency. Gradually, this doctrine came to legitimize any *de facto* authority. Despots, autocrats and dictators (including Napoleon in 1799) easily co-opted the *ulama* to gain political legitimacy for the status quo, however unjust or whatever the means of succession to power.

Closing the 'Gate of Knowledge'

Perhaps the single most damaging blow to Islamic knowledge came in the tenth century under the Abbasids when the 'Gate of *Ijtihad*', knowledge based on reasoning, was declared closed (Esposito 1984: 19). The consensus of *ulama* was that the Islamic way of life had been adequately delineated by previous scholarship. Henceforth there could be no justification for independent judgement or rational inquiry. Future generations were bound to *taqlid*, unquestioned acceptance and memorization of precedents and interpretations of past authority. With the gates of rational inquiry thus closed, no scholar in future could ever qualify as *mujtahid*, i.e. those entitled to original thinking.

Closing the gates of rational knowledge and independent reasoning has had a disastrous effect on Islamic science and education. Secular science was replaced by theology and dogma, and public education, which had flourished in the first two centuries of the Abbasid dynasty, lost its dynamism and creativity. It became institutionalized around the dysfunctional *taqlid* system of learning by memorizing and blind imitation. Gradually, the reactionary *mullahs* and *ulama* assumed a monopoly control of public education, morality and opinion, and, in the process, advanced the cause of *jahiliyya* (mass ignorance), fatalism and underdevelopment as effectively as imperialism and colonial exploitation.

The Gate of *Ijtihad* remained closed until the nineteenth century when Islamic modernists, notably Afghani, Abduh and Iqbal, clamoured for freeing Islamic knowledge from its 'dogmatic slumber' as a precondition for adapting it to the requirements of life in a modern world (Iqbal quoted in Esposito 1988: 142). During the preceding nine centuries only a few notable Islamic scholars dared to conduct independent reasoning and claim authority as *mujtahid*. Ibn Taimiya (1262–1328) and Jalal ad-Din as-Suyuti (1445–1505) were the notable original thinkers along with non-conformists such as Ibn Khaldun (1332–1406).

Following the Reformation and Renaissance in Europe, the distance between Islamic and European science and technology increasingly widened. By the age of imperialism, the internal weaknesses of the Muslim societies had become so endemic that they were no match for external domination and exploitation. The *ulama* contributed to this process by resisting technological inventions such as the printing press as un-Islamic. Here is an account of the reaction surrounding the introduction of printing into the Ottoman Empire which occurred as late as 1728:

> At the first rumor of the proposed innovation alarm spread throughout Constantinople. The many thousands of scribes, living by copying books, saw their profession in peril. The theologians found the new project profane; the emanations of human intelligence, they alleged, having always been handed down to posterity by writing, ought not to be subjected to any less carefully made transmission. A third party, the scholars and those who cherished literature for its own sake, were disturbed by fears lest the precious art of caligraphy, which shed glory even on the noblest thoughts . . . should be lost to mankind.
>
> (Emin 1914: 22)

Islamic education

Islam has always put great emphasis on knowledge, *ilm*, and its acquisition through learning. One of the key sayings of the Prophet was an injunction to the believers to seek knowledge, even if it meant travelling to far-away China. The importance of knowledge in Islam is symbolized by the fact that the very first word of the first revelation is 'Read', a command given to Muhammad in his sleep at the age of forty:

> Read: In the name of thy Lord who created
> Created man from a clot
> Read: And thy Lord is the Most Bounteous,
> Who taught by the pen,
> Taught man that which he knew not.
>
> (XCVI: 1–5)

But what exactly is meant by 'knowledge'? In early Islam, there was no public education. Al-Azhar in Cairo, the first university in the world, was started in the tenth century. Before then, Islamic centres of learning, notably in Persia, were built around persons of eminence, and emphasized memorizing the Qu'ran, copying down traditions from the Prophet and deriving legal interpretations from them. Mass Islamic education in *medreses* did not emerge until medieval times. Although in the meantime the Islamic scholars had rediscovered Greek rational sciences and philosophy, Islamic law and theology remained the central part of the educational system in the *medreses*.

After the closure of the Gate of *Ijtihad*, rational and secular knowledge was suppressed in favour of theological learning. This has been well put by Fazlur Rahman (1982: 34–5):

> But the most fateful distinction that came to be made in the course of time was between the 'religious sciences' (*'ulūm shar'iya*) or 'traditional sciences' (*'ulum naqlīya*), and the 'rational or secular sciences' (*'ulūm 'aqlīya* or *ghayr shar'īya*), toward which a gradually stiffening and stifling attitude was adopted. There are several reasons for this perilous development. First of all, the view is expressed recurrently that, since knowledge is vast while life is short, one must fix priorities; and these will naturally be in favour of the religious sciences, upon whose acquisition one's success in the hereafter depends. . . . The spread of Sufism, which – in the interests of cultivating an internal spiritual life and direct religious experience – was generally inimical not only to rational sciences but to all intellectualism. . . . The third important reason for the gradual decline of science and philosophy was, of course, that while higher degree holders of religious sciences could get jobs as qadis or muftis a philosopher or a scientist was limited to court employment.
>
> (Rahman 1982: 33–4)

Thus the *ulama*, the moral voice of society, became increasingly reactionary and anti-intellectual, avoiding concern for human problems, suppressing creativity and preaching the virtues of patience and fatalism even in the face of injustice and tyranny. One of the most famous Islamic philosophers was Hamid al-Ghazali (1059–1111), whose book *Tahafut al-Falasifa* (The Incoherence of the Philosophers) had a tremendous influence. It was an attack on rationalism and secular knowledge. Al-Ghazali, who began by placing great virtue on self-doubt as a precondition of man's yearning for knowledge, concluded by sacrificing original thinking to theological dogma. He argued that the reason why faith in Islam was declining was due to the respect people showed for pre-Islamic philosophers such as Socrates, Hippocrates, Plato and Aristotle. He attempted to discredit their secularism by demonstrating the incoherence of their arguments. Ibn Rushd, known as Averroes, criticized and rejected al-Ghazali's arguments (Guillaume 1956: 136–8). However, it was too late: Islamic theology, and the reactionary *ulama*, won easily over secular knowledge. *Taqlid*, blind imitation, became the leading Islamic paradigm of learning.

The nonconformists

There were, however, exceptional and nonconformist Islamic scholars as well. Ibn Khaldun's *Muqaddimah* written in 1377, can be compared to Adam Smith's *Wealth of Nations*, which was written four centuries later and represented the start of modern economics. Many economic principles, including price theory and labour value theory of production, were expounded in amazingly clear language in the *Muqaddimah*, but unfortunately, because Khaldun was a nonconformist in his emphasis on rationalism, his influence on Islamic scholarship was minimal. He has been 'discovered' in more recent years only after widespread recognition and admiration in the west (Rosenthal 1984). Ibn Khaldun is discussed in more detail in Chapter 4.

Ibn Khaldun seems to have had some belated influence among sixteenth-century Ottoman scholars, in particular Mustafa Ali (1541–1600) who, like Khaldun, glorified the principle of royal authority. The central problem for Ali, as for Khaldun, was to explain why empires decline. Ali was writing at the time of Murad III (1574–95) when the Ottoman Empire was already showing signs of decline due to abuse of authority, corruption among the state officials, lack of responsibility and economic disruption. He believed, as did Ibn Khaldun, that 'ultimately only restoration of royal authority and responsibility could solve these difficulties'. (Fleischer in Lawrence 1984: 52).

Mustafa Ali's intellectual peers were Naima and Kinalizade Ali

Celebi who cite Khaldun more explicitly. This is evident in the case of the Circle of Equity, the eight interconnected principles of good government which represented the benchmark for these early Ottoman reformers:

> There can be no royal authority without the military
> There can be no military without wealth
> The subjects produce the wealth
> Justice preserves the subjects' loyalty to the sovereign
> Justice requires harmony in the world
> The world is a garden, its walls are the state
> The Holy Law [*shari'ah*] orders the state
> There is no support for the *shari'ah* except through royal authority
>
> (Fleischer, ibid.: 49)

Ali, who served as district governor in Jeddah and, therefore, had practical experience with the emerging weaknesses of the Empire, fixed the date of Ottoman decline with the reign of Selim the Sot (1566−74) when the pursuit of pleasure replaced responsibility as the primary duty of the Sultan. Up to and including the reign of Suleyman the Lawgiver, Ottoman power and success rested on meritocracy and commitment to the pursuit of justice:

> for Ali the hallmarks of Ottoman success and the determinants of Ottoman legitimacy [were]; impartial justice, meritocracy, administrative morality, and loyalty to the dynasty.
>
> (Fleischer, ibid.: 61)

These qualities ensured legitimacy and loyalty among both the Muslim and non-Muslim subjects. The most successful sultans had achieved secular reforms: Mehmet the Conqueror was a great patron of higher education, starting the imperial university in Istanbul; Suleyman the Lawgiver, consolidating and codifying man-made laws, *kanun*. These reforms benefited the people and, as stated in the Circle of Equity, guaranteed loyalty, harmony, and survival of the state.

> 'A state', Ali writes, 'has two treasures: one its silver and gold; the other its subjects. The latter must be won and kept by justice, and is the more important, for without it the momentary treasure will pass to another.'
>
> (Fleischer, ibid.: 55)

The reactionaries and traditionalists

But such views were like voices of strangers in the dark. The dominant view has belonged to the traditionalists and conformist *ulama* who, while fatalistically submitting to unjust rulers, preached patience and obedience to the masses. While claiming to be the moral voice of society, they intepreted these values as the law of Islam, *shari'ah*. Implicitly, and sometimes explicitly, they argued that God's Law was constant and unchangeable.

Reactionaries and traditionalists reject any separation of state and religion. Their views in the Malay and Turkish contexts were discussed in Chapter 2. They yearn for the restoration of some past ideal state, not according to man-made legislation, but strictly in conformity with the *shari'ah*. The Shaikh of Al-Azhar, one of the major voices of Islamic orthodoxy, recently warned the Egyptian prime minister and the speaker of the People's Assembly that 'no *ijtihad* is allowed to any human if a *shari'ah* text exists' (Ayubi 1980: 490–1).

Traditionalists and reactionaries are undemocratic. They dream of a theocracy along the lines of Ayatollah Khomeini or some feudal model for guiding the Islamic society backwards along the straight and narrow path of Islam in the name of Islamization as purification. Maududi from Pakistan is one of the most influential proponents of this school. He founded the Jama'at-i Islami to implement his programme in Pakistan. While he recognizes *jahiliyya*, mass ignorance, as a principal source of Islamic backwardness, he is clearly undemocratic and considers capitalism and secular democracy as the first delusion of mankind (Maududi 1984: 100). His strong preference is for a theocracy of the *ulama*:

> Islam will become an operative reality in our times when men possessed of faith and integrity and a clear vision of the Islamic Order, people who are in the vanguard of man's intellectual life and have the competence to run the affairs of the world assume the reins of leadership.
>
> (Ahmad and Ansari 1979: 378)

The modernists and progressives

The reopening of the Gate of *Ijtihad* began in the mid-nineteenth century. It was pioneered, in particular, by the Islamic reformer and Pan-Islamic activist Jamal al-Din al-Afghani (1838–99). Afghani, who viewed religion in instrumentalist terms, was highly

critical of Islamic scholars who wished to divide scientific knowledge on religious lines as 'Muslim science' and 'European science'
and he argued that there is no incompatibility between science and
knowledge and the Islamic faith. The contradiction was between
dogma and free human enquiry based on reason. Thus, he put
reason on at least equal footing with divine inspiration (Keddie
1972).

The compatibility between Islam and rationalism was central in
the ideas of Muhammad Abduh (1849–1905), the Egyptian
philosopher who was greatly influenced by Afghani. Abduh drew a
clear distinction between duties to God, *ibadah*, and social duties
arising from interpersonal relations, *muamalat*. As a social
reformer, his particular concern was the latter sphere and he was
especially critical of the Muslim practice of polygamy and the low
social status of women:

> To be sure, the Muslims have been at fault in the education and
> training of women, and of acquainting them with their rights;
> and we acknowledge that we have failed to follow the guidance
> of our religion, so that we have become an argument against it.
>
> (quoted in Esposito 1984: 49)

In more general terms, Abduh was a social relativist who believed
that every generation had the moral duty to interpret scripture for
itself. He stated that the

> Qur'an and *hadith* laid down specific rules about worship; about
> relations with other men, they laid down for the most part
> general principles, leaving it to men to apply to all the circum-
> stances of life. This was the legitimate sphere of *ijtihad*.
>
> (Hourani 1970: 148)

Another notable Islamic reformer was Muhammad Iqbal (1875–
1938), co-worker of Ali Jinnah, founder of Pakistan. He was a
great poet, admired by Hindu and Muslim alike. His romanticism
was tempered with realism and it moved him to abandon the idea of
a united India in favour of Muslim nationalism and join forces with
Jinnah, the secularist leader of the movement to create Pakistan.
As a modernist, Iqbal believed that the Muslims must once again
reassert their right to *ijtihad*, and he argued that this right should
be transferred from conservative *ulama* to a national assembly or
legislature acting for the community.

A major theme with these progressives and modernists was the
view that a synthesis of Islamic and western law is warranted as a
necessity for adapting to change. They regarded Islam not as an

absolute, constant system but as a dynamic and creative force quite compatible with modernization. They saw Islam's encouragement of individual reasoning, *ijtihad* and rational investigation as being necessary for contemporary reform. Their greatest contribution lay in their efforts to reopen the 'Gate of *Ijtihad*'.

Yet, these Islamic progressives were essentially *ad hoc* reformers and political activists, rather than thinkers proposing coherent social and political theories. Their thoughts contained several inconsistencies. Though anti-western, they nevertheless admired western civilization and saw Islamic reform in largely western terms. While critical of *taqlid*, they idealized the west and sought to imitate European ideas of liberty and freedom. They correctly drew a causal link between Reformation and rational knowledge, but they ignored the historic shift of economic centre of gravity from the Middle East to the west as a result of the discovery of the New World and alternative trade routes to the Old Silk Road. In short, they missed the simple, but crucial, link between civilization and economic prosperity. As a result, their reforms related to political and social, but regrettably not to economic, aspects of public policy.

The secularists

Secularists make a clear distinction between faith and politics. This life matters, therefore the human condition here must be improved by legislation and man's deliberate action.

An underrated thinker of this school is Ziya Gokalp, the intellectual father of Turkish nationalist identity who endorsed Ataturk's move to abolish the Caliphate in 1924 (Berkes 1959). Gokalp (quoted in Ozbudun 1984: 42) stated:

> Theocracy is the system in which laws are made by Caliphs and Sultans who are regarded as the Shadows of God on earth. Clericalism refers to the acceptance of traditions, claimed to be originally instituted by God, as unchangeable laws and to the belief that these laws can be interpreted only by spiritual authorities, believed to be the interpreters of God. . . . The state that is completely freed from these two characteristics of the medieval state is called the Modern State. In a modern state the right to legislate and to administer directly belongs to the people.

For secularists like Gokalp, as for limited rationalists like Abduh, *ibadah* (prayer) is a personal duty of man to God. Social relations, *muamalah*, need to be updated and modernized by man-made legislation to fit changing social conditions. Legislation is also necessary to regulate civil, commercial and criminal cases. A secular state is the instrument of such legislation, and there is nothing wrong in patterning legislation or the state on the western constitutional model to provide responsible government responding to human needs and problems.

Yusuf Akurca, another influential rationalist of the Young Turk era, was even more emphatic than Gokalp about the need for westernization by adopting western civilization in its entirety. He argued that civilization is a whole and should be adopted *in toto*. Contrary to those Islamic reformers who were willing to borrow only western technology, but not European ways of thought, Akurca declared that it would be absurd to try and separate thought from material aspects of civilization (Ozbudun in Evin *et al.* 1984: 33).

Is there still an Islamic social contract?

Despite these sharp differences between the traditionalists, progressives and secularists, the promise of an Islamic social justice persists as a social phenomenon. It exists in all Islamic societies, traditional, progressive or secular, although in different forms. The Islamic social contract remains socially relevant, existing in the Muslim mind as a binding 'Covenant with God' (Al-Attas 1978: 80). In practice, it is always subject to arbitrary interpretation, and yet it constitutes an Islamic 'core' belief defining personal and group identity. At the highest level of generality, it serves as a common bond among the Muslim community, the *Umma*.

Despite dissenting and conflicting opinion, certain key elements of the Islamic social contract can be identified. In general, normative terms, four elements can be distinguished.

First, power and sovereignty belong to God. The ruler holds power in trust of God to whom alone he is answerable.

Second, the basis of power is divine legitimacy rather than popular support. The ruler's legitimacy derives from his trusteeship of God. Hence acquisition of power by force of arms is fatalistically accepted and legitimized, provided only that the ruler does God's will. What counts is the quality of the ruler.

Third, the ruler's quality is judged according to the criterion of righteousness, i.e. how wisely and justly he implements God's will.

Fourth, God is the ultimate judge of the ruler's justice but during this life judgement is given by the *ulama*, the learned Islamic scholars who then instruct, but do not require consent from, the people.

The Islamic social contract can be reduced to an archaic but pragmatic trade-off: an exchange of ruler's justice and protection in return for the subjects' obedience. In this simple trade-off, how the ruler acquires his power is irrelevant; neither is his authority challengeable. The faithful subjects are merely expected to submit to the existing political status quo, whether formed legally or illegally, peacefully or by force of arms.

Cultural relativity

The Islamic social contract is far from a monolithic covenant. In theory, divine law, *shari'ah*, may be viewed as constant, firm belief in the truth of Islam. But, as demonstrated by the Prophet himself with the Constitution of Medina, this constant truth has to be applied to the specific circumstances of particular times and places which, unlike truth, change. In other words, divine law requires adaptation in order to fit cultural relativity.

Cultural relativity reflects the fact that, although all Muslims are equal members of the *Umma*, individual circumstances nevertheless differ reflecting differing needs, constraints and potentials. Thus, an Indonesian rice farmer in Java, say, can hardly have aspirations and constraints identical to those of a peasant in the Egyptian desert. Their spiritual and material needs are shaped not only by Islam but also by their respective cultural environments. These cultural differences entail different human needs which, in turn, necessitate culture-specific formulations of public policy based on man-made legislation ready-made to fit culture-specific circumstances.

Some parts of the Muslim world have coped with cultural relativity better than others. This can be illustrated with reference to the Arab, Turkish and Malay conceptions of legislation. As regards the Arab and Turkish conceptions, these have been succinctly put by Count Ostrorog, the legal advisor to the last Ottoman Sultan, some fifty years ago:

> The Arab mind remained inviolably faithful to the following fundamental conception [of legislation]: Legislative power belongs to God; Executive Power belongs to the Calife; the Doctors of the Law, who interpret the Law, are the indispensable intermediaries between God and the Calife. The consequence of that conception was that no such thing as a Statute, an Edict, drafted in systematic legal shape and promulgated as binding, is to be found in the whole of Arab Mohammedan history.

Not so with the Turks. The Turkish Hans professed to be, and certainly were, very good Moslems, but from the outset they asserted their right to enact regulations that were to be obeyed because they so willed, because at the top of the document they deigned to write in their purple Imperial ink: *Mujebinje'amel oluna*! which I think may be adequately translated by, 'Be it acted as enacted' – or because they caused their sign-manual *Tughra*, figuring the impression of their open hand, to head the document as a mark of its Imperial origin.

(Ostrorog 1927: 42)

This Turkish cultural variation can be traced to their pre-Islamic tradition of *yasa*, supreme law, which manifested itself in the Ottoman practice of *kanun*, man-made law, as well as more particular edicts such as *firmans* and *irades* (Shaw 1976: 134–5; Shaw and Shaw 1977: 37–9). Paralleling this Turkish civil law tradition, the Ottomans had a highly developed system of canon law culminating in the office of *Sheyh-ul-Islam* (the chief of the clergy) managing a large subordinate religious bureaucracy consisting of *muftis*, *kadis* etc., in each *sanjak* (province of the Empire), rendering Islamic justice by such means as *fetvas* (legal opinions). The *fetvas* of the *Sheyh-ul-Islam* had absolute effect even during the reign of the most powerful sultans such as Suleyman the Magnificent (Lybyer 1913). As the Ottoman Empire declined, so did the quality of their legislation.

In the Malay conception of law and legislation, there is not only *shari'ah*, divine law, but highly localized *adat* (customary laws), some written, some oral, and many tracing back to pre-Islamic times. *Adat* laws are subject to great regional variation as, for example, among Negeri Sembilan, Perak, Malacca and elsewhere (Hooker 1970). The administration of *shari'ah*, always mixed with local *adat* laws, has been the primary responsibility of the local sultan popularly regarded as the guardian of Islam in his domain. The British, however, left behind a legacy of western, secular legislation which has continued to regulate public policy at the federal level very much on secular lines. This fact has been a major cause of the rapid economic growth and prosperity of post-independence Malaysia, as discussed in Chapter 7.

Deficiencies of the Islamic social contract

As a theory of state, the Islamic social contract is clearly inadequate. The roots of its inadequacy lie in its feudalistic simplicity. This is a reflection of the historical fact that as a theory it has been largely dormant since the age of feudalism when it was last articulated by the great Islamic scholars such as Al-Mawardi and Al-Ghazali. It remained untouched by European Enlightenment, and it continued to justify tyranny and usurption of power by illegal or immoral means. Thus, for example the tenth-century authority, Ibn Batta, compels the faithful to be submissive and patient, even in the face of oppression:

> You must not rise in arms against the Imams, even if they be unjust. Umar ibn as-Khattab said, may God be pleased with him. 'If he oppress you be patient; if he dispossesses you, be patient'.
>
> (Lewis 1987: I, 170−1)

The traditional Islamic social contract was essentially a marriage of convenience between the ruler and the *ulama*. The ruler gained legitimacy, the *ulama* acquired status. The people, by contrast, got precious little. The *ulama*, in charge of public morality, had every interest in the maintenance of the status quo and hence preached a conservative ideology of submission, patience and fatalism. They idealized the past, centred around some 'golden age', glorified history at the expense of the present; and they prescribed obedience and respect for the elders, discouraging the young to do better than their fathers.

On the plane of pure theory, there are two principal inadequacies with the Islamic social contract. In the first place, there is a problem of precise, enforceable definitions, and second, there is the absence of checks or balances. Thus, what exactly is meant by 'justice', 'protection' and 'loyalty'? How are they to be enforced? Is there no remedy even against an usurper or a tyrannical ruler? How can such a ruler be replaced non-violently?

On these questions, there is no clear consensus. By tradition, Islamic consensus − that is, legitimization of legislation − has been the monopoly of the *ulama*, as already pointed out. But who checks the *ulama*? To whom are they accountable? Not to the people. This is the missing link, the fundamental gap, in the Islamic theory of social contract.

The contemporary search for a new Islamic social contract is by no means a monolithic movement. In fact, Islamic resurgence displays a bewildering range of diversity among, as well as within, fundamentalists, modernists, progressives, and militants and extremists (Shepard 1987). These differences, however, are differences of prescription, not of diagnosis; there is common consensus regarding the central fact that the Islamic societies are in a state of crisis generated by relative backwardness. While countries in the Islamic Periphery have taken major steps in reopening the 'Gate of *Ijtihad*', the Islamic Core lags behind. It is in the Core that Islamic fundamentalism carries its greatest force.

An important exponent of Islamic fundamentalism is the deceased Pakistani Syed Abdul A'ala Maududi (Ahmad and Ansari 1979: 35), who held that the cause of Islamic decline is deviation of the believers from the True Path, and therefore salvation lies in the restoration of a purified Islamic theocracy based exclusively on the fundamentals of Islam freed from any western influence. But Maududi seems unwilling to face the modern reality of nation-states; his ideal state is theocracy in which *hakimiyya* (sovereignty) is entrusted to a Moghul-style ruler. Maududi's ruler is a just and righteous monarch aided by an elite group of *ulama* dedicated to justice. There is no accountability to the people because 'man's position in the universe is that of a subject and a subordinate' (Maududi 1984: 103). Clearly, Maududi is anti-democratic and anti-populist, and regards Islam as a Third Way, which is the only true way of achieving justice, fundamentally different from capitalism as well as communism which are merely 'delusions' (Maududi 1984: 100–1).

Maududi has had great influence not only in Pakistan, but on extremists and militants in the Arab Middle East, in particular on such groups as the Egyptian Ikhwan al-Muslimun (the Muslim Brotherhood). Sayyid Qutb, the author of *Social Justice in Islam*, originally published in 1948 and the major ideologue of the Muslim Brothers, was also greatly influenced by Maududi. But Qutb differs from Maududi in at least one important respect. While wishing to purify Islam from western ideological influences, he recognizes the need for modern legislation as the means of Islamic social justice (Qutb 1970: 267–76). Other Islamic militants and extremists, such as Shari'ati and Jalal Al-i Ahmed put the blame for Islam's decline on the corrupting influences of western culture generally equated with decadence (Piscatori 1986: 23). This anti-western xenophobia, termed *westoxication*, singles out the negative aspects of western culture such as alcoholism and drug addiction as a justification for Islamic purification.

On the other hand, the progressives, such as Afghani and Abduh, as we saw before, see the causes of Islam's decline in Islam itself, in particular its lack of any analytical or scientific tradition. Accordingly, the way to Islamic development is through a pragmatic blend of Islamic tradition with modern technology and know-how. These early progressives, however, overlooked the fact that western science and technology were the product of not only liberty and freedom, but of economic and social progress implemented by a secular state. Secularism was a challenge left to men of action like Kemal Ataturk, Ali Jinnah and Sukarno. Secularists attribute Islamic underdevelopment to reactionary theocracy and argue that Islam must first be disestablished so that the secular state can become the unchallenged instrument of development. For secularists Islam is a private religion, requiring personal submission of man to God.

The problem of accountability

In classical Islamic statecraft, the *ulama* provided the sole checks and balances on the ruler. So long as their scholarship was genuine and creative, the *ulama* were able to enjoy independence and limit legitimate authority.

Such a system of checks and balances is neither feasible or desirable. It is too elitist. It runs contrary to the Islamic principles of egalitarianism and populism. It therefore needs to be replaced by a new system of checks and balances limiting political authority: 'people's power', or the accountability of the ruler directly to the subjects.

A major theme of this book is that the Muslim dilemma today is a question of accountability. By accountability we mean answerability of the rulers to the ruled in social, political and economic terms. Spiritual needs, as matters of conscience, deserve to be respected as fundamental human rights. The proper domain of Islamic public policy must be the social and economic needs of the people, and the major criterion of good government must be the degree to which these needs are satisfied. When the policies and performance of rulers satisfy the needs of the ruled, and such satisfaction is popularly and freely confirmed, then the accountability test is duly met.

The major challenge facing Islamic societies is internal socio-economic reconstruction to deal with poverty and basic human needs. This challenge has to be pursued by updating the Islamic social contract whereby the rulers become answerable to the ruled. For this, neither total reliance on western models, nor total withdrawal from the world in search of purification, is sufficient. Accountability requires public policy responsive to human needs, both material and spiritual. It also requires checks and balances to prevent abuses and excesses. Therefore public policy designed for public good must provide for legally enforceable standards and safeguards to protect public interest. In view of mass poverty and economic underdevelopment in Islamic societies, the primary aim of public policy in these societies must be the construction of an efficient and just economy in harmony with Islamic social justice. In essence, this is Islamic capitalism, a system in which the surplus created by economic growth is not all appropriated as capitalists' profit but also helps promote social justice and ecological replenishment (see Chapter 11).

The imperfect economy: the necessity of intervention

The Islamic economic principles, to be analysed in detail in Chapter 4, approximate the capitalist ideal of perfect competition. Unfortunately, no such system exists in reality. In technical terms, the ideal capitalist economy – known as Pareto optimal – is supposed to reconcile efficiency and equity conditions. According to the Pareto optimality theorem, an economic change (for example a development project) which met the efficiency conditions would also be judged socially equitable if it increased the standard of living of at least one individual while harming no one. However, if it caused a loss in welfare for some individuals while benefiting others, then the gainers ought to be *potentially* capable of compensating the losers. But theoretical compensation is not the same thing as actual compensation.

Islamic economic theory, as we shall see in the next chapter, is not entirely inconsistent with Pareto optimum. Islam, too, requires an ideal balancing of equity and efficiency. In the Islamic ideal, as in a Pareto optimal economy, production is perfectly harmonized with consumption. This harmony is achieved through rational behaviour which is the common underlying behavioural pattern in both the Islamic and capitalist economy. Nevertheless, there are some significant differences, especially in terms of distribution (due to *zakat*) and pricing (due to *riba*). This subject is discussed further in the next chapter.

Turning from theory to practice, a major weakness of the capitalist economy is the existence of widespread exploitation. The majority of citizens may find that their welfare is sacrificed in the pursuit of profit maximization by a relatively few monopolists and oligopolists. The pursuit of profits, unchecked by appropriate social policy, creates excessive income differentials causing deprivation and poverty for the majority as a necessary condition for wealth and income concentration for the few. While reasonable incentives are necessary as rewards for productive effort, excessive disparities in incomes and economic opportunities create social injustice and disharmony. That is why government intervention in the economy with socially sound policies is necessary to promote economic justice together with productive efficiency (Okun 1975).

Responsible public policies need, therefore, to start from the pragmatic point that the socio-economic status quo is unjust and imperfect. Accordingly, the proper rule of public policy is to guide an imperfect economy in order to minimize economic injustice and market failures. This means not banning but regulating monopolies, oligopolies and cartels in order to protect the public interest. This is true for domestic markets as well as for international trade. Islamic societies have to come to terms with an increasingly integrated and competitive world economy dominated by monopolies and oligopolies which exploit markets and resources unless prevented from doing so by means of effective rules and regulations. The pursuit of social justice, i.e. the elimination of economic exploitation, requires the adoption of legally enforceable rules against unfair trade practices, inappropriate technology, ecological damage and rules in favour of redistributive policies designed to provide an effective safety net for the needy and the disadvantaged.

Chapter four

Islam and economic development
The problem of compatibility

This chapter has two aims. First, it shows that, at the level of pure theory, the ideal Muslim economy is remarkably similar to a capitalist economy, for both are based on private property and market competition in which production and exchange are profit driven. Unfortunately, however, Islamic economic theory failed to progress beyond the ideal of perfect competition. This failure is primarily attributable to Islamic scholarship which rejected the pioneering contributions of such early economic thinkers as Ibn Khaldun. Islamic economics, as a guide to Islamic public policy, never advanced beyond infancy.

Second, the chapter argues that Muslim countries need an Islamic theory of imperfect competition to guide legislation and public policy to cope with the complexities of modern economy in an increasingly competitive world.

The chapter is organized in two sections. In the first section it is shown that Islamic doctrine is, to a large extent, quite compatible with capitalist economic theory inasmuch as it recognizes rational economic behaviour. In the second section there is a brief survey of economic policy challenges in Islamic societies.

Islam and the economic man

Is Islam compatible with economic development and modernization? There is a widespread opinion, both inside and outside the Muslim world, that would answer this question with a resounding 'no' (Parkinson, Wilder in Lim 1975). This negative opinion can be supported by empirical evidence and doctrinal injunction. Empirically, Muslim underdevelopment is readily observable and easily verified on the basis of standard quality-of-life indicators (World Bank 1988). Doctrinally, this relative underdevelopment is typically attributed to Muslim fatalism and low aspirations, which, in turn, are ascribed to the presumption that the true Muslim withdraws from this material and temporal world in favour of the next life. Thus, the correct Islamic way of life here in this life is pictured as a rejection of materialism, risk-taking and energy to improve the human condition in favour of spiritualism and contentment.

These misconceptions stem from two main sources: orientalism (Said 1979), which promoted stereotyping intended to misrepresent Islam both as religion and culture, and Islamists who have chosen to emphasize the mystical and ritualistic aspects of Islam over its positive and action-oriented aspects. The combined influence of these orientalists and Islamists on public opinion in Muslim societies has been so inordinately powerful that their advocacy was often as uncritically accepted as, for example, was the *Myth of the Lazy Native* (Alatas 1977a).

Rational behaviour axiom

In theory, Islamic values are consistent with the rational behaviour axiom. But Islamic rationality is not pure self-interest; it is a delicate balance of ethical responsibility and economic self-interest.

Man (inclusive of women) is a free agent endowed by God with intellect and freedom of choice. Thanks to these divine gifts, man is an action-oriented agent. He has a dual mission. Materially, he is expected to initiate action to use and control resources for his material advantage. As a moral agent, man is endowed with freedom which entails moral responsibility of choosing between good and evil guiding man's progress along the True Path leading him to God (Esposito 1988). It also obliges man to act with justice and moderation in his social and market relations, always avoiding excess.

Islam and perfect competition

In terms of market relations Islamic economic doctrines are most compatible with perfect competition based on private property ownership and private enterprise. Islam instructs man, as a worker, to be productive, industrious, thrifty and altruistic. As a producer he is a perfect competitor earning only normal profits since monopoly or oligopoly profits are exploitative. Sellers are prohibited from cornering markets through hoarding and speculation. Trade of *haram*, i.e. harmful goods and services (such as pork, prostitution and alcohol), as well as interest are banned. Good Muslim consumers are prudent and thrifty saving part of their current income for future requirements. They avoid excesses such as conspicuous consumption and resist greed. Ethically minded sellers and consumers are ecologically responsible for avoiding environmental degradation, and they willingly share their income and wealth with the poor through *zakat* and other redistributive means (Maududi 1984, Siddiqi 1981, Kahf 1978).

Pricing under perfect competition and Islam

In Islamic economics, pricing occupies a central place. Unfortunately, how prices of products and inputs should be determined is not spelled out as a self-contained theory of prices; instead, the answer is scattered in fragments and has to be pieced together. When this is done, the outcome is a rational choice model of perfect competition, i.e. absence of market imperfections.

In the theory of perfect competition, prices are determined through competitive market forces. The interaction of supply and demand determines an 'equilibrium price' which also clears the market. This equilibrium price is the outcome of a process, known as Adam Smith's 'Invisible Hand', which is unregulated by any government or authority. It comes about purely as a result of rational behaviour on the part of many buyers and sellers acting independently in pursuit of their own interests on the basis of full information.

In Islam there are two central pricing concepts: Just Price and Zero Price. The former is an ethical norm consistent with Islamic equity, while the latter is a special case. Both of these price concepts can be reconciled with the concept of equilibrium price determined in a competitive market.

Riba: the problem of the interest rate

Take, for example, the idea of Zero Price. An important example of this is *riba*, generally referred to as interest rate contrary to Islam. Strictly speaking, however, *riba* means 'addition', as in additional value. It is quite plausible that *riba* may refer to extra value over and above a just price for capital. It is, therefore, open to debate as to whether the Islamic prohibition refers to the interest rate (as the opportunity cost of capital) or usury (as an unjustified extra value in excess of the allowable opportunity cost of capital). Thus, Qureshi cites several verses from the Qur'an using the term *riba* and in all these cases he translates it as usury, although later on he mixes the two (Qureshi 1974: 40–5).

More recently, Chapra has distinguished between real and

nominal monetary values and has argued that the ban on *riba* may refer to *real* rate of interest as under a gold standard. It is important to recall that when *riba* was banned, gold and silver were the media of exchange. The ban was imposed to ensure justice and fair play between lender and borrower. To this end, exact equivalence between value loaned and countervalue repaid was required. Six commodities were specified (i.e. gold, silver, wheat, barley, dates and salt) for purposes of ensuring equality of value loaned and repaid. As Chapra has put it, 'if one scale has one of these commodities, the other scale also must have the same commodity, "like for like and equal for equal" ' (Chapra 1985: 59). This would imply that the Islamic injunction regarding *riba* is in real, not nominal, terms. Accordingly, in an economy based on paper currency and exposed to inflation, it may be argued that Islam would allow indexation – i.e. nominal interest charges on loans and deposits exactly equivalent to the rate of inflation – in order to prevent erosion of the value of money and hence unfair losses suffered by borrowers or lenders.

Theory aside, however, in practice *riba* has been interpreted as a total ban on interest without any distinction between usury and cost of credit. Thus, Qureshi equates interest with usury on the grounds that it is difficult to establish what is an exorbitant rate of interest: 'A rate of interest which is considered as very moderate and reasonable today may be considered as very exorbitant and excessive tomorrow.' (Qureshi 1974: 101). This is a faulty argument based on poor theory. That prices move up or down over time is true for all markets since fluctuations are the dynamics of market adjustment. If a price is too high at one point in time, this is due to excess demand in relation to supply and this situation will generate its own corrective dynamic so that in due course the price will fall back towards equilibrium where supply and demand are in balance. If, however, this corrective dynamic is blocked by fixing the price at zero, the market – whether of labour, land, capital or some commodity or service – simply disappears.

Thus, the practice of zero interest rate has had a disastrous consequence on economic development in the Muslim world. It prevented the creation of Islamic banking until very recently by which time the global supremacy of western banks and financial institutions was a foregone conclusion. Even in Muslim lands, banking, insurance and essential financial services were in foreign hands. Thus, investment in Islamic development was often subject to foreign veto. In addition, the zero interest injunction contributed to capital flight, discouraged accumulation of savings and promoted excessive depreciation. If and when the interest rate is zero, no saver would voluntarily loan his funds to an investor any more than a worker would voluntarily work for zero wages. Even when investment is financed from own savings, the implicit price of these funds is the interest rate foregone. Indeed, savings will be zero since a zero interest rate would provide no incentive to save. Where an alternative banking system with positive interest rate exists, there will be capital flight in search of interest earnings. As a result, aggregate saving will decline towards zero and there will be no provision for depreciation. Thus, housing stock or infrastructural facilities will simply deteriorate into obsolescence. Overall, the practice of zero interest rate policy constitutes one of the most important explanations for Islamic underdevelopment in the world.

Some may argue, however, that interest can be charged under a different name such as 'dividend' or 'bonus'. This is evident in the Islamic banking innovation which has recently been initiated under Saudi Arabian sponsorship (Ahmad *et al.* 1979). The Islamic concepts of *sharakah* and *mudarabah* have been utilized for risk-sharing arrangements between Islamic banking institutions and private investors. This is similar to conventional merchant banking. There is no reason why they cannot succeed under special conditions similar to merchant banking. More generally, serious disputes and problems can be expected to arise over the terms of risk-sharing, distribution of profits, and the division of managerial and executive responsibilities. Doctrinally, however, these new Islamic innovations indicate that the prohibition of *riba* is not inconsistent with the notion of some positive interest rate as the cost of credit.

Just Price

The Islamic concept of Just Price may at first sight suggest an 'administered price' or some regime of price control fixed arbitrarily by an administrator or official. In practice, there are many examples of such 'administered' prices in regulated public industries including utilities, in agricultural support programmes, in foreign exchange control systems or in minimum wage legislation. Administered prices differ from equilibrium prices and they are inefficient and wasteful because they generate shortages or surpluses. If the Islamic concept of Just Price meant administered prices in all markets it would be a regressive concept justifying price controls which, almost inevitably, spill into black markets, speculation and hoarding.

The Islamic concept of Just Price is closer to a market-determined equilibrium price than administered prices. Many references in the Qur'an indicate that market prices normally fluctuate: 'The rise and fall of prices is in the hand of Allah (i.e. is subject to natural laws)' (Maududi 1984: 293). What is condemned is malicious withholding of supplies from markets for speculative gains: 'He who withholds the stock of grain for forty days with the purpose of effecting an increase in prices, Allah has nothing to do with him and he is no man of Allah.' (Maududi 1984: 293). In the same manner the injunction against *riba* can best be regarded as a ban on usury, i.e. excessive charge of interest over a fair cost of capital. For what is interest but the cost of capital, just as the wage-rate is the cost of a unit of hired labour, or rent the cost of using a piece of real estate? Just as it would be unthinkable that labour and land, as development resources, should have zero prices, so it must be with the cost of capital.

But what exactly is a Just Price? While there is no consensus on this question, Islamic scholars, both old and new, tend to regard it as equilibrium price. Ibn Taimiya (1262–1328) who wished to establish a norm for legal settlement of financial damages, used the term 'price of equivalent' intended to guide a judge. By the term 'price' he meant 'a price determined in a market free of imperfections' (quoted in M.N. Siddiqi 1981: 59). Kahf, a contemporary specialist of Islamic economics, states that 'All prices, whether of factors of production or of products . . . are looked at as just or fair prices' and endorses Ibn Taimiya's definition (ibid.).

On this point, Ibn Khaldun, the greatest economist of Islam, is even more definitive and significant. Indeed, Ibn Khaldun, writing some four centuries before Adam Smith, can be credited as one of the original fathers of the modern economic theory, including the concept of equilibrium price determined competitively by forces of supply and demand (Boulakia 1971). Yet Ibn Khaldun was largely dismissed by subsequent Islamic scholars. For example, his *Muqaddimah* was long banned as too secular at Al-Azhar, the centre of Islamic learning (Rahman 1982: 68). Thus, Ibn Khaldun's economics were never developed by subsequent Islamic scholars in the way which Ricardo, Marshall, Walras and Robinson, among others, developed Adam Smith's theories in the west. We shall now provide a synopsis of Ibn Khaldun's economics.

A synopsis of the economics of Ibn Khaldun

Ibn Khaldun (1332–1406) was interested in the same question as concerned Adam Smith: what are the causes of the rise and decline of nations (or 'dynasties', *dawlah*, to use his own term)? Ibn Khaldun, impressed with ancient Greek empiricism, was a rationalist who believed in the power of human intellect. His research agenda was the physical and natural environment in all its historical, economic, political and social aspects. The basis of his analytical technique was the inductive method of observation and historical confirmation.

Although the *Muqaddimah* was written as a book of history, it contains all the major elements of modern economics, including a theory of production, a theory of prices and markets, and theories of distribution, public finance, business cycles and international trade, all of which are combined into a coherent general economic theory logically integrated into history.

Ibn Khaldun's economics rest solidly on rational behaviour. He starts in a very Aristotelian manner by asserting that man is a political animal, 'That is, he cannot do without social organization, for which the philosophers use the term "town" (polis)' (Dawood 1981: 45). He then develops the theme of man as an economic animal. 'God created and fashioned man in a form that can live and subsist only with the help of food. He guided man to a natural desire for food and instilled in him the power that enables him to obtain it' (ibid.). Among all animals, man alone is endowed by God with the gift of intellect, 'ability to think, and the hand' (ibid.: 46). Thus, by his intellect and creativity, man as economic animal engages in production and exchange. Man does not live alone, however. He needs the skills and productive creativity of others for mutual trade and co-operation. Thus, through specialization and exchange, growth and prosperity evolved and sedentary civilization developed. Differences in levels of civilization originate from differences in man's efforts.

Labour is the main factor of production and profit is the motivating force of human labour and free men. 'Every man tries to get things; in this all men are alike. . . . When he has control of himself . . . he strives to make a profit.' Profit is a reward for human labour. It represents that part of income 'that is obtained by a person through his own effort and strength'. (Dawood 1981: 297). Ibn Khaldun lists three sources of profit-making: (1) appropriation, i.e. forceably taking it from others, such as by imposts and taxation or by exploiting domesticated animals or trees in the forest; (2) profit realized from the practice of a craft or profession; and (3) commerce. For Ibn Khaldun, commerce is the most advanced form of earning a profit, but one which is naturally full of tricks intended to maximize the profit margin between purchase prices and selling prices. He regards this as natural and legal. 'The law permits cunning in commerce, since (commerce) contains an element of gambling' (ibid.: 300). What Ibn Khaldun refers to is the risk-taking function of the entrepreneur for which residual profit represents a fair and legal return. But he is also aware of profiteering as a result of stockpiling or speculation. For commerce means 'buying goods at a low price and selling them at a high price' and sometimes large profits may be earned 'by storing goods and holding them until the market has fluctuated from low prices to high prices'. (ibid.: 310).

Prices are determined by the laws of supply and demand. All goods, with the exception of gold and silver, fluctuate in prices in response to changing conditions of supply and demand. High prices tend to increase supply, while increasing supply decreases prices. Production of goods is organized according to a division of labour and skill specialization characterized by crafts. The larger the city the greater the diversity of crafts. Thus, the greater the degree of sedentary civilization, the larger the size of the market; hence the greater is the division of labour and hence the more diverse the range of production of goods.

Just as there is domestic division of labour within a state, there is also an international division of labour reflecting differences in crafts and skills (hence productivity) among states. International trade provides an outlet for trading surplus production for imports of luxury. The basis of international trade is to be found in differences in crafts (i.e. skills and productivity) and the size of markets, whereas the motive of international trade, as in domestic trade, is profit. Merchants who specialize in international trade can expect to make higher profits the higher the risks and costs of such trade. Thus, the market has its own adjustment mechanism for restoring equilibrium between supply and demand without any intervention by government authority.

Economic growth, through urbanization and international trade, which is the path to sedentary civilization that Ibn Khaldun regarded as the highest form of civilization, also contains the seeds of its own decay and disintegration. This happens when the ruling class acquires an insatiable taste for power and prosperity at the expense of social justice. 'Civilization and its well-being as well as business prosperity depend on productivity and people's efforts in all directions in their own interest and profit. When people no longer do business in order to make a living, and when they cease all gainful activity, the business of civilization slumps, and everything decays.' (Dawood 1981: 238). Citizens depart in an exodus to other more agreeable territories, while competing groups seek military support from outside sources to take over and set up a new dynasty.

Ibn Khaldun placed great importance on human capital formation, not only as a means of stimulating economic development, but also as an essential recipe for stability. While his conception of history had an element of Marxist inevitability of growth and decline of nations, he also believed that decay and disintegration could be averted by means of education and training designed to develop proper aptitudes, *malakah*. Ibn Khaldun rejected traditionalism in favour of adaptation and dynamic adjustment to changing circumstances. He regarded education and training as creative paths whereby each generation could achieve a better and higher civilization. It is a great loss for Islamic scholarship that Ibn Khaldun was dismissed almost totally by subsequent *ulama*.

Naqvi's Islamic general equilibrium model

Islamic economic theorizing remained virtually dormant until very recently. A few authors in what is now Pakistan were the first to revive interest in Islamic economics. Here Syed Abdul A'ala Maududi and Anwar Iqbal Qureshi are the notable examples. Their works, however, were more in the nature of advocacy pieces rather than coherent and rigorous contributions. Serious theoretical works began only in the last ten to fifteen years, e.g. Monzer Kahf (1978), M. Umer Chapra (1985), Masul Alam Choudhury (1986), and Syed Nawab Haider Naqvi (1981). An essential characteristic of these contributions is the synthesis of economics with Islamic ethics. While the result, known as Islamic economics, contains too many inconsistencies to justify the claim that it would be capable of delivering greater economic justice than alternative systems (Kuran 1989), the analytical approach of this school is meritorious. This will now be illustrated with reference to Naqvi's work.

In an outstanding example of rigorous scholarship, Syed Nawab Haider Naqvi recently put forward an Islamic general equilibrium model representing a synthesis of Islamic ethics and neo-classical welfare economics. The chief merit of this work lies in its demonstration of the correspondence of Islamic economic principles with the theory of perfect competition. Naqvi begins his economics from Islamic ethics. His overall objective is to derive from a set of four ethical axioms – unity, equilibrium, free will and responsibility – an ideal system of Islamic economy in which Islamic ethics serve as 'the point of departure' for constructing a general equilibrium model (Naqvi 1981: 80).

Naqvi's four ethical axioms are: (1) the unity axiom, whereby economic activity is indissolubly linked with man's ethical environment; (2) the equilibrium axiom, which requires that there must be a just balance amongst the basic production, consumption, and distribution relations; (3) the free will axiom, which reflects the idea that 'individual economic freedom and state control be suitably combined to reflect the distinctive Islamic concept of human freedom' (Naqvi 1981: 62); and (4) the responsibility axiom which dictates a conscious policy of redistribution in society in conformity with Islamic egalitarianism and which similarly regulates relations between lenders and borrowers under conditions of risk and uncertainty. Notable in his system, as will be shown below, is the critical role of Islamic exchange of private sacrifice for divine merit.

Naqvi's ideal economy is essentially a modified Pareto optimum general equilibrium, fulfilling both efficiency and equity conditions in production, consumption and distribution relations. It is constructed on rational behaviour and perfect competition assumptions. Naqvi's producers and consumers, as in the Pareto model, are rational decision-makers, optimizing profits or utilities subject to technical, budgetary and taste constraints. However, in Naqvi's Islamic ideal economy social welfare functions are interdependent; this is consistent with the Islamic norm that the welfare of one depends not just on one's own actions and decisions but on others' as well. Man is a co-operative agent, an instrument of others' welfare as well as of his own. Hence Islamic producers do not blindly pursue maximum profits – according to the neo-classical first-order condition of marginal revenue product equals marginal cost. Instead, in accordance with the responsibility axiom, they refrain from producing goods and services that are environmentally damaging and those that are banned by Islamic ethics. Consumers and producers, consistent with the equilibrium axiom, willingly share (for example through *zakat*) a portion of their wealth and income in a socially responsible way which maximizes total social welfare. Naqvi's concept of 'total' welfare maximization requires absolute income equality. Any deviation from this condition will generate corrective individual sacrifices, through charity and other transfers, to restore such equality because 'a rise in the degree of income inequality will tend to diminish overall happiness and satisfaction' (Naqvi 1981: 65). Thus, in Naqvi's ideal economy, individuals are less than entirely selfish decision-makers because they put positive value on the preferences of others, but they are maximizers nevertheless because of the psychic and vicarious benefits of divine merit earned from doing God's will.

Thus, for Naqvi the ideal Islamic economy is built solidly on rational behaviour. But this is not, as in the neo-classical model, narrowly channelled into excessive pursuit of selfish ends at the expense of others. Rather it is a system based on a double exchange.

In addition to the standard exchange of cash for goods and services in ordinary market transactions, there is a second implicit exchange of private sacrifice for vicarious benefits derived from altruistic behaviour. Private sacrifice for altruism is an Islamic requirement for charity and social responsibility; but in return for this the sacrificer is compensated in terms of divine merit.

Naqvi's rigorous analysis is impressive and insightful. It is a significant contribution towards a modern articulation of Islamic norms. As with any ideal system, however, it suffers from certain deficiencies. For example, what if not all individuals are honest, sincere and well-meaning? What if perfect competition conditions are violated? In particular, what corrective measures and remedies should be applied to deal with monopolies, cartels and unfair trade practices? By operating strictly within a perfectly competitive system, Naqvi ignores these critical issues. He states that his ideal system is meant only for 'well-meaning people, to whom alone this book is addressed' (Naqvi 1981: 169). This is hardly satisfactory. If, in fact, every person was perfectly endowed with honesty, sincerity and good intentions, then surely there would be no injustice or exploitation to worry about.

Economics and public policy in Islam

Perfect competition is an ideal which does not exist in practice. Public policy in western market economies is not based on *laissez-faire*, but on the existence of imperfect competition characterized by monopolies, oligopolies, cartels and all kinds of unfair trade practices which exploit the weak and powerless. In these economies, public economic policy provides a *protective* service, consistent with the idea of state as an instrument serving the public. Economic policy is intended to protect the public interest. It does this in two principal ways: first by providing guidelines and standards to restrain unfair trade practices (such as collusion and price fixing), and second, by determining remedies for compensation for injury caused by violation of those standards. The overall effect of such public policy is to improve economic fairness and, by so doing, move society a step closer to the ideal of perfect competition.

An Islamic economic system built as if perfect competition were a practical reality amounts to public policy nihilism. It corresponds to a *laissez-faire* regime of non-intervention in the economy. How then can deviations from the ideal of perfect competition be handled in the Islamic economy? For example, how are monopolists, speculators, profiteers and exploiters to be restrained or punished? What are required, relative to a specific time and place, are policy rules to guide implementation, performance and effectiveness evaluation.

Islamic fiscal policy

In western economies, taxation and expenditure policies have been utilized as deliberate tools of public policy in order to provide essential public goods and services (such as education, health, low-cost housing, etc.) as well as to promote industrial development. Under Keynesianism, fiscal policy became an instrument of deficit financing and aggregate demand management to ensure full employment, while income transfers have been relied upon as income stabilizers to provide an economic and social safety net for the unemployed and the needy.

Fiscal policy as a tool of meeting human needs is nothing new to Islam. Unfortunately it remained underdeveloped, as if frozen in time, since medieval times. Take for example *zakat*. While there is a specific obligation to pay 2.5 per cent of one's annual wealth, authorities differ on whether it is a compulsory tax levied by the state for purposes of public goods (Qureshi 1974: 146), or whether it is a 'form of devotion, in fact like *namaz*' (Maududi 1984: 92–3). There are even greater ambiguities in regards to the collection, administration and utilization of *zakat*. To whom is it payable? Charitable trusts, legacies and endowments, known as *waqfs*, are regarded as highly meritorious in Islam, but the terms and conditions have conventionally been left to the discretion of the deceased. Historically, the practice was abused to accumulate familial landed endowments or the benefits were restricted to ruling classes or leaders of such religious orders as the Bektasi, Naksebendi, Kadiriye and Mevleviye (Barnes 1987). Contrary to the original intent, *waqfs* did little for the poor or peasantry. A socially efficient system would be to regulate *waqfs* under public law, channelling the revenues into low-cost housing, education, welfare and other social services for the needy.

Islamic monetary policy

The primary objective of monetary policy is the control of money supply and the regulation of banking and credit. In Islam, these objectives have traditionally been ignored in favour of the single-issue debate over the question of *riba*. Only in recent years, have money, banking and Islamic monetary policy emerged as important issues of Islamic policy (Ahmad *et al.* 1979; Chapra 1985).

Historically, as discussed above, the practice of zero interest was directly responsible for the underdevelopment of monetary institutions and monetary policy in Islamic societies. It resulted in monetary repression. The only banks in Islamic countries were foreign banks, and saving and investment were almost exclusively in the hands of foreigners. Thus the British and the Chinese in Malaysia, and the Europeans and ethnic minorities of Greeks, Armenians and Jews in the Ottoman Empire, controlled and owned the financial and corporate assets. The Malays and the Turks viewed banking, saving and investment as un-Islamic.

Monetary repression is contrary to the (pro-capitalist) spirit of Islam. Take the case of Islamic obligation to be thrifty and save for a 'rainy day'. This clearly implies deferred consumption at the expense of current consumption for the sake of the future. But what is the incentive for compressing current consumption for the sake of saving at zero rate of interest? Even if this is a real rate of interest, so that no depreciation of the principal is suffered, what is the most appropriate form of savings thus generated: liquid cash (hoarding)? real estate? bank deposit? government bond? How should these funds be used in the most productive manner? Should they be entrusted with the government? in a public trust agency? invested in stocks and shares? These are complex questions requiring highly trained expertise in charge of modern, sophisticated monetary policy. Such a monetary policy should be designed and operated by personnel trained on both the Islamic and western monetary theories. This is essential to adapt to the evolving world monetary system which, thanks to modern technology, is rapidly moving towards an integrated global system.

A globally integrated financial system effectively precludes the creation of a separate Islamic monetary and banking system. Innovations such as the profit-sharing *muradabah* investments may be feasible under special circumstances, but, as the experience of OPEC oil surpluses demonstrates, investible savings (both long-term and 'hot money') move globally in search of the highest return. Since there is a direct correlation between risk and return, it is not surprising that large sums from oil-surplus Arab countries were recycled into bad projects which contributed to the Third World debt crisis.

Human resources policy

Islam places the highest value on knowledge (*ilm*). According to Kurshid Ahmad (in Ahmad and Ansari 1979: 232), human resource development should be 'the first objective' of an Islamic society.

Why, then, have Muslim societies so long been victimized by *jahiliyya*, mass ignorance? Why are the levels of literacy in Muslim lands still the lowest in the world? Why, in particular, is the position of women so inferior? Who is responsible for this discrepancy? The blame rests on two interrelated groups: the *ulama* who have stressed theological education at the expense of scientific and empirical knowledge, and those in charge of policy-making who abandoned their accountability to the masses.

The development experience of western countries and the more recent achievements of Japan, South Korea, Taiwan and Singapore, show an astonishing similarity in their early recognition of the importance of practical, skill-oriented education. In Taiwan, for example, practical farmer education was stressed in the 1950s at the time of major land reform in order to increase the productivity of the farmer. In Singapore, university education was curtailed in order to reallocate investment in polytechnics and on-the-job skill development (Mehmet 1989).

By contrast, human resource development priorities in Islamic countries have been unclear and wasteful. In Turkey and Malaysia there has been over-investment in classical education, while there have been persistent shortages of technical and vocational skills required for self-employment. In some countries, like Bangladesh, there is not even a coherent education policy in force. Instead, there is a great multiplicity of non-governmental organizations, mostly foreign, pursuing their own objectives. In the oil-surplus Middle Eastern countries, imports of expensive expatriate manpower are substituted for the development of indigenous technology and knowledge (Shaw 1983).

International trade policy

Trade and commerce have always been important in Islam. After all, the Prophet himself was a trader. The Constitution of Medina was the first set of man-made rules regulating trade and commerce. But, in subsequent periods, these precedents were either ignored or abandoned by the *ulama*. The political elites collaborated with foreign interests to the detriment of national welfare. The Ottomans initiated the system of *capitulations* at the height of their power in 1536 (Shaw 1976: 97). The Malay sultans willingly accepted the British Residency system. Both of these methods of European penetration paved the way for the economic subordination of Muslim societies to western financial interests. The Ottoman trade was always in the hands of Christian minorities, while the Turks remained shut out, this exclusion being rationalized by such stereotyping as the 'ignorant Turk' with no interest in or capacity for trade and industry. In Malaysia, 'the lazy Malay' stereotyping by the British justified preferential treatment of the Chinese to emerge as the dominant business class.

The development of indigenous trade and industry in Malaysia and Turkey had to await the advent of a nationalist, secularist development strategy. But, as we shall see in subsequent chapters, the creation of a viable indigenous business class has been frustrated by lack of competition. Political elites at the top have chosen to rely on protection rather than competition as their strategy of developing indigenous trade and industry. They relied on sponsorship and nepotism rather than market forces in resource allocation. In the end, this approach encouraged rent-seeking behaviour.

This does not invalidate a national, secular development strategy. It merely demonstrates the inherent selfishness of man everywhere and the need to limit this tendency by appropriate rules enacted in the public interest. The Turkish or the Malay entrepreneur, like his American, Japanese or European counterpart, is motivated by his own interest, and will always attempt to maximize his gain especially if laws and regulations encourage him to do so. Trade rules and regulations must, first and foremost, ensure fair competition in the public interest. But how is a competition policy to be formulated? How is it to be implemented? What criteria and standards are needed? These questions necessitate a thorough knowledge of the theory of imperfect competition – something that Islamic scholarship has yet to develop.

Imperfect and monopolistic competition

The theory of imperfect competition, pioneered by Joan Robinson (1933) and the theory of monopolistic competition developed by Edward Chamberlain (1950), are major contributions to modern economic theory. These theories have great practical and policy relevance. They describe how the monopolies, oligopolies and cartels that dominate modern economies work, and thus provide essential guidelines for their regulation via public policy. Thanks to these theories, evils of monopoly, advertising, price discrimination, collusion and various forms of economic exploitation are brought within the domain of legally enforceable rules. More recently, these theories have been extended to international trade to throw light on how multinational corporations operate, and how governments with public policies can regulate their harmful activities such as transfer pricing and inappropriate technology transfers.

Unfortunately, the theory of monopolistic and imperfect competition has yet to be reconciled with Islamic norms.

Rationality, self-interest and altruism

As with perfect competition, the central logic of the theory of imperfect competition is the rational behaviour assumption. Rational man is driven by self-interest, first and foremost; altruistic tendencies, while compatible with rationality, are subsidiary. The fundamental difference between perfect and imperfect competition is the presence of market power.

What is true for a rational individual holds also for nations. The pursuit of national interest is consistent with the rationality principle. Old and new forms of mercantilism continue to define national interest, both for Islamic and non-Islamic countries. In the age of colonialism, imperial powers were motivated by the pursuit of wealth and power at the expense of the rest of the world. Socialist and communist countries pursue their vision of national interest first and foremost. Altruism enters these calculations, if at all, only secondarily. Foreign aid programmes are not exercises in altruism; in reality they are instruments of foreign economic or military policies of the donors. Belatedly, Islamic countries are discovering the paramountcy of national economic interest. By forming the OPEC cartel, Muslim countries like Saudi Arabia and other Islamic oil-producers finally discovered the relative importance of market power. In the process, they realized unprecedented wealth, and they have continued to earn huge returns from interest collected on their deposits in western banks.

But the pursuit of self-interest, while rational and beneficial in many respects, may sometimes lead to excesses such as greed and corruption. Imperfect competition is a world of collusion, exploitation and unfair trade practices. What is the best way of dealing with such undesirable consequences of imperfect competition? A ban on imperfect competition would be both impractical and socially undesirable. It would be impractical to attempt to replace it with the ideal of perfect competition; and it would be undesirable since many price and non-price advantages would be lost. A more rational approach would be to regulate excesses of imperfect competition by means of effective policies aimed against the evils of monopolistic domination and unfair trade practices. Guidelines for such policy formulation are readily provided in the theory of imperfect competition.

The deficiency of Islamic economic policy is that it is not sufficiently based on the theory of imperfect competition. Even in such secularized Islamic countries as Malaysia and Turkey, public economic policies are underdeveloped with respect to regulation of monopolies, patents and copyrights, and unfair trade practices. As a result, economic exploitation goes unchecked. In fact with the increasing price of privatization the risk of economic injustice is greatly increased. The important task ahead is not to stop privatization or ban imperfect competition; that would be totally unrealistic. Rather the challenge is to design and implement effective public policies to monitor and cope with imperfect competition, aimed at its regulation in the public's interest.

Privatization, profit maximization and quasi-rents

Privatized development (i.e. reliance on the private sector as the engine of growth in place of government-led growth) now being implemented vigorously in Turkey and Malaysia is part of a global trend which can be expected to accelerate elsewhere in the Islamic world. Unfortunately, its full implications are often unclear. What are its objectives and benefits? What are the implicit risks and uncertainties? How can these best be dealt with?

At first sight, privatization implies a shift from public to private monopolies or oligopolies. In terms of pricing strategy, it implies a transition from regulated pricing to profit-maximizing pricing. In more practical terms, it means going from lower to higher retail prices and from larger to smaller levels of output. Potentially, consumers stand to suffer lost consumer surplus, whereas producers and groups with market power gain in super-normal profits and quasi-rents. If not checked, these quasi-rents enrich monopolistic corporate interests, worsen income and wealth distribution, and increase the cost of living for the ordinary consumers. In Islamic societies the transition to monopolistic pricing under privatization is especially risky and is likely to increase the influence of Islamic fundamentalists because higher retail prices, super-normal profits and quasi-rents seem to be contrary to Islamic norms of fairness and social justice. These unfair consequences, however, may be checked by means of effective legal safeguards and protective measures.

Privatization is not without its advantages. In fact these advantages may outweigh the disadvantages. Dismantling inefficient state economic enterprises would reduce deficits financed out of tax revenues. It would make bureaucratic and political elites more accountable. Privatization and economic liberalization would get rid of endemic shortages and black markets caused by artificially low retail prices of essential goods and services. Liberalization of investment and tax regulations would provide greater incentives to private investors and might lead to more investment and jobs. The privatization question is analyzed in greater detail in Chapter 8.

Public policy to regulate privatization

These advantages of privatization would not come about automatically. Only deliberate action and public policy can ensure that the excesses of market power are regulated in the same way that excesses of state capitalism or socialism need to be weeded out. If unfair trade practices are not regulated by clear and responsible legislation, then privatization would indeed result in monopolies and oligopolies charging excessive prices. If the consumer and environmental groups are not given adequate representation in the drafting of health and safety regulations, public interest would not be properly safeguarded. If the tax, investment and technology policies reflect only the wishes of lobbies and special interests, but not those of the workers and consumers, then such policies would be biased and unfair. To be fair and responsible, public policy needs to be constantly adapted and modernized in order that it remains efficient, accountable and responsive to human needs.

Is it inevitable that such a public policy would lead to materialism and gradual erosion of Islamic values? The fundamentalists would, of course, answer affirmatively. They would likely condemn it as cultural rot introduced by 'westoxication' (Jalal Al-i Ahmad 1984), focusing only on the negative influences of advertising and materialism. Such views are confused and regressive, based on misinformation and half truths. Any religious and moral system which can only be preserved in pure form and sustained on the right path if, and only if, it is 'bottled up' and insulated behind a 'Great Wall', must be inherently weak. Islam is a religion of humanism, placing man in a unique central position in the universal order, in direct relationship with God, allowing him to find tranquility within himself, to satisfy his needs responsibly and in harmony with nature. As an egalitarian system in which all men are equal before one God, irrespective of race, colour or status, Islam teaches the universal values of tolerance, brotherhood and social justice. These are very powerful values. It won the hearts and minds of people in the Middle East, Africa, Asia, Europe and North America, and continues to do so. Islam does not need to be 'bottled up' to be kept pure against westernization or any other alien influences.

What this chapter has shown is that Islamic economics stopped flourishing after Ibn Khaldun. It did not proceed beyond the abstract, ideal theory of perfect competition. As a result, Islamic economics and public policy are severely deficient and in urgent need of reconciliation with the realities of imperfect competition. This is essential especially in an age of privatized development.

Part three

Development in the Islamic Periphery: the nationalist phase

Part II has shown that the Islamic promise of social justice for the masses has generally met failure. Historically, the primary responsibility for this failure rested with the *ulama* who abandoned the precedent of the Constitution of Medina and failed to develop a tradition of Islamic public policy responsive to changing social, political and economic issues. The *ulama*, monarchical at heart, interspaced themselves between the sovereign and the masses and institutionalized a self-serving 'gate-keeping' role. They frustrated the evolution of an organic, or symbiotic, relationship between the ruler and the ruled, and through their advisory role they monopolized access and information flow from the bottom to the top. The *ulama* denigrated the Aristotelian dictum 'Man is a political animal' into the politics of sponsorship and expediency, all buried underneath a rigid form of scripturalism. Their anti-democratic sympathies blocked the evolution of a 'bottom-up' public policy tradition. Thus, Islamic societies have long been 'segmented' (Gellner 1981: 33–6) into a *high culture* of the centrist ruling elites and the *low culture* of the peasantry with little symbiotic relationship between them, and certainly no functional accountability between the rulers and the ruled.

Public policy requires a theory of the state to articulate the rationale, to identify the tools and targets of policy-making and to determine the criteria for evaluating the performance of policies and policy-makers. The *ulama*, especially after the fourteenth century, adopted an increasingly regressive, anti-secular stance suppressing rational inquiry into human affairs. Rationalism was abandoned to European scholarship, even though Muslim teachers had been instrumental in transmitting it to the west. As a consequence, the positivist concept of the nation-state as an instrument of improving the quality of life, could not emerge from within; nor did it penetrate the world of Islam until quite recently.

Such a progressive evolution had to await the advent of a

nationalist revolution in the Muslim world. When nationalism finally reached Islamic societies in the late nineteenth and early twentieth centuries, it resulted in a long and bitter confrontation with the traditionalists, the age-old custodians of Islamic knowledge and morality. This confrontation is the modernization debate in Islam. The modernizers achieved their first major success in the Islamic Periphery (i.e. in the Turkish and Malay worlds). They utilized the same tool: the new ideology of nationalism; and the same popular promise: a modern age of shared prosperity based on national reconstruction.

However, the ruling elites in charge of nationalist development in Turkey and Malaysia shared one fundamental weakness with the traditional elites: they lacked populist roots. If not monarchical they were aristocratic, convinced by virtue of superior ideology to lead, without any accountability, the ignorant and backward masses into the age of modernity. In the end the nationalists, too, failed to deliver the promised benefits to the grass roots. The post-Ataturk Kemalists in Turkey, and the *Bumiputera* leadership in post-independence Malaysia, sustained the 'cultural gap' between the ruling elites and the masses (Toprak 1981: 122). Their priorities and policy instruments were inappropriate. Instead of responding to the needs of the peasantry these elites opted for urban-biased, capital-intensive industrialization, causing a massive rural exodus in the process. Islamic resurgence was, above all, a grass-roots response to a top-down cultural and economic restructuring imposed by authoritarian national elites. Untrue to their own ideology, the nationalist elites suffered from the same drawback as did the traditional *ulema*: a deep mistrust in the inherent capacity of the masses to make intelligent choices. Accordingly, the nationalists, too, failed to forge the organic relationship necessary to resolve the age-old Islamic identity crisis.

Chapter five

Nationalism confronts Islam
The modernization debate in Malaysia and Turkey

In both Malaysia and Turkey modernization has long been a hotly debated subject between the Islamic traditionalists and the modernists. The *Kaum Tua–Kaum Muda* (Old Order–New Order) controversy in Malaysia, and the *laiklik* (secularism) debate in Turkey are but national manifestations of the same issue concerning the proper place of Islam in a modern society.

Modernists are nationalists. Nationalism, not religion, is their ideology. They reject theocracy as being incompatible with development and modernity. They insist on a clear, formal separation of religion and politics. For them the modern world is a rapidly changing world of technology, science and knowledge, and politics must be secular, utilitarian and flexible to cope with new challenges, whereas theocracy requires an unchanging, constant world-view. The modernists hold the traditionalist *ulama* – who controlled public education and morality and who resisted such innovations as the printing of books as being un-Islamic – primarily responsible for the age of *jahiliyya*, the age of mass ignorance, which characterized the world of Islam from the fifteenth century onwards when Europe experienced the Renaissance, the Industrial Revolution and the French Revolution. Europe advanced, the modernists argue, because of individual freedom and scientific knowledge. The former made the electorate the real political masters while the latter put technology at the service of man. Secularization of politics gradually created the instrumentalist state, while political accountability gave content and meaning to the utilitarian concept of a public policy as the function of a sovereign acting to maximize the greatest happiness of the greatest possible number.

The Islamic traditionalists reject outright the concept of national sovereignty as meaningless and preposterous. They argue that sovereignty belongs only to God. They therefore call for the rule of *shari'ah* (God's law) in a non-national state uniting all Muslims the world over through one Islamic community, the *Umma*, under submission to God. In this traditional world-view there is no room for the idea of a nation (Figure 5.1) and nationalism is regarded as a source of disunity among the *Umma*, a dangerous obstacle which must first be removed before any real transformation can occur to restore Islamic purity.

Figure 5.1 The Islamic world-view

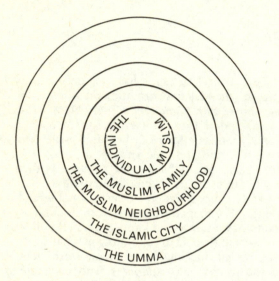

Source: Sardar (1987: 110)

Sometimes, calls for Islamic purity are phrased in terms of total isolation from the west. In the words of Dr Kalim Siddiqui, Director of the Muslim Institute in London,

> we cannot even begin to think about the total transformation of the *ummah* without first taking up the position that there is no compatibility whatsoever between Islam and the west. It is only when we have taken this step that we have created the necessary spiritual, material and historical situation in which the total transformation of the *ummah* becomes a logical necessity. . . . This declaration of incompatibility forces us . . . to define our civilizational goals in terms of Islam and Islam alone.

The Islamic traditionalists aspire to a theocracy under the rule of the *ulama*. They reject secularization of politics and hide their true political ambitions behind undemonstrable promises. Thus, they denounce the pursuit of either monetary objectives or momentary pleasures as deviations from man's mission in this world in God's service. They promise that the real rewards for the faithful are not in this temporal world, but in the other; to gain entry into the other world, man's divine duty is to do God's will. Although God's will, and the individual's divine duty are constant, they must be revealed and interpreted by the *ulama* to ensure that the people remain 'on the straight path'. Islam is the total source of knowledge and any departure from its teachings can only lead to confusion, regression and degeneracy. The way to avoid these dangers is through the restoration of the rule of the *ulama*. The assumption of power in Iran by Ayatollah Khomeini was seen by the traditionalists as a contemporary demonstration of the righteousness of their cause and of a worthy model to be imitated.

An example of the traditionalist's action programme is that of Cemalletin Kaplan, leader of an ultra-right faction of Turkish guest-workers in West Berlin.

Our Objective: Islamic State
Sovereignty: Belongs to Allah
Constitution: The Holy Qur'an
Rule: *sheri'at*
Source: Again, the Holy Qur'an
The Leader and Example: The Prophet Muhammad
The Method: Proclamation
The Subject: The supremacy of Justice
Instruments of Proclamation: Every legal means
The authority of Proclamation: Divine sanction
The style of Proclamation: Open, clear, and succinct
Weapon: Knowledge (Holy verses, *hadith*, mind and logic).
    (Quoted in Mumcu 1987: 9 – author's translation)

The debate between the traditionalists and modernists is a power struggle over 'the moral leadership' of the people (Gungor 1987: 222). In the first half of the twentieth century, Turkish and Malay modernists won because, in an age of relativism, the nationalist ideology proved more appealing than the universalism of Islam. But this was not any easy victory, nor was it entirely non-violent. Indeed, what the nationalist modernizers in Turkey and Malaysia won was not a knock-out, but a round in the battle.

Our comparative survey leads to the conclusion that the nationalists who prevailed over the Islamists shared a common trait with the traditional *ulama*: they mistrusted the masses. Although both aspired to a leadership role, theirs was an elitist concept of 'leader-follower' leadership. The nationalist modernizers did not seriously attempt to eradicate the age-old polarization between the centre and periphery (Mardin 1973). Both the Turkish and the Malaysian development strategy in the nationalist phase lacked accountability to the masses and, consequently, it institutionalized a new socio-economic order of structured inequality: income concentration at the top and mass poverty at the bottom.

The chapter is organized in two sections. In the first the Malaysian modernization debate will be discussed and in the second the Turkish case will be examined. This order is chosen partly because the Malaysian debate is more recent and is, histori-cally speaking, less complex. Also, the *Kaum Tua–Kaum Muda* debate was significantly influenced by the Turkish nationalist revolution at the other end of the Islamic Periphery.

The Malay *Kaum Tua–Kaum Muda* debate

The Malay modernization debate was shaped by European colonial-ism. Decades of colonial rule generated a feeling of cultural insecurity and economic resignation among the Malays. The British administration adopted a policy of benign neglect of the Malays, concentrated in their *kampongs* (rural villages), while they exploited the rich natural resources of the country with the cheap labour of the Chinese and Indian workers imported for this purpose. The colonial attitude regarding the Malays was typified by the harsh judgement of Sir Frank Swettenham that: 'The leading characteristic of the Malay of every class is a disinclination to work' (quoted in Alatas 1977a: 44).

Views such as Swettenham's, while legitimizing colonialism, con-tributed to stereotyping the Malays as lazy and always resisting progress and radical change (Parkinson in Lim 1975). In fact, as the numerous Malay rebellions demonstrate, many Malays wished to share in the new wealth created during and after the rubber boom, but were prevented from doing so by colonial interests and bureaucrats who preferred Malays to remain as rice growers while the Europeans monopolized the profits of the plantations (Bauer 1948, Talib in Hairi and Dahlan 1982).

Colonialism influenced Malay nationalism in a second funda-mental way. It was responsible for the creation of a multiracial society. When the British imported large numbers of Indian and Chinese workers under the cheap-labour policy, their motive was profit. But it produced a comparative sense of identity crisis among the Malays. This crisis alarmed them to the emerging reality that they were becoming a minority. They were in danger of losing their country. But was this a spiritual or a national awakening? Where did salvation lie?

Both the *Kaum Tua* and the *Kaum Muda* ideologies were differential responses to these central questions. The advocates in both camps were motivated by the same broad objective: that the cultural insecurity of the Malays could only be cured by overcoming their relative 'backwardness'. But their prescriptions, based on religion and nationalism respectively, differed. Both camps defined Malay identity in some mixture of Islam, race and ethnicity. While Islam was always a constant source of identification in a multiracial society, its status as personal or collective morality, and, in particular, its relationship to Malay nationalism, were ambiguous.

The *Kaum Tua* traditionalists viewed salvation in spiritual terms. Their political views were feudal, justifying uncritical submission to rulers (Syed H. Ali 1975). For them the ideal was in the past, in some Islamic golden age, before the arrival of European colonialists. Malays were Muslim, pure and simple, part of the universal *Umma*. They argued that any foreign education other than Arabic had a damaging influence on youth, by corrupting the spiritual values of Islam. They preached strict attachment to Islam and the rule of the *shari'ah* and *adat* and rejected nationalism in favour of Pan Islam. Some *ulama*, such as the mystical *sufi*, put other-worldliness and serving God first and foremost, and shunned profitable commercial pursuits (Mahathir 1970: chap. 8). The traditionalists suffered a major setback in 1924 when Kemalist Turkey suddenly abolished the Caliphate, the symbol of Pan-Islamic unity and 'the focal point of Islamic life' (Milner 1986: 120).

The *Kaum Muda* modernists, educated in Cairo and the Ottoman Middle East and exposed to progressive Islamist thinkers like Adbuh and Afghani, were the real forerunners of Malay nationalism. They implicitly believed that the Malays had their destiny in their own hands, that leaving it to Allah was insufficient. They chose nationalism over Pan-Islam both as the means to get rid of colonialism and to achieve progress and development. They attacked both the traditional practice of Islam in Malaya, adulterated by impurities of custom and superstition, such as belief in *bomohs* (the spirit doctors), as well as the reactionary *ulama*, whose archaic and erroneous teaching they considered inimical to progress and development.

The modernists were in favour of modern, scientific education in English and of foreign study. Not surprisingly, they were condemned by the traditionalists 'as worse than idolators and Christians' (Thomson quoted in Soenarno 1960: 8). In turn, the

modernists described the traditionalists as ' "hawkers of religion,",
obstacles to progress, and destroyers of the true faith' (Roff 1967:
65). For these modernists, the root cause of Malay backwardness
was the lack of freedom due to oppressive traditionalism perpetuated by the reactionary *ulama* and to colonial exploitation and
domination. They therefore stressed advocacy writing and pam-
phleteering in order to educate the Malay masses on the ideas of
nationalism. Both the technique and the ideas were modelled on the
Ottoman Middle East. But in the beginning Malay nationalism was
nationalism within an Islamic framework; it lacked the spark of
Kemalist secularism.

One of the earliest and most influential instruments of Malay
national awakening was the periodical *Al-Imam* (The Leader)
started in 1906 in Singapore, then the centre of Malay nationalism.
It was started by a group of Malay-Muslim intellectuals with
extensive family and trading connections to the Ottoman Middle
East. The more prominent organizers were: Shayk Modh. Tahir b.
Jalaluddin Al-Azhari, the first editor, born in West Sumatra,
raised in Mecca and educated in Al-Azhar in Cairo where he was
greatly influenced by the great minds of the day, Abduh and Rida;
Sayyid Shayk b. Ahmad Hadi, a Malacca-born Malay-Arab of
Hadhrami descent; Hajji Abbas b. Modh. Taha of Singapore; and
Shaykh Mohd. Salim Al-Kalali, an Atjehenese merchant and
director of *Al-Imam* during its first two years. During the next
thirty years, *Al-Imam* played a key role as a vehicle of radical
Malay nationalism, directing its editorial policy both against the
regressive *ulama* as well as the colonial powers who exploited and
subordinated the Malays.

The *Al-Imam* variety of Malay nationalism reflected its intellectual and political links with the Middle East. It was outward-
rather than inward-oriented nationalism. It stemmed from the fact
that among the original group of four creative minds behind the
project, only one (Hajji Abbas) could be considered to be a
'peninsular Malay'. With this outward orientation, the *Al-Imam*
Malay nationalism aimed at persuading the Malays, as *Umma*, to
recognize allegiances outside their state and local sultan. Pan-Islam,
then the grand policy of the Ottoman Sultan Hamid, was a major
influence. In fact, in this formative stage Malay nationalism was
financially and politically aided by the sponsorship of such figures
as Hajji Attaullah Effendi and Muhammad Alsagoff, who acted as
representatives of the Ottoman Sultan in the colony, and
Muhammad Kamil Bey, the first and only Ottoman Ambassador to
Batavia who, when dismissed by the Dutch in 1899 for these Pan-
Islamic activities, ended up in Singapore (Reid 1967: 271, 279–80).

The colonialists took the Pan-Islamic threat very seriously in view of its widespread appeal among all levels of the Malay society. Thus, in 1891 when the Turkish warship *Ertogroul* visited Singapore *en route* to Japan, it created considerable excitement among the Malay and Indian Muslims. Petitions of grievances were drafted, and letters from the Raja of Selangor and the ruler of Atjeh were written to the captain appealing for the help of the Ottoman Sultan-Caliph. The ship, however, had sailed off before these could be submitted (Reid 1969b: 258).

Abdul Hamid's Pan-Islamic policies were highly influential in shaping nationalism among the Malays as well as the Idonesians. At a time when colonialism was at its zenith, Islam served a double political function: it united the world of the faithful against the injustices of colonial rule and, at the same time, it preserved ethnic identity in a multiracial society. The Ottoman Empire, though literally on its death-bed, was nevertheless the sole independent Islamic power at the time, and, as such, its policy of Pan-Islam could, and did, inspire the nascent nationalism of Muslims in the Malay world. Thus, *Al-Imam* carried extensive coverage of news from the Ottoman Empire and the Islamic Middle East. For example, there were articles on the Turkish navy in the issue of January 1907, on the Hijaz railway in July 1907, and on the Turkish system of government in October 1907 (Roff 1967: footnote, 59).

The *Al-Imam* was soon followed by numerous other papers and periodicals, such as *Neracha*, *Warta Malaya*, *Al-Ikhwan* and *Saudara*. All these publications played an important role in promoting Malay nationalism. But this early form of nationalism was primarily religious, closely tied to Pan-Islamic ideology. It demonstrated to the Malays the wider world of Islam, the common experience of Muslim societies under colonial rule and injustice, and the need to identify with the cause of their co-religionists. In this scheme, Turkey occupied a special place and the Ottoman Sultan, however despotic at home, was widely revered as the Caliph. The Malays readily sympathized with the Turks in all their wars including the Libyan campaign against the Italians, the Balkan wars and the First World War. They took special pride in the Turkish victories at Gallipoli and over the Greeks. Popular books about Mustafa Kemal, the Turkish War of Independence and the establishment of the Republic at Ankara were published and widely read (Za'ba 1939: 160–1).

The transition from a wider Pan-Islamic brand of Malay nationalism towards a more inward-looking, anti-colonial, political independence movement emerged gradually. Until 1926, Malay nationalism lacked a political orientation. In that year, the Singapore Malay Union (SMU) was formed. It was the forerunner of the Malay political parties of the 1940s. It marked the transition from a religious to a secular brand of Malay nationalism. To what extent the abolition of the Caliphate in 1924 influenced such a transition is an interesting topic for future study. With the formation of the SMU, the Malay intellectual elite began increasingly to realize the necessity of political action and effective leadership through clubs and associations in order to achieve Malay progress.

Political mobilization became indispensable to protect Malay interests both against colonialism and against other races in Malaya. The Chinese and Indians, brought into Malaya by the British for cheap labour to work on plantations and mines, were increasingly threatening the domain of the Malays. A Chinese Legislative Councillor, in a speech in 1931, declared:

> Who said this is a Malay country? When Captain Light came here did he find any Malays or kampongs? Our forefathers came here and had worked as labourers and they did not remit money back to China. They spent their money here and by this means the Government was able to open up this Country into a civilised one. We have become one with the Country. This is ours, our country.
>
> (Quoted in Soenarno 1960: 11)

But the Malays were no longer slumbering politically. They became fully alive to the full implications of the colonial immigration policy. Any encroachment upon Malay rights and privileges as *Bumiputera* (sons of the soil), brought a quick retort. The *Singapore Free Press* in its editorial on 22 March 1938 wrote:

> The Malays have awakened to the problem of western civilisation which they have to face and already there is a realisation that, if they are to succeed against the encroachment of other races in Malaya, they must combine for their own and the welfare of succeeding generations.
>
> (Quoted in Soenarno 1960: 15)

It was with the formation of the United Malays National Organization (UMNO) in 1946 that Malay nationalism and identity merged. UMNO represents the political maturation of Malay nationalism. It was an act whereby the Malays took charge of their destiny, asserted their identity, and in the process shaped the future of the country. Without UMNO in 1946, it is almost certain that the Malaysia of today, based on the supremacy of the Malays, would not have been possible.

The trigger for the formation of UMNO was the threat by the British to establish a Malayan Union, consolidating all the Malay states and the Straits Settlements of Penang and Singapore into one administration headed by a British governor. In short, Malaya would become a British colony at the expense of the Malay sultans, the traditional symbols of Malay identity and guardians of Islam within their jurisdiction. Under the Malayan Union proposal, all non-Malays would be granted equal rights and the Malays would become a minority in their own land.

In early March 1946, forty-six Malay associations gathered in Kuala Lumpur to protest against the Malayan Union, and on 11 May 1946 they formally established UMNO to fight for Malay rights and oppose the Malay Union. Dato Onn bin Jaafar, son of the Chief Minister of Johore, was elected as President. Dato Onn was of Turkish descent (see Chapter 1, p. 28).

UMNO was a secular, Ataturk-style political party, patterned explicitly on the nationalist model of Kemalists then in power in Turkey (Za'ba quoted in Milner 1986: 124). It was the creation of the 'ultra-progressive' wing of Malay nationalists, known as the 'Turkish-style party' which, while borrowing Kemalist nationalism, avoided its secularism. Besides Onn, it included Tunku Abdul Rahman, who subsequently became the father and first Prime Minister of Malaysia. Later, Zainal Abidin bin Wahid, the historian of Malay nationalism, wrote approvingly of Ataturk 'for freeing the Turkish nation not only from foreign influence but also from feudal government' (Milner 1986: 122).

In 1951 Dato Onn left UMNO in a bitter dispute over the citizenship status of non-Malays. He wanted to open UMNO membership to all citizens of Malaya and change it into a multiracial party. This was unacceptable to the Malays. Tunku Abdul Rahman took over from Onn. In 1952 Tunku Abdul Rahman was able to patch up an alliance between UMNO and the Malayan Chinese Association (MCA) and this proved a great political success. The Malayan Indian Congress (MIC) subsequently joined the alliance, and the UMNO–MCA–MIC alliance paved the way to *Merdeka*, national independence, on 31 August 1957 (Hashim 1983).

The basis of the UMNO–MCA–MIC alliance was an inter-ethnic political compromise: the Malays agreed to grant citizenship rights to non-Malays in return for their agreement to entrench special rights for the Malays as the indigeneous people of the country. This was Article 153 of the Constitution which authorized the Yang Di Pertuan Agong, King of Malaysia, to safeguard the special rights and privileges of the Malays by reserving certain positions in the federal public service, by granting special scholarships and by providing licenses under federal law for the operation of trade and businesses.

Post-independence: the May 1969 turning point

UMNO has been the dominant ruling party since *Merdeka*, but its role since independence has undergone significant changes. Up to May 1969 it was merely a senior partner in a multiracial political coalition government. After May 1969 Malays were in political command and UMNO exemplified this fact until the constitutional crisis in 1987 which led to the demise of UMNO.

During the first thirteen years of *Merdeka*, from 1957 to May 1969, Malaysia was ruled by the UMNO–MCA–MIC alliance under the leadership of Tunku Abdul Rahman. But increasingly he was perceived among the Malays as too soft and liberal with the non-Malays and insufficiently sensitive to the Malays' special rights. Malay nationalists – including future Prime Minister Mahathir, who disagreed with the Tunku – were forced out of UMNO.

On 13 May 1969 the country was the scene of bloody race riots, coming at the heels of a hotly contested general election in which the Chinese had scored major political gains at the expense of the Malays (Slimming 1969; Vorys 1975). May 1969 was a turning point in post-independence Malaysia. It directly resulted in the adoption of the New Economic Policy (NEP), a large-scale pro-Malay affirmative action policy intended to implement the special rights of the Malays. It was designed and implemented under the leadership of another Malay nationalist, Tun Razak, the Tunku's deputy, who took over the reins of power in a silent *coup d'état* immediately after the May 13 incident. The NEP was launched as a twenty-year socio-economic plan to urbanize, industrialize and modernize the Malays and to eliminate, once and for all, inter-racial inequalities in incomes and economic opportunity in the country. To this end, it was assigned two major aims, or 'prongs': first, to eradicate poverty, which was especially widespread among the rural Malays; and second, to restructure the ownership of industrial and corporate capital in the country on the basis of a racial quota of 30 per cent for Malays, 30 per cent for resident non-Malays and 40 per cent for foreign investors. In 1970, the Malays owned about 2 per cent of the total industrial and corporate capital in Malaysia, the foreigners owning about 70 per cent and the Chinese the balance.

The effectiveness of NEP, which expired in May 1990, is examined in greater detail in Chapter 7. While it was less successful on the poverty eradication front than on equity restructuring, there is little doubt that it catapulted the Malays from the backwaters into the mainstream of the Malaysian economy. It urbanized them, it created an expanding middle class, and it considerably narrowed down inter-ethnic disparities. In short, the NEP drastically upset the old Malay order of feudalism and conservatism.

The NEP upset the old order, but did not destroy it. It gave a new direction to the old debate between the modernists and the traditionalists. It did so because the NEP strategy created a new form of inequality in Malaysia: growing intra-Malay inequality. It polarized the Malays not only into rich and poor, but also along political and religious party lines. Malay politics became patronage politics in which rewards such as subsidies and scholarships were distributed, not by merit, but by influence and favouritism. As the nationalist modernizers emerged as managers of 'money politics' at the national as well as the local village level (Shamsul 1986), Islamists reappeared, in the new environment of the NEP, claiming legitimacy as the true moral custodians of the *rakyat* (Malay subjects).

Islamic resurgence

What complicates the politics of Malaysia is the fact that the country is, officially, non-secular. Islam is the official religion. This is a reflection of the historical fact that, unlike in Turkey, Islam played a largely positive role in the evolution of Malay nationalism.

Malaysia is a federal country. Until 1982, the political significance of Islam was generally limited to the states where the local sultan is the head of Islam under his jurisdiction. In the east-coast states in Peninsular Malaysia, the most underdeveloped and heavily Malay regions, Islamic parties held power. On the other hand, at the federal level, policy-making had been, at least unofficially, secular, especially in economic and industrial development. As a result, the Malaysian economy has continued to grow and prosper thanks to its strong trade-orientation. While maintaining and expanding the rubber and oil palm plantations, the federal leadership chose industrialization, relying on cheap (especially female) labour, as its main modernizing strategy.

Two major factors contributed to the resurgence of Islam in Malaysia after May 1969. The first, and foremost, was urbanization. It replaced traditional Malay rural homogeneity with urban-based pluralism. One key organization in this process was the Malaysian Islamic Youth Movement (ABIM) established in 1972.

It coincided with the dramatic increase in scholarships and educational opportunities available to Malay youth under the NEP. It gave rise to campus politics and the emergence of such leaders as Anwar Ibrahim. At the same time, the rising volume of Malay exodus from *kampongs* into new land schemes, industrial estates and urban centres upset the traditional values and institutions of the Malays. Islamists criticized the employment of women in factories and shopping centres; parents and elders complained of declining morality; and the migrants themselves complained of low wages, slum landlords, poverty and alienation (Chandra 1987).

The second major factor was the Islamic revolution in Iran and the success of Ayatollah Khomeini in restoring theocracy. It confirmed the convictions of the Islamic fundamentalists, strengthened the arguments of the militants and it seemed to demonstrate to the rank and file that 'Islam is the best'. The growth and proliferation of numerous Islamic missionary and voluntary organizations, some with outside funding and leadership, began to win new converts. The Dakwah movement and the headwear movement (women wearing the veil and Muslim clothing), which was most visible on university campuses, began to gather momentum. Some academics began to write about the 'reflowering of Islam' (Nagata 1984). Most significant of all, political inclinations among the rural Malays, the backbone of UMNO leadership at the federal level, began to shift radically towards its opponent, the Parti Islam SeMalaysia (PAS). In the late 1970s, PAS entered into a tacit alliance with ABIM while in Iran Ayatollah Khomeini took power in 1979 (Sundaram and Cheek 1988).

The reaction of UMNO leadership was to try and outflank its Islamic opposition. In July 1981 Mahathir took over as Prime Minister; and in March 1982, just before the general election, Anwar Ibrahim, the president of ABIM, was co-opted into UMNO. Shortly after the election, the PAS leader Mohammad Asri, decided to join the Mahathir-Anwar faction, surrendering PAS to the *ulama*. UMNO began to lose its secularist character and moved along the slippery path of Islamization, ostensibly to introduce 'discipline through Islam' (Mauzy and Milne in Gale 1987). Since 1982, Islamic banking has been introduced, an Islamic university established, a Department of Islamic Affairs and a large religious bureaucracy have been created, and, most recently, there have been moves in the direction of introducing elements of *shari'ah* laws in the federal jurisdiction.

The Turkish secularization debate

The Turkish secularization debate in the Kemalist period is a more complex topic than its Malaysian counterpart because it needs to be placed in its proper historical, i.e. Ottoman, context. This historical context, spanning some two centuries, has been the subject of extensive debate in and outside Turkey and can only be described here in a very brief outline.

The Ottoman legacy

For centuries Islam, not Turkification, had been the leading objective of the 'non-national Ottoman state' (Haddad and Ochsenwald 1977). The basis of the state was a theocratic structure which explicitly subdivided the subjects into two major religious categories: Muslims and non-Muslims. The Ottomans recognized Christians and Jews as 'people of the Book' and granted each religious community a high degree of autonomy under the celebrated *millet* system. The Qur'an commanded:

Dispute not with the People of the Book
save in the fairer manner, except for
those of them that do wrong; and say,
'We believe in what has been sent down
to us, and what has been sent down to you;
Our God and your God is One, and to Him
we have surrendered'.

(XXIX: 46)

The *millet* system, unintentionally, promoted nationalism among non-Muslims. It did so by allowing subdivision of non-Muslims along both ethnic as well as religious lines, for example the Armenian, Greek, and the Jewish *millets*, and hence these ethnic groups were able to flourish along national lines. On the other hand, no such possibility existed for the Muslim subjects: the Turks, Arabs, Albanians, and Kurds were an undifferentiated category, all equal members of the *ummet*, the global community of the believers. As such, Arabic and Turkish nationalism emerged later than nationalism among non-Muslim ethnic groups, and Turkish nationalism itself emerged last of all (Berkes 1959, Ozbudun in Evin 1984).

In the century before the First World War, European powers became increasingly aware that the Ottoman Empire was a 'Sick Man of Europe' and took advantage of the *millet* system to raise the national consciousness of the non-Muslims in a more or less systematic method of destabilizing the Empire from within. This was the paramount objective of the Eurocentric Eastern Question.

111

Reform, ostensibly on behalf of the non-Muslim ethnic groups, was the diplomatic leverage utilized, but often the European powers pursued their own hidden economic and territorial ambitions. During this period of Ottoman decline, public policy of the Empire was split into two slices. European powers and western missionaries emerged as protectors of the Christian minorities providing them with superior education, legal and citizenship privileges, while the decaying Ottoman state left the Turkish and Muslim masses under the charge of the retrograde *ulema*, especially the village *mullahs*.

Economic decline in the age of European colonialism was the key factor in the demise of the Ottoman public policy. At the start of the nineteenth century, the Ottoman multinational state received two mortal blows from Europe. The first was the Industrial Revolution. It upset the old trading routes on which the economic equilibrium of the Empire had been based. It reduced the revenue base of the state, and especially hurt the ethnic minorities such as the Greeks, Jews and Armenians who had long controlled Ottoman trade and, through their ability to bribe officials and inter-mediaries, had dominated the palace politics of the Ottoman government. As the revenue basis of the Empire shrank, the Sultan started foreign borrowing, beginning with a secret convention with the British in 1839 (the year of the Tanzimat – Reform – edict), mortgaging tax sources (such as tobacco and railways concessions) or land (such as Cyprus and Egypt) in order to raise loans and finance wars (including the Crimean War) and for other unproductive purposes such as royal weddings and palaces. Finally, in 1876, the Ottoman state declared bankruptcy and became the first defaulter on foreign debt. Thereafter an Ottoman Debt Administration, run by European bankers, controlled the economic policy of the Empire putting their interest ahead of Turkish national interest (Earle 1966, Blaisdell 1966, Pamuk 1987).

The second mortal blow from Europe was the new religion of nationalism. As put by Carlton Hayes:

> 'Nationalism as a religion inculcates neither charity nor justice; it is proud not humble; and it signally fails to universalize human aims. . . . Nationalism's kingdom is frankly of this world, and its attainment involved tribal selfishness and vainglory, a particularly ignorant and tyrannical intolerance – and war. . . . Nationalism brings not peace but war.'
>
> (Quoted in Haddad and Ochsenwald 1977: 8)

European nationalism destroyed the Ottoman *millet* system. As the economic base of the Empire declined, so did its capacity to govern. As a result the quality of life deteriorated, far more so in the case of the Turkish and Muslim majority than in the case of non-Muslim minorities. Thanks to the protection of western powers and of numerous missionaries and philanthropists, the Greek, Jewish and Armenian minorities maintained superior economic standards of living, while also enjoying first-class schools and welfare institutions in the country. Gradually, but surely, these minorities shifted their loyalties to the enemies of the Empire and some, like the Ottoman Armenians, ended up bringing great suffering upon themselves as well as Turks and Muslims (Oke 1988). First the Greeks achieved their independence with active European support; the Bulgarians, Romanians, Serbs and others followed. By the end of the nineteenth century, Arab nationalism, sparked by Europeans, especially the French, began to fragment the Muslim *millet* (Antonius 1938). Still the Turkish intellectual elite resisted Turkish nationalism, and such patriots as Namik Kemal kept on preaching the virtues of Ottomanism (Lewis 1968: 140−2).

Thus, the Turkish masses were the last of the Ottoman *millets* to be exposed to nationalism. In the Turkish Anatolian heartland, away from the degenerate and cosmopolitan world of Istanbul where the intellectual elite resided isolated from the masses, Turkish consciousness was the monopoly of the ignorant *mullahs* and other-wordly *ulema*. The Sultan, as the Caliph, was, of course, the symbolic head of all Muslims everywhere, and the *Sheyh-ul-Islam*, the Chief Religious Officer, was similarly the head of the large non-national Islamic clergy within and outside the Empire. The religious establishment had, by long tradition, a tremendous power base, and enjoyed a great influence over public morality. Under *sheri'at*, the entire judicial system was controlled by the *ulema*, the Islamic clergy. Legislation was enacted by them, and they administered the laws, including the large body of unwritten, customary laws known as *adet* laws. They also controlled public education in Qur'anic schools using Arabic, God's chosen language, in a pedagogical method known as *taqlid* (rote learning). By the early twentieth century, the quality of government service provided by the state and moral leadership by the *ulema* was miserable; corruption, misrule and chaos prevailed everywhere.

The paradoxes of the Ottoman legacy

The Kemalist break with the Ottoman past was so sharp (similar to that of Maoist China) that it is necessary to spell out the reasons behind it. In theory, the Turks were in charge of the Ottoman Empire; in fact, control over public policy had, during the course of the century before 1914, passed into the hands of Europeans and

Christian minorities who functioned as middlemen. This is why, in the end, the Turkish majority was virtually the most disadvantaged *millet* in this cosmopolitan Empire. The explanation for this astonishing fact lies in the paradoxes of Ottoman statecraft of which three, in particular, deserve comment.

First, the Ottomans had a strong sense of territory as an object of conquest, but they had no sense of territoriality, i.e. the exercise of sovereignty within a well-defined territory. At the height of their power, they began compromising their sovereign authority by giving away extra-territorial concessions, known as *capitulations*, granted to European powers. Originally conceived as trade concessions to forge diplomatic alliances with particular powers (such as France and Venice), over time capitulations were extended to other powers under the most-favoured-nation clause. Not only did the Ottoman state lose control over trade, tariff and taxation, but its legal authority also gradually diminished as Christian subjects could thus claim foreign citizenship and protection.

Second, the Ottomans had a highly developed concept of power as military might, but this power was devoid of dominance. Turkification, or even Islamization, were never the Ottoman objectives. Their military might was constrained by Islamic rules of warfare which prescribed strict limits on the rights of conquered people. Thus, time after time, they would conquer, but impose no cultural or political assimilation of the conquered people. Their *millet* system of ethnic autonomy contrasts sharply with the Russian policy in regards to other ethnic groups such as the Crimean Tartars after the annexation of 1774, or the actions of the *conquistadors* in the New World or the opening of the West in North America.

Third, the Ottomans had a highly sophisticated idea of ethnicity but applied it only to the Christian *millets*. Thanks to this Ottoman formula, the ethnic identities of numerous non-Muslim national groups in the Empire were preserved. They granted ethnic autonomy to conquered ethnic groups; they practised tolerance towards Jews fleeing the Inquisition in Europe; and permitted western missionaries to aid, educate and awaken the nationalist aspirations of the Christian minorities of the Empire. True, these minorities paid taxes whereas Muslim subjects did not, but such taxes exempted Christians from military service. Thus, while able-bodied Turks were away on military duty, agriculture was left in care of their womenfolk, and trade and commerce passed into the hands of the Christian minorities.

Even in the age of nationalism, after the French Revolution, the Ottomans resisted the emergence of a Turkish sense of national identity paralleling national awakening among the Christian minorities. The ordinary Turks did not have a sense of belonging to a ruling ethnic group. In particular, they had a confused sense of self-image. Who were they: Turks, Muslims or Ottomans? Their literature was sometimes Persian, sometimes Arabic, but always courtly and elitist. There was always a huge social and cultural distance between the Imperial centre and the Anatolian periphery. As Bernard Lewis expressed it:

> in the Imperial society of the Ottomans the ethnic term Turk was little used, and then chiefly in a rather derogatory sense, to designate the Turcoman nomads or, later, the ignorant and uncouth Turkish-speaking peasants of the Anatolian villages.
>
> (Lewis 1968: 1)

In the words of a British observer of the Ottoman values and institutions at the start of the twentieth century:

> [The] surest way to insult an Ottoman gentleman is to call him a 'Turk'. His face will straightway wear the expression a Londoner's assumes, when he hears himself frankly styled a Cockney. He is no Turk, no savage, he will assure you, but an Ottoman subject of the Sultan, by no means to be confounded with certain barbarians styled Turcomans, and from whom indeed, on the male side, he may possibly be descended.
>
> (Davey 1907: 209)

The leaders of the *Tanzimat* (reform) period (1839–76), men like Rashid and Midhat who believed that European ideas of constitutional monarchy and equality of all citizens regardless of ethnicity and religion could be introduced top-down, were idealists aiming at not a Turkish but an Ottoman identity. The 'Ottoman nation' (*tabiyet-i Osmani*) was a legal fiction of a citizenship law enacted in 1869 in a desperate Ottoman attempt to preserve the Empire's integrity in the face of growing secessionist movements. It was an empty label:

> Could this 'Ottoman nation' be a delusion? For example, was not the army fighting a part of this Ottoman nation in Macedonia? Were not we at war within the Ottoman country with our Bulgarian, Serbian and Greek citizens? Were we not fighting against Ottoman citizens in Crete? Did we fight interminably against the Druises in Syria? Why were we fighting tooth and nail against the Armenian citizens?
>
> (Aydemir quoted in Oke 1988: 55)

At its death-bed, the Ottoman state was not only militarily weak and financially broke, its soul was utterly lost. The Ottomans had betrayed their Turkish identity.

Kemalism confronts the Ottoman–Islamic legacy

Not surprisingly, therefore, Kemalism reached out to the pre-Islamic populist roots of the Turks to unearth the lost Turkish national identity. As Kushner expressed it, the Turks had gone further than other Islamic people

> . . . in submerging their identity in the wider Islamic one, embodied in the principle of the *Umma* – the all-embracing community of believers – recognizing no political or ethnic barrier between them. . . . The essential division in the population of the Empire was between believers and non-believers. Turks did not enjoy any more privileges than Arabs or other Muslim citizens. In fact, the government hierarchy, for example, appeared to favor non-Turks, so great was the number of functionaries brought into the service of the State from non-Turkish peoples.
>
> (Kushner quoted in Ozbudun 1984: 26)

Culturally, the Ottomans elevated Persian and Arabic to the literary pinnacle, so that, as these languages developed, Turkish arts and literature remained stagnant. Many Turkish scholars and men of letters are still renowned as Muslim rather than Turkish authors. In jurisprudence, the Ottomans gave the *sheri'at*,

> . . . a loftier place than most of their predecessors had done, and fully integrated their religious institutions into the state apparatus. This was done by organizing the *ulema* (Islamic scholars) into a systematic official hierarchy culminating in the office of the *Seyhulislam* (the chief *mufti* or juriconsult) who enjoyed a power and standing second only to these of the Grand Vizier.
>
> (Ozbudun in Evin 1984: 26)

To the very end the Ottomans fought for Pan-Islamic ideals at the expense of Turkish national identity. They did this even when, as in the First World War, it had been abandoned by Arab nationalists and when Turkish national existence was itself in mortal danger. Thus, Mustafa Kemal Ataturk, the 'saviour' of modern Turkey (Volkan and Itzkowitz 1986), liberated Turkish national identity as much from the clutches of great power imperialism as from an anti-national Ottoman–Islamic past.

The Kemalist disestablishment

Once the National War of Independence (1919–22) was successfully completed, the Kemalist nationalists hit back at the Ottoman–Islamic past with a vengeance. The Sultanate was abolished and replaced by a Republic declared in the new national capital of Ankara in the Anatolian heartland. In an amazingly rapid series of reforms in 1924–5 Kemalist Turkey disestablished the Islamic religion and institutions, thus destroying the power base of the traditional *ulema*.

In March 1924, two momentous reforms were enacted: the Qur'anic schools were closed down and public education was secularized under a Ministry of Education; and, at the same time, the Caliphate was abolished. In April 1924 the *sheri'at* courts and laws were replaced by the European legal system. These reforms had a shock effect in the rest of the Muslim world; in Europe, long used to repeated but futile Turkish reforms since the nineteenth century, they were little noticed, or dismissed with the cynical remark: 'Swiss Codes for Turkey, how very funny!' (Ostrorog 1927: 13).

In 1925, not content with legal and institutional reform, Ataturk determined to change the self-image of the Turks as a prelude to the creation of a modern Turkey. He introduced his Hat Law whereby the traditional turban, or fez, was replaced by a hat. Dress in Ottoman society had been a mark of social as well as official status. Thus, the *ulema* and the clergy were distinguished no less by their traditional garb than by education; without his turban and gown a Muslim clergy was a nobody, as immortalized in one of the stories of the popular folk hero, Nasreddin Hodja. Mustafa Kemal chose Kastomonu, one of the most conservative towns in Anatolia, for his hat reform. He entered the town, wearing a panama hat and European dress, but such was his fame and reputation as the *Ghazi* (victor) over the Allies in Gallipoli, and most recently over the Greeks, that the townspeople took to his reform as fish to water. Kemal wanted to shake his countrymen out of their centuries-old habits of traditionalism, superstition and fatalism. The manner in which he would introduce his reforms had a great deal to do with his personality organization, shaped by a grieving mother symbolizing Turkey in travail (Volkan and Itzkowitz 1986).

Ataturk pushed on with his reforms. The European calendar and clock became legal and, in December 1925, Sunday was declared as the weekly rest day. *Tekkes* were declared illegal and ordered to cease operations at the end of October 1925. *Vakfs*, the Islamic trusts and charities, which had traditionally supported the religious orders, were taken over by the state. Large numbers of teachers in

Qur'anic schools, judicial officials in the *sheri'at* courts and *sheyks*, *sufis* and *dervishes* in *tekkes* and mosques lost their sources of livelihood and became unemployed, many with no alternative skills or job prospects. They simply sank into poverty and destitution, some disappearing into obscurity but many joining the forces of resistance against Kemalism.

These initial reforms in 1924–5, far-reaching and revolutionary though they were, represented only a start. Secularism was officially declared in 1928, when by an amendment, the second article of the 1924 constitution stating that 'the religion of the Turkish state is Islam' was deleted. On 1 November 1928, the Latin alphabet was officially introduced and a major national literacy campaign launched. Kemal Ataturk himself became the 'Chief Instructor' in this campaign. The replacement of the Arabic alphabet represented a fundamental mental revolution; it changed the mode of reasoning of the Turks and thrust them into a contemporary world of culture. It was a cornerstone in Kemalist cultural restructuring imposed from above.

In 1930 Turkish women were granted modern civil rights, including political equality with men, and the right to vote and hold public office. The veil, long the symbol of female subordination, was banned, and the seclusion of women was officially ended, though not till 1935. Henceforth, they could walk in public, dressed in European fashions, and take part in public life – at least in major cities and towns.

In 1934 another major reform of Turkish identity took place. All Turkish citizens were required by law to adopt a surname, Mustafa Kemal himself becoming Ataturk (father of Turks). Henceforth there could be no ambiguity about the family origins of Turkish citizens. Unfortunately, in Turkish communities outside Turkey where Kemalist reforms could be adopted only voluntarily, some confusion over self-identity persisted. In Cyprus, for example, the traditional system of using the father's name in place of surname (as in the author's case) remained in force.

Kemalist reforms were revolutionary reforms. They shook the traditional Turkish society to its very foundations. While they were generally accepted as a necessary condition for modernization – or westernization – the masses had little understanding of these terms, but they were willing, by and large, to accept them as an article of their faith in the great leader Ataturk. But dissent was not lacking, even among the circles closest to Ataturk. For example, Halide Edib Adivar, a well-known female reformer and associate of Ataturk, was dubious about slavish imitation of everything western:

Total and slavish imitation of a model is the very opposite of the spirit of Western civilization. This point needs special attention from late-comers to this civilization.

(Adivar quoted in Lewis 1968: 279)

There was also reaction from the masses. For example, the cost of a hat was as much as a third of the salary of a lowly-paid official, and many a peasant had to borrow in order to comply with the new dress regulations.

But the really serious threat to Kemalist reforms came from the traditionalists. They organized conspiracies and violent resistance. In 1925, in the wake of abolition of the Caliphate and the introduction of the Hat Law, the Kurdish leader Sheyk Said revolted, charging that Islam without the Caliph was not Islam. He captured Elazig and beseiged Diyarbakir, 'on the road to God' (Kinross 1971: 399). It took a full-scale military operation to put down this rebellion. No less threatening were the sporadic acts of revolts and conspiracy, and often secret resistance movements, led by the unemployed and disestablished *ulema*. The Islamic clergy, consisting of the *mullahs*, *kadis*, *muftis*, *vaizes*, *muezzins*, *sheyks*, *dervishes*, etc. now displaced and powerless, condemned the Kemalist reforms as the work of the godless betrayers of Islam. They called for the restoration of *sheri'at*. They conspired, sometimes openly but mostly secretly, for the overthrow of the 'infidels' now in power in Ankara.

The Kubilay incident

A major and violent confrontation between the Kemalist nationalists and the Islamic traditionalists occurred at the village of Menemen in Aydin province in December 1930. On this occasion, a sizeable band of Muslim fanatics, hired by a Naksebendi leader, Sheyk Esat, incited a riot and murdered a young nationalist school teacher, Kubilay, son of an *emigré* family from Crete. The leader of the hired band, one Giritli Mehmet, declared himself a Mahdi, boasting vainly that bullets could not penetrate his body, and that he was on a divine mission to save Islam from the hands of Kemalist infidels and restore *sheri'at* in Turkey. Following Kubilay's cold-blooded murder a military force was sent to restore order. Giritli Mehmet and some of his followers were killed in action, and the rest were captured in flight. In March 1931 a military court found thirty-six individuals involved in this incident guilty of treason, and sentenced them to death. In the end, twenty-eight adults were hanged in the public square in Menemen (Cetinkaya 1986: especially 24–6).

The Kubilay incident created a shock effect in Turkey. It ushered in a policy of strong, often brutal oppression and de-Islamization. Religious freedom was suppressed, *tarikats* were banned and pushed underground, and mosques and religious institutions were left in a state of decay and disrepair. Any dissent or resistance to Kemalist reforms was liable to severe punishment through the notorious Independence Tribunals (Albayrak 1984: 210–13).

The de-Islamization policy was strictly enforced throughout the 1930s and during the Inonu years until the late 1940s. In several cases, de-Islamization was carried out in an oppressive manner, as for example in the case of Sheyk Said Nursi, the leader of the Nurcu *tarikat*, who was systematically persecuted and repeatedly charged by the state prosecutor for treason only to be acquitted each time. In 1923, Nursi visited Ankara, the seat of the new Republic, but he did not conceal his contempt for Kemalist secularism. In a speech at that time he declared that

> the morale of the people of faith was extremely high as a result of the victory of Islam over the Greeks. But I saw that an abominable current of atheism was treacherously attempting to subvert, poison and destroy their morale.

(Nursi quoted in Algar,
in Kurshid Ahmad and Ansari 1979: 319)

These were harsh words. In particular, to brand the War of Independence of the Turkish nation, 'victory of Islam' was not only insulting, it was a candid admission of the chasm which separated the Kemalists and traditionalists. The fight between them was bitter, nasty and brutal, but not short.

The return of Islam and counter-response

Then in the mid-1940s a reversal set in initiated, surprisingly, by none other than Inonu, Ataturk's right-hand man and his successor. This reversal was occasioned by concern about growing atheism and loose public morality; and by villagers' complaints that they could not bury the dead or circumcise their children for lack of clergy. There were heated debates in parliament. Then Inonu decided to act. In 1947 new legislation was introduced creating a system of religious middle schools, *imam hatip*, to train Islamic clergy; making Qur'anic instruction in elementary schools compulsory, and shortly afterwards opening a Faculty of Religion (Albayrak 1984: 250–76). The pace of Islamic restoration quickened after 1950 when Democrats under Menderes won a stunning election victory against Inonu. The Democrats restored the Arabic *ezan* (call to prayers), and began lifting the ban on *tekkes* and *tarikats*. While the original intent behind this limited Islamic revival might have been to correct the excesses of the 1930s and 1940s, the Democrats soon discovered that Islam could be exploited as a powerful vote-getting tool (Albayrak 1984: 284 *et seq.*). However, abusing Islam for political ends was anti-Kemalist and unacceptable, in particular, to the military elite who regarded themselves as the ultimate guardian of Kemalism.

Menderes went too far or perhaps he went too far too soon for the centrist elites. By mixing religion and politics, however, Menderes undermined the basic Kemalist tenet. He increasingly appeared to the bureaucratic, military and political elites at the centre as an opportunist who would even dismantle Kemalism to stay in power. When, in addition, he began to mismanage the economy, squandered the large western aid and caused inflation, he prepared the ground for his personal tragedy (Hale 1981: chap. 5). A major setback for the nascent Turkish democracy occurred when the first military *coup d'état* took place in 1960 (Feroz Ahmad 1977).

The 1960 coup checked the Islamization trend and restored Kemalist secularism. But this was a partial and temporary limitation. In 1963, civilian rule was restored, an event which marked the end of authoritarian cultural restructuring imposed from above. It brought in a highly liberal constitution which guaranteed personal freedoms. Rapid industrialization and urbanization began to change the traditional values and attitudes of the rapidly expanding Turkish population. In particular, *gecekondus* (urban shanty towns), became the fertile breeding grounds of a new Islamic revival, centred on the *tekkes* and *tarikats* – a process which assumed a new, and international, aspect in the 1970s.

The growth of 'parallel' Islam

In Turkey there are two versions of Islam: 'official' Islam created by the nationalists under the control of the Republic; and a 'parallel' Islam (Dumont in Akural 1987), a kind of underground religious movement. Islamic resurgence involves primarily 'parallel' Islam centred around *tarikats* and *tekkes* which, legally speaking, are banned. In theory, *tarikats* are non-political, religious orders devoted to a mystical 'search of divine truth'. They function under the total authority of a leader, *sheyk* or *halife*. The organizational unit of each *tarikat* is the *tekke* (convent), which acts both as a place of prayers and also as a community centre providing social, educational and mutual aid services funded by contributions from the membership and revenue from *vakfs* (Saylan 1987).

The Kemalists had abolished the *tekkes* and *tarikats* because they represented centres of authority competing with the Republic. Members of a particular *tarikat* owed total allegiance to the *sheyk* who was the absolute ruler of the movement. In any situation of conflicting loyalties, the *tarikat*, which represented a 'philosophy of life' and required total commitment, could be expected to win out over the national government (Gungor 1987: 37–9). Since there were numerous *tarikats* with large followings, Kemalists could not implement their policy of national reconstruction with a population fragmented into various religious sects and split by conflicting loyalties.

There was a second powerful reason. *Tekkes* and *tarikats* represented potential obstacles to Kemalist cultural restructuring. Over the centuries, they had lost their character as centres of mysticism and Sufi learning to become nests of superstitious beliefs and rituals. Along with the *taqlid* system of Qur'anic education, the *tekkes* had contributed to the mass ignorance (*cehalet*) that characterized the Turkish masses. This *cehalet* suited the *sheyks*, *dervishes*, and *mullahs*, who, basking under the traditional respect owed to learned teachers identified by the Islamic garb, enjoyed a monopoly over public opinion and collective morality. Kemalist secularism and cultural transformation could only be implemented if the superstitions of the old system could be thrown out in their entirety.

But the *tekkes* and *tarikats* had other useful social roles as well. They provided membership in a mutual aid society. The *tarikat* functioned along the lines of a classic feudal patron–client relationship. In exchange for obedience and loyalty to the *sheyk*, the followers of the *tarikat* could claim valuable benefits ranging from financial assistance to access to education, medical care and job placement.

The rapid urbanization after 1960 changed the Turkish urban–rural equilibrium. Urban-based industrialization caused a rural exodus into *gecekondus* (Karpat 1976). The mutual aid services of the *tarikats* proved increasingly valuable to the migrants in *gecekondus*. The squatters had no secure land titles and could not claim official protection from the authorities. They were physically and psychologically outside the jurisdiction of the government. Always faced with the threat of eviction at short notice, they were in desperate need of protection and sponsorship. Hence the *gecekondus* were ideal recruiting grounds for the *tarikats*. This explains their reappearance in the 1960s and 1970s.

There were, as well, other contributing factors. One was the relative liberalism and greater tolerance during the Second Republic towards Islamic political parties. Religious movements forged open alliances with a particular party in search of political protection and rewards. Consistent with their traditional conservatism, these *tarikats* favoured parties on the ideological right. Examples of this were the Nurcu and Naksebendi support for the Justice Party, successor of the Democratic Party of Menderes. The party which gained the greatest support of the Islamic resurgence at this time was the National Salvation Party (NSP) led by Necmettin Erbakan (Saribay 1985). The NSP, established in October 1972, espoused an Islamist political philosophy centred on 'morals and virtue' with a particular appeal to small traders and low-income groups in contrast to big business (Margulies and Yildizoglu 1988). It emerged as the party with the third largest block of seats in the general elections one year later, gaining about 12 per cent of the total votes cast. This was a period of great political instability, economic chaos and ideological violence in Turkey (Karpat 1981; MERIP Reports 1984). In this crucial period, the NSP held the balance of power and was able to forge coalitions of expediency with the two major parties: the Republican People's Party led by the social democrat Ecevit and the Justice party led by Demirel and closely allied to big business interests. For the Islamists, the long days of banishment had now ended; they emerged to occupy the centre-stage in Turkish politics. Taking advantage of the situation, the NSP exercised an inordinate degree of Islamic influence over public policy. Thus, several Islamic measures were enacted, including compulsory religious instruction in all primary and middle schools, anti-pornography laws, more religious broadcasts on state radio and television, and a major expansion in the size of the religious bureaucracy (Landau 1981). Ironically, the power of the Islamists in the period of political instability was matched by the ascendancy of the Turkish left (Samin 1981). However, left and right were both hopelessly fragmented with an astonishing degree of inter-faction rivalry and strong inclination to resort to ideological violence.

The third military *coup d'état* in September 1980, was successful in ending the reign of ideological violence into which Turkey had plunged, but it was not able to stop *irtica*, Islamic reaction. *Tarikats* became bigger and more prosperous, their publications multiplied (Saylan 1987), and the Islamic extremists' call for a *sheri'at* regime in Turkey became louder, though not more popular. During 1984–7, the number of people tried by the state for attempting to change the character of the secular Turkish republic rose from 2 to 128 (Feroz Ahmad 1988). A new and significant trend in the Turkish *tarikats* was the fact that they began to go international, developing funding and ideological links with like-minded organizations in Saudi Arabia and Iran as well as with the Turkish guest-workers in Western Europe. The most notorious activity of this international Islamic network was the so-called Rabita Affair, which exposed that Turkish *imams* (prayer-leaders) in Germany and Belgium were in the pay of the Saudi-based World Islamic League (Rabit'at al-Alam al-Islami) advocating the overthrow of Kemalist secularism in Turkey in favour of *sheri'at* (Mumcu 1987).

The emergence of patron—client type *tarikats* among Turkish migrant settlements in Western Europe, especially in West Berlin, reveals another interesting dimension of the Turkish identity crisis (Abadan—Unat in Basgoz and Furniss 1985). It is an understandable phenomenon for at least two reasons. In the first place the *tarikat* functions as an adjustment mechanism easing entry and survival in an alien environment. Thus the migrant worker is often provided with assisted passage, a job and protection and help against bureaucracies, landlords, etc. Second, the *tarikat* provides cultural confirmation and belongingness to an in-group of like-minded Muslims facing discrimination and hostility in a Christian setting. Thus, the membership in the *tarikat* allows the migrant worker to regain his sense of identity. It has been observed by social scientists studying Turkish migrant women that even the more 'modern' migrants become more Islamic after arrival:

> Turkish women who arrived dressed in skirts or pants, shifted over after a couple of years to the typical Turkish dress abroad — meaning headscarf, wide pants under the dress — in order to demonstrate their belongingness and identity to the in-group. They admitted that in Ankara or Istanbul they would reject this way of dressing by qualifying it as reactionary and conservative. However, they underlined that the manifold deprivations and discriminations they encountered abroad, forced them to adhere symbolically to their in-group.
>
> (G. Elwert quoted in Abadan-Unat ibid: 18)

The *tarikats* among Turkish settlements in western Europe have also acquired considerable wealth from membership dues. Thus, they finance schools, mosques, publications and community services. They have developed close links with Turkish political parties back in Turkey, typically with the ultra-Islamic National Salvation Party and with the extreme neo-fascist party of Alparslan Turkes and those *irtica* groups working for a Khomeini-style theocracy in Turkey. The Rabita Affair, mentioned above, has doubly embarrassed the Turkish government, by forcing it to admit that foreign exchange constraints had obliged it to go along with a scheme whereby the clergy ministering to Turkish workers in Europe were placed on the Saudi Arabian payroll, and, even more embarrassingly, that some of these clergy were rabid anti-Kemalists working for a Khomeini-style Islamic state in Turkey.

Thus, Islam among the Turks, both at home and abroad, remains a strong reassertion of identity. If ever there was a Kemalist wish for Islam to wither away, it has not done so and is unlikely to do so in the future when human rights are expected to flourish rather than diminish. The elusive search for an optimal balancing of Islam and Turkish politics remains as a continuing challenge, but one that pluralism and development are rending increasingly manageable.

Conclusion

What emerges from the above survey of the confrontation between the nationalist modernizers and the traditionalists is a strong image of two sets of actors (or better still combatants) vying with each other to seek power, and speak as the 'moral voice' of society. In this confrontation the modernizers, playing the role of western-izers, attempted to win over the hearts and souls of the grass roots with the magic of nationalism, charging the traditionalist camp as the voice of superstition and regression.

Did the nationalist modernizers succeed? Clearly not. Their failure is all the more remarkable in view of the initial success of the Malay and Turkish nationalist ideology to win a considerable measure of popular consensus for economic development and cultural restructuring imposed from the top. At first, it looked as if the modernizers would win hands down. But, after decades of top-down national leadership, it is evident that the nationalist elites of the Islamic Periphery have failed to score a knock-out. How do we explain their failure? We now turn to examine this question.

Chapter six

Turkish etatism
Creation of a non-competitive economy

From its formation in 1923 until 1980, the Turkish Republic followed a national economic policy that was intended to open a new era of prosperity for the Turkish people. The chosen development strategy, however, conflicted with the populist objectives of Kemalism. Under this strategy, known as etatism (*Devletcilik*), the state assumed direct control of resource allocation by means of economic planning and public enterprise. The result was a non-competitive, corporatist economy (Tachau 1984) with a strong capital and pro-urban bias. Etatism also failed to promote equity in income distribution. The roots of the Islamic resurgence in Turkey are to be found in the failure of the nationalist development strategy to deliver social justice.

The national economic policy of the Republic can be sub-divided into three periods: first, the one-party phase of early etatism; second, the false start during the Menderes decade; and third, the import substitution industrialization between 1960 and 1980. Throughout all three periods, however, etatism remained the dominant economic philosophy.

This chapter is organized in two main sections. The first provides a historical survey of the etatist strategy under the management of centrist elites. Its main conclusion is that the economic and political crisis that culminated in the coup of 1980 was the result of a systemic failure characterized by elite mismanagement. The second section contains an assessment of the ideological determinants of elite mismanagement and the rise of Islamic resurgence as a response to it.

Etatism and rent-seeking behaviour

All phases of etatism need to be analysed against the commanding ideology of Kemalism. It shaped the development strategy following the establishment of the Republic of Turkey in 1923 which was briefly surveyed in the second section of Chapter 5.

The economic strategy of Kemalism

The paramount objective of Kemalism is national independence through development, or in Ataturk's words, 'complete independence'. By 'complete independence' he meant 'complete freedom in political, financial, economic, judicial, military and all other matters'. (UNESCO 1963: 185). Even before the military victory in the National War of Independence, Ataturk fixed his sight on a long-term 'economic victory' and declared a new

economic era in which our country will become developed, prosperous and rich . . .

Friends, from now on we shall win new important victories, but those will not be won by the bayonet; they will be economic, scientific and educational victories. One cannot say that the victory won by our armies has brought true salvation to our country. This victory provides valuable ground on which our future victories will be won. Let us not pride ourselves on our military victory, but rather prepare ourselves for new scientific and economic victories.

(UNESCO 1963: 188)

Ataturk was a populist who believed that 'economic victory' should benefit the Turkish peasantry whom he regarded as the real 'owner and master of Turkey'. In a speech on 1 March 1922, before the War of Independence had ended, he described the place of the peasantry in the national economy as follows:

Who is the owner and the master of Turkey? We can all give an immediate answer to this question. The real owner and master of Turkey is the peasant, the producer. It follows that the peasant has a greater claim to prosperity, happiness and wealth than anyone esle.

(UNESCO 1963: 187)

In this speech, he outlined his own economic priorities:

1. To revive agriculture which has been ruined by European competition and re-equip it with modern means.
2. To maintain the forests in a good condition and make, the most of them.
3. To nationalise, to the extent allowed by the country's resources, the institutions and economic enterprises of direct public concern.

4. To exploit the country's mineral resources, permitting and protecting private capital investments.
5. While agriculture and agricultural industries provided the economic basis of the country, other existing industries, such as the textile industry, should be developed and protected, and serious efforts should be made to establish industries in other parts of the country.
6. To ensure the financial independence of the country. This, in turn, meant having a budget proportionate to the country's economic resources.

(UNESCO 1963: 189)

Although Ataturk shared this generation's rejection of capitulations, he recognized the need for foreign investment so long as it respected Turkish laws. At the Economic Congress in Izmir in early 1923, he announced a liberal economic policy welcoming foreign investment so long as it respected Turkish laws and sovereignty:

Our country has not sufficient capital to develop its resources in a short space of time. It is therefore in our interests to make use of outside capital and resources. . . . Let it not be thought that we are hostile to foreign capital. No, ours is a vast country requiring much capital and great efforts. Provided that our laws are respected, we are always ready to give the necessary assurances to foreign capital.

(UNESCO 1963: 191)

Yet, within a decade, the national economic strategy became autarkic and etatist. In the process a populist, agrarian strategy was abandoned, as was a policy of economic liberalism promoting private enterprise. Gradually, but surely, the young Turkish Republic adopted an authoritarian strategy of state capitalism under the direct control and management of centrist elites. At the outset these elites consisted of the top political/military/bureaucratic leadership which shared a conviction of having saved the nation and was now dedicated to the task of leading it. After 1960, in the period of high economic growth under import substitution industrialization, a new state-sponsored capitalist class emerged into the ranks of the centrist elites. The etatist strategy remained in force until 1980. Although it underwent several policy shifts in the preceding half century, it never lost its highly centralized, 'top-down' character: the frequent policy shifts merely reflected power struggles within these centrist elites.

Building the etatist economy: the early phase

In view of frequent policy shifts which marked its history, it is not surprising that etatism has been variously described as 'a modernized form of mercantilism', 'an advanced type of socialism', 'a third way outside capitalism and socialism', or more aptly, 'a poorly managed capitalist economy' controlled by the government (Hale 1981: 55). At the outset, it was shaped as much by the Ottoman legacy, and the world economic situation confronting the new Turkish Republic, as by Kemalist ideology.

Structurally the Turkish economy in 1923 was in ruins, caused by years of war and having virtually no manufacturing base. Capital and entrepreneurship were lacking as a result of the departure of Greeks and Armenians who had controlled Ottoman trade and industry. Legally, the capitulations were to remain in force until 1927 as provided under the Treaty of Lausanne. Thus, at the outset, Ataturk endorsed a pragmatic 'mixed' economy policy. While allowing room for private enterprise and espousing economic liberalism, he gave top priority to the creation of a national financial system. In 1924, the Is Bank was established to provide finance for private business undertaking. In 1925, the Industrial and Mining Bank was set up as a purely state bank to finance public ventures. In 1927, a law was passed to promote private enterprise in conformity with the early Kemalist commitment to a 'mixed economy' model.

The Wall Street Crash in 1929 and the ensuing world economic depression provided the occasion for the transition from a 'mixed economy' to an etatist model. The collapse of commodity prices in the aftermath of the 1929 Crash, and rising fascism in Europe, were ominous external signals of an impending international crisis, and they quickly led the nascent Turkish national leadership to adopt autarkical controls (Tekeli and Ilkin 1977). Politically, the etatist transition was relatively easy in view of the ideological homogeneity of the messianic, centrist elites backed by a strong grassroot consensus for the Kemalist dream of a strong national economy. If the 1929 Crash had spawned etatism, it was the Kemalist economic nationalism which legitimized its institutionalization and entrenchment at the centre well beyond the 1930s.

Kemalism was more than Ataturk's own ideas. It was shaped by intellectuals before and others after Ataturk. For example, the highly influential Turkish nationalist Ziya Gokalp firmly believed in a national economy as a necessary condition for the viability of the Turkish state. Gokalp rejected Ricardo's free trade theory of comparative advantage, dismissing it as 'nothing but the national economics of Britain' (quoted in Walsted 1977: 67), and relying instead on the protectionist theories of Frederich List. Gokalp's economic nationalism had won a great convert in Ataturk's right-hand man and successor, Ismet Inonu, as we shall discuss later.

The official launching of etatism occurred in 1933. It was marked with the creation of Sumerbank as a combined state bank and national holding company. In that year, too, five-year economic planning began with Russian economic and technical assistance. An interest-free $18 million loan for industrial development was negotiated and, even more significantly, Russian technicians were invited to Turkey to set up an economic planning machinery. In announcing the first five-year plan, Prime Minister Inonu made this point very clear in justifying his etatist strategy:

> The purpose of making Turkey an independent nation finds its expression in the will to change her into a self-sufficient body . . . and to entrust either the State or some national concerns with the building up of such industries as, it was thought, private capital was unable to establish . . .
>
> (Inonu quoted in Thornburg *et al*. 1949: 35)

In the following period, etatism was vigorously implemented through waves of state economic enterprises (SEEs) built as state monopolies and financed by subsidies and low-interest bearing borrowings from the state. SEEs mushroomed in every sector of the economy: in railways, shipping, heavy industry, physical infrastructure, banking, mining, manufacturing, agriculture, tourism, services, etc. (Hale 1981: chaps 4–5).

For administrative purposes SEEs were granted considerable autonomy. They were placed under the jurisdiction of a General Economic Commission, chaired by the Prime Minister, and were allowed to operate as off-budget agencies. Their expenditures were excluded from the national budget, and their revenues were not required to be turned over to the Treasury.

In the circumstances of the 1920s and 1930s, it is not difficult to make an 'infant industry' argument in support of the claim that the SEEs filled an economic vacuum in the young, war-torn Turkish Republic. The SEEs spearheaded the construction of basic industries, provided useful training ground for future managerial and skilled manpower, and they supplied infrastructural facilities which the country desperately needed. It can even be argued that by under-pricing such goods and services, the SEEs helped promote private entrepreneurial activity in later years although, of course, this was not cost free.

But after 1936 etatism became the official dogma of the single party led by Inonu. Industry, physical infrastructure and urban growth were pursued at the expense of the welfare of the Anatolian peasantry. Rural development, village needs and land reform were systematically ignored. In 1945 agricultural production was what it had been in 1929 (Alexander in Pepelasis *et al.* 1961: 474).

How the villagers lived?

The backbone of the Turkish nation was the *koylu* (village folk) in Anatolia, depending on traditional agriculture structured in a localized version of patron—client feudalism dominated by the landowning *agas* (Kiray 1982). The injustices of this system have been vividly portrayed in the epic novel by Yashar Kemal *Memed My Hawk* (1984). Anatolian trade and commerce had been in the hands of the Armenians, the Jews and the Greeks who, as in the case of the Chinese in Malaysia, also performed the role of money-lenders to the *koylu* with the inevitable results of indebtedness and interethnic conflict. Ottoman policies of military service imposed on the Turkish males meant that agriculture was left in care of the women, while trade and commerce passed into the hands of non-Muslim ethnic minorities. While the Christian *millets* prospered, especially in the nineteenth century when the Ottoman Empire was incorporated into the European capitalist system, the Turkish *millet* was impoverished (Kasaba 1988; Pamuk 1987). Education and social services for the *koylu* were either not available or inadequate; western missionaries had educational and welfare centres in several places in Anatolia, but these were only for the benefit of Christian minorities. At the end of the Turkish War of Independence, most of these minorities had gone, but the etatist leadership made little attempt to develop substitute Turkish human capital. In 1924 a *koy kanunu* (village law) was passed providing for *koy enstitusu* (village institutes) in order to provide basic primary education, but it was a short-lived experiment which was terminated for political reasons, and the 1924 law, as with several promises of land reform, remained dormant. As late as the 1950s, little had altered, structurally or qualitatively, in the life of the *koylu*. When a pioneering British anthropologist went in 1949 to study village life in the Kayseri province in central Turkey, he was entirely correct in his observation that 'the greatest gap in our knowledge of Turkey was, and still is, how the villagers live' (Sterling 1965: 3).

Social change and economic development did not reach the *koylu* until the Menderes decade of the 1950s. Even villages close to the new national capital were relatively untouched by early etatism. Daniel Lerner's classic modernization study (1958) was focused on

Balgat, then a village eight kilometres outside, but now well inside, Ankara. His study is more remarkable in its demonstration of the glaring social and economic distance which separated the *koylu* and the urban elites a full three decades after the establishment of the Republic, than the symbols and indexes of the 'passing of traditional society'. The sad fact was that the etatist mind-set quickly reverted back to the Ottoman mentality of mistrusting the *koylu*, centralizing in its own hands all the decision-making concerning resource allocation and priorities, and adopting an urban-biased development strategy.

Inonu: the chief architect of etatism

Inonu had the most decisive influence on etatism. His authority was second only to that of Ataturk, whom he succeeded and attempted to style himself as *Milli Sef* (National Chief), but with limited success. In 1936, at the height of the one-party rule and Ataturk a dying man, he made etatism a state dogma by including it in the constitution and then adopted it as the ideology of the Republican People's Party. After Ataturk's death in 1938, etatism 'degenerated' (Berkes 1965: 106); but the war years and, after 1950, the transfer of power to the Menderes Democrats helped conceal its fundamental flaws.

The 'degeneracy' of etatism arose from the fact its chief architect, Inonu, had a poor understanding of economics. At the Lausanne Conference, where he was the chief Turkish delegate, he was given high marks for his negotiating skills. In fact, he can be criticized for his handling of the economic issues. His absorbing aim at Lausanne had been to obtain the agreement of the western powers to end the capitulations. To achieve this he traded the Turkish trump card of the Middle Eastern oilfields, which were in the Ottoman Empire, for a mere 10 per cent share in British Petroleum. Subsequently, he was to sell this share for just £500,000, in order to finance the construction of Ankara's Cubuk Baraj dam (Kinross 1964: 410). While giving up 80 per cent of the pre-1914 Ottoman Empire, Inonu had agreed to burden the war-ravaged Turkish Republic with the Ottoman Debt, a burden that was not discharged until 1954 (Kepenek 1987: 35).

Inonu was a military man, an excellent chief of staff. Living in a fascist period, he espoused economic nationalism and authoritarianism. For Inonu, etatism was a matter of necessity justified on grounds of national security and survival: 'The policy of economic etatism, above all, by being a policy of defense, appears to be a necessity in itself' (quoted in IBRD 1951: 7).

Inonu's world-view was one of autarky. His objective was a self-reliant economy freed from external dependence on finance and trade. As a Kemalist, Inonu was an economic nationalist; he had a great mistrust of foreign bankers and financiers, whom he blamed for the financial ruin of the Ottoman Empire (Aydemir 1966). Inonu regarded self-sufficiency as a matter of national security and justified heavy investments in railroads and infrastructure on the basis of his popular slogan, 'three whites and three blacks', that is, self-sufficiency in flour, sugar and cotton textiles, and in coal, iron and petroleum (quoted in Walsted 1977: 66). But Inonu, like Ataturk, was no economist. He knew little, if anything at all, about the rules of allocative efficiency, marginal productivity and opportunity cost. He dismissed the possibility that a corporatist economy might become uncompetitive and wasteful. His development strategy was not based on efficiency but on nationalism. It was anti-rural, anti-populist and highly corporatist.

Inonu's inclination for etatism was reinforced by the then influential group of ideologues formed around the magazine *Kadro* owned by Yakup Kardi Karaosmanoglu and edited by the Soviet-trained Sevket Aydemir (Sadiq 1986). The *Kadro* group was quite well-informed about the world economy. Its judgement in favour of national reconstruction via self-reliant industrialization was not without justification when it is appraised against the background of the Wall Street Crash of 1929, and the onset of the Great Depression (Tekeli and Ilkin 1977, Boratov 1974). Clearly, in the specific circumstances of the early 1930s, an export-oriented growth with foreign capital did not look like a realistic alternative to protectionist industrialization. Western capital was unavailable and domestic savings, through demand compression and forced savings, were the major means of mobilizing finance for infrastructural projects. Therefore, national economic reconstruction could only mean state capitalism. The economic welfare of the *koylu* had to be sacrificed on the altar of corporatism.

Cost aside, in this early phase of etatism, Turkey did indeed make 'substantial progress' as judged by a World Bank mission which also observed: 'It is doubtful if comparable accomplishment would have taken place in this period under domestic private enterprise with the handicap of the Ottoman heritage' (IBRD 1951: 9).

On the other hand, another team of foreign experts, less aware of the historical constraints of the case, dismissed the national development strategy of etatism arguing that it had 'deliberately discouraged' private enterprise which was 'hardly given a fair trial'. (Thornburg *et al.* 1949: 33–4).

Etatism: the later years

While etatist philosophy could be justified in the circumstances of the inter-war era, it is hard to do so subsequently, especially in the post-war period. At the end of the Second World War, thanks to her neutrality in the war, Turkey possessed a functioning, if still inadequate, economic infrastructure, and a balance-of-payments surplus. The economy overall compared favourably with such neighbouring countries as Greece, as well as with Japan, South Korea and many war-devastated European countries. Politically, the country had moved to a multi-party system in 1950 (Karpat 1959). These favourable circumstances were further reinforced by the huge American and western financial inflows as a result of Turkish entry into NATO, OECD and the Korean War (Hale 1981: chap. 5). If the Turkish economy, like Turkish politics, had been placed on a competitive and trade-oriented footing at this time, it is quite likely that, by 1980, Turkey would have become the Japan, or at least the South Korea, of the Middle East.

Etatism survived the Menderes decade. In fact, in 1959 the SEE sector was larger than it had been in 1950 despite the fact that the Democrats boasted of being a party of economic liberalism and free enterprise. After the military coup of May 1960, etatism was restored with central planning and SEEs as key elements of the national economic policy. Successive governments led by Inonu, Ecevit and Demirel kept on expanding the SEEs, wasting economic resources and ignoring the basic structural deficiencies of the etatist model. By so doing, these politicians in effect sacrificed national economic interest for short-term political gains. In so doing they all helped bring about the economic crisis and political chaos of 1979–80.

The Menderes false start

In retrospect, it seems that the decade of the 1950s was the proper time for the restoration of a competitive, trade-oriented Turkish economy. This is what actually happened in Japan and, shortly afterwards, in South Korea, Taiwan, Hong Kong and Singapore (Mehmet 1989). Such an economic restructuring would have required promoting the private sector by gradually privatizing the SEEs, offering appropriate incentives to investors and undertaking monetary and trade reforms to develop a competitive, export-oriented industry.

To be sure, the Menderes Democrats began with promises along these lines, boasting to turn the country into 'little America within thirty years' (Celal Bayar quoted in Hale 1981: 88). However, they quickly abandoned not only economic planning – Menderes argued that 'the budget is the Plan' (quoted in Hale 1981: 88) – but also economic rationality itself. Discretionary and costly policy shifts became the rule of the times (Singer 1977), generating rapid inflation, huge deficits and a crippling external imbalance which fuelled the political crisis which, in turn, resulted in the military coup of May 1960.

In the early 1950s agricultural output had risen impressively thanks to a combination of good weather and dramatic gains in labour productivity which were due to imported farm technology based on tractors. But this was highly capital-intensive technology which generated a huge labour surplus. The Democrats' agricultural strategy was uneven; while mechanizing traditional agriculture to boost output, it neither adopted a labour-intensive strategy, nor pushed through a programme of major land redistribution and complementary innovations as happened, for example, in Taiwan and South Korea. As a result, no significant alternative employment opportunities in rural areas were generated. The mechanization of agriculture increased economic inequalities and upset the tradition rural equilibrium. There was a huge, chaotic rural exodus into towns where housing and other amenities did not exist. The result was the mushrooming of urban shanty towns; the *gecekondus* (squatter settlements, literally meaning 'landed at night') were to become the breeding grounds of new social movements in later years.

The Democrats' industrial strategy was no better. Again, capital-intensity was emphasized despite emerging excess labour pressures. With no coherent plan or policy, factories and industries were built without any concern for cost, efficiency or locational advantage. Only political advantage seemed to matter. Redundant sugar and cement factories built by Democrats were notorious. As Hale expressed it:

> examples of badly planned and located plants abounded in the 1950's. The Democrats' primary purpose was to win votes. Accordingly, they were frequently prepared to establish factories in politically sensitive areas, even if the production costs were unnecessarily high, or there was no demand for their products. . . . Overall, the production of cement rose at an average of around 17.8 per cent during the 1950's, so that domestic production exceeded demand by 1959. To keep the plants operating at near capacity, Turkey was forced to dump cement, at a loss, on foreign markets during 1959–60.

A similar pattern emerged in the case of sugar, where production had overtaken consumption by a substantial margin by 1955. In spite of this, the state-controlled Turkish Sugar Factories continued to open new plants, so that by 1960 the surplus of production stood at over 345,000 tonnes, or almost 54 per cent of total output. Of this, just under 200,000 tonnes was exported – again, at a substantial loss.

(Hale 1981: 92–3)

In other industries, the Democrats followed the same misguided pricing and investment policies. In iron and steel, they attempted to expand domestic productive capacity by building a second plant at Eregli to supplement the high-cost plant at Karabuk; yet they failed to protect the Karabuk plant against lower-priced imported steel, thereby generating costly unused capacity. In textile manufacturing, despite rapid expansion of a private sector, they not only maintained the giant Sumerbank, but they crippled it by price controls that kept its prices well below its private competitors, generating excess capacity and large operating deficits (Singer 1977: 265–80).

Untrue to their own economic philosophy, the Menderes Democrats kept on expanding the size of the public sector. In manufacturing, the SEEs accounted for 57 per cent of total fixed capital formation in 1958 compared with 54.4 per cent in 1950 (Hale 1981: 91). Most importantly, the SEEs became objects of patronage politics. Loss-making SEEs multiplied as favouritism, featherbedding and political interference in their management became political tools.

Systemic mismanagement in the SEE sector

At the beginning, the SEEs were not expected to operate as state monopolies stifling private enterprise and depending upon subsidies. In fact, law no. 3460 enacted in 1938 provided for the possibility that SEEs would be reconstituted as joint-stock companies in which shares, either wholly or in part, could be transferred to the private sector. They were also expected to operate as profit-making (if not profit-maximizing) entities. But in practice this provision was discarded. Privileged arms-length relations with the state and protective policies turned SEEs into permanent and non-competitive state monopolies. They were provided with loans from the Central Bank at 1 per cent interest, whereas private borrowers had to pay 8.5–12 per cent on commercial loans. Not only were the SEEs free from domestic competition, they were generally insulated fom international competition by protective tariffs and an over-valued Turkish lira which encouraged import substitution at the expense of exports (Krueger 1974a).

Thus there was a lack of the profit motive in the SEE model. Successful management was not based on profitability. An operating loss did not mean corporate bankruptcy or personal disgrace. Pricing and investment policies were centralized in the hands of bureaucrats and politicians. Administered prices had no relation to either production costs or market conditions. Under the circumstances, loss-making SEEs multiplied with relative ease. Political connections sheltered operational losses and managerial incompetence. In short, the SEE sector became the centre of patronage politics dominated by featherbedding and favouritism. As losses and deficits mounted, mismanagement had a cancerous effect on professional standards and worker morale (Walsted 1977: 66 and 76–7). Patronage politics spawned rent-seeking behaviour.

Post-1960 import substitution industrialization

The heyday of rent-seeking behaviour in the etatist economy was not the Menderes decade. It was the period from 1960 to 1980, following the restoration of parliamentary democracy after the military coup against Menderes in 1960. This was the period when import substitution industrialization (ISI) was adopted as the principal development strategy. It was also a period of unprecedented growth of civil and constitutional liberties thanks to the provisions of the Constitution of the Second Republic. In particular, Turkish workers for the first time won the right to form trade unions, bargain collectively and strike.

The adoption of ISI signalled the rising importance of the Turkish capitalist class. Still dependent on state protection and subsidy, the Turkish capitalists joined the centrist political, bureaucratic and military elites. The result was a non-competitive industrial strategy based on a mixture of private and public enterprise. On the one hand, private 'infant' industries, owned and operated by the emerging class of industrialists, were encouraged by a variety of protective policies. On the other hand, state planning and etatist intervention in the economy were restored. 'Infant' industries did not replace SEEs; there was little attempt to privatize or denationalize state economic enterprises. Most tellingly, resource allocation became even more non-competitive than before.

Not surprisingly, therefore, the ISI strategy exacerbated the structural imbalance of the Turkish economy. On the one hand, private 'infant' industries were heavily subsidized by tariffs and other measures which amounted to effective rates of protection of up to 400 per cent or higher (Krueger 1974a). On the other hand, the role of the SEE sector began to change. It began to act as supplier of underpriced inputs to private 'infant' industries. Under the weight of these indirect subsidies, the SEE operating losses sky-rocketed, necessitating matching fiscal replenishment from the national budget. The profits of the capitalist class were matched by rents collected by middlemen arranging licenses, obtaining permits or simply peddling influence. Rent-seeking and accumulating budget deficits directly contributed to the economic crisis of 1979–80.

Macro trends

In macro-economic terms, however, the period from 1960 to 1980 was one of rapid economic growth. Income per capita rose five-fold, industry's share of GNP surpassed that of agriculture, and no less than half of the GNP originated in services (Hale 1981: 129–31). But, on the other hand, the Turkish economy was highly insular; in 1977 exports accounted for just 4 per cent of the GDP compared to 20 per cent for a sample of middle income countries (MICs). Furthermore, the Turkish industry was highly capital intensive and created too few jobs. For example, employment in industry absorbed only 14 per cent of the labour force compared to 22 per cent for the same sample of MICs (World Bank 1980: 6). Anne Krueger, after an extensive review of the industrialization strategy under the first and second plans, concluded that a more labour-intensive and export-oriented strategy would have been con-siderably more efficient. Thus, at identical levels of investment, the Turkish economy could have generated a total of 300,000 more jobs, along with lower import costs and higher levels of output (Krueger 1974a).

The rapid growth of industry in the ISI period was inflationary. It was financed by monetary expansion caused by deficit spending and short-term foreign borrowing on highly unfavourable terms. The general price level in 1979 was some twelve times higher than in 1963. Declining real wages and higher cost of living caused increas-ing economic hardship for the masses. In the 1963–73 decade, the income share of the bottom 40 per cent declined from 13 per cent to 11.5 per cent (State Planning Organization quoted in Hale 1981: 137). By 1983, it is estimated that it had shrunk to just 9.6 per cent (Celasun 1986: 207).

Rent-seeking behaviour

The ISI strategy encouraged rent-seeking behaviour through cor-ruption, inefficiency and mismanagement. Import and exchange controls, licensing regulations and protective tariff policies provided the ideal environment for 'distributional coalitions' (Olson 1982). These coalitions and networks, made up of powerful bureaucrats with 'gate-keeping' roles or influential politicians with access to potentially profitable information about government contracts and projects, were able to extract 'transaction costs' and margins from collusion, corruption and influence-peddling. These rent-seeking behaviour patterns paralleled similar trends within the Malaysian New Economic Policy atmosphere discussed in Chapter 7. In the case of the Turkish ISI environment, there was so much graft and corruption in the SEEs during the period of hectic invest-ment under the first plan (1963–7), that several watchdog agencies in the Ministry of Finance and the High Control Board were created, but to no avail (Walsted 1977: 77).

While quasi-rents generated in the ISI phase enriched the centrist elites, it brought increasing economic distress for the masses victim-ized by falling real wages and incomes. The operating losses of the SEEs, financed by transfers from the national budget, generated an unprecedented monetary expansion which, in turn, led to spiralling inflation. Despite these heavy losses, almost half the total public sector investment in 1977 was earmarked for the SEEs; yet, the total SEE contribution to the GDP in 1977 was a mere 7 per cent, exactly the same proportion as a decade earlier in 1967. Feather-bedding swelled the size of the SEEs: during 1973–7, employment in the SEEs jumped by an incredible 52 per cent, going from 425,862 to 646,157. Overall in 1978 the state subsidies and transfers to cover the operating losses of the SEE sector equalled half the total current expenditure in the national consolidated budget (World Bank 1980: Tables 5.1 and 5.4). Chronic mismanagement of the SEEs was a major cause of the economic crisis in which Turkey found itself in 1979–80.

The emergence of competing ideologies

In the post-1960 period, the Kemalist national economic ideology came under increasing attack by competing ideologies, not only from the political right and left, but also from Islam. Rapid economic transformation, increased pluralism, and in particular a highly liberal constitutional environment unleashed a bewildering array of new ideologies, some neo-fascists, some anarchists, some religious, some ethnic or regional and several militant (Keyder 1987: esp. chap. VIII). These new ideologies shared one common aim: to confront the old authoritarian 'leader–follower' ideology, change the nature of the state and redefine the national agenda

139

(Weiker 1981). Monolithic Kemalist nationalism began to be fragmented as new interest groups emerged. The new capitalist was now
confronted with a class struggle as class-consciousness began to
take root among the industrial workers and the trade union leadership bargained for a new deal. The intellectual and the new
ideologies operated in two principal theatres: the university campus
and the *gecekondus*. The former was the breeding ground for
abstract, futuristic ideologies in which the cadres were the typical
university graduates co-opted by the relevant ideological faction by
offers of jobs or bribes. On the other hand, the *gecekondus*, the
home of the underdog, became the battleground for the rights of
the marginalized and the alienated. It proved fertile ground in
particular for the more traditional religious ideologies.

Competing new ideologies inevitably affected the centrist civilian
and military elites. The military brass, seeing itself as the custodian
of Kemalism, regarded the emerging pluralism as a source of
instability and a threat to Kemalist conformity. The civilian elites
became increasingly fragmented and polarized as technocrats and
politicians attempted to redeem their roles in new and conflicting
domains. The end was clear: etatism had outlived its usefulness.

SPO planning: technocrats versus political elites

The final, costly episode of etatism was conducted within the
framework of Five-Year Plans introduced in the aftermath of the
1960 military coup. Lack of planning was then regarded as a major
cause of the economic mismanagement under Menderes. In June
1960, a month after the coup, Professors Tinbergen and Koopman
were commissioned to advise the new leadership on the best form
of planning appropriate for Turkey, and the result was the establishment of the State Planning Organization (SPO). Tinbergen and
Koopman tended to opt for the French-style indicative planning.
Despite this, however, the Kemalist forces wanted to restore central
planning and the SPO emerged as a powerful instrument of
etatism. The prescription chosen was the ISI strategy based on the
usual menu of protective tariffs, overvalued currency and a wide
range of direct and indirect public subsidies for infant industries.
This was the wrong prescription which failed to take into account
the great structural changes that had occurred in the economy since
the 1930s. What was required was more, not less, competition.

As a consequence, the SPO planning had little relevance to the
rules of economic efficiency. It was pseudo-planning. Investment
and allocation decisions were frequently subject to political interference. Hence there was a clash between the planning technocrats

and the political leaders. This came to a head in October 1962, when there was mass resignation of the planners triggered by the insistence of the political leadership to adopt a 7 per cent growth rate despite the planners' warning that available resources could only sustain a 6.5 per cent growth rate.

The politicians had won a hollow victory and prepared their ultimate demise. They manipulated planning and relied on deficit financing to boost the growth rate; they followed a highly protectionist ISI strategy, they mismanaged the SEEs by featherbedding and low administered prices, and they covered operating losses with state subsidies financed partly by monetary expansion and short-term external borrowing. This was a recipe for short-term political gain and for long-term economic disaster. In the short term, the economy performed quite well, achieving an annual growth rate of 6.4 per cent during the First Plan period, 1963–7, and 6.7 per cent per annum during the Second Plan, 1968–72 (World Bank 1980: 1).

The delayed social costs of economic mismanagement became apparent in the early 1970s. Inflation began to emerge as an increasingly serious problem. But the crunch came with the OPEC crisis in October 1973. External disequilibrium, which in the late 1960s had been concealed with short-term borrowing and rising remittances from Turkish guest-workers in Europe, was no longer manageable after the quadrupled oil prices exposed the structural imbalances in the Turkish economy.

The political process, which had enjoyed an unprecedented growth and expansion in the 1960s thanks to liberalization measures introduced under the new Constitution, became increasingly fragmented. Kemalist forces became increasingly alarmed. On 12 March 1971 the military staged another coup; this time indirectly by memorandum. Effective power passed to the high command of the armed forces. However, both the political instability and the economic crisis worsened.

The balance of payments crisis

The major cause of the economic crisis of 1979–80 was the foreign exchange constraint. It took OPEC to expose the basic structural imbalance of the Turkish economy. The ISI strategy, based on cheap imported oil and producing for the highly uncompetitive domestic market, had crippled the economy since Turkish export earnings could barely cover the country's oil import bill. From 1974, external disequilibrium pushed the Turkish economy inexorably towards financial bankruptcy.

The culprit was the non-competitive, anti-trade etatist industrial strategy. Under this strategy, the necessity for export earnings was consistently ignored. Traditionally, any shortfall in foreign exchange earned from traditional agricultural exports was offset by foreign aid and military transfers from the United States or European allies. The Kemalist elites in charge of etatism consistently failed to recognize that Turkish exports were essential to pay for imports, and that Turkey's ability to earn foreign exchange depended on a competitive industrial strategy. There was no attempt to learn from the experience of Japan, South Korea, Taiwan, Hong Kong and Singapore.

The foreign exchange constraint was exacerbated by highly inappropriate fiscal and monetary policies. Fiscal policy had been, as we have seen, customarily mismanaged to write off the SEE deficits which after 1973 began to fuel hyper-inflation. Between 1970 and 1972 the annual inflation rate was a tolerable 14 per cent, but by the end of the decade it had reached an unprecedented rate of well in excess of 100 per cent. Monetary policy which was based on an over-valued Turkish lira, a negative real rate of interest, and expensive short-term foreign borrowing, sheltered a non-competitive, high-cost inward-looking industry. The origin of the external payments crisis after the mid-1970s lies in the 1960s, but this structural weakness was temporarily offset by significant inflows of remittances from Turkish workers in Europe.

In the mid-1970s, especially after the Cyprus intervention, the Turkish political system was too fragmented to cope with the deteriorating economic crisis. It sought remedy in short-term external borrowing. In the space of just six years, between 1972 and 1978, the Turkish foreign debt ratio jumped from 13.1 per cent to 26.7 per cent, most of it being in short-term borrowings (World Bank 1980: 31). In the meantime, political violence escalated to civil war proportions (MERIP 1984).

The final nail was put in the etatist coffin in early 1978. At that time the Turkish government, in a *de facto* state of bankruptcy, was obliged to seek financial relief from OECD countries while negotiating debt rescheduling with its external creditors. This was a humiliating pill for the etatist elites to swallow, recalling the Ottoman debt crisis of a century before. After bitter and protracted negotiations with the IMF a large standby agreement was reached in 1979 based on the usual IMF 'medicine' of deflationary stabilization and structural adjustment. Central in this package was a commitment to phase out etatism in favour of economic liberalization and an export-oriented strategy. The Turkish government undertook to cut the SEE subsidies, to privatize state monopolies and public enterprises, to devalue the Turkish lira to switch to a more open, competitive and free enterprise economy, and to encourage the private sector. Thus, after more than half a century, the ideology of etatism entered history. The politicians who could claim credit for this achievement were Demirel, the prime minister in 1979–80, who negotiated the IMF economic reform package, and Ozal, the prime minister after 1983, who actually implemented these reforms.

With the passing of etatism, the Turkish identity, nurtured on the ideology of nationalism, had received a new shock treatment. Threatened from the left as well as from a resurgent Islam, the Kemalist elites, with World Bank encouragement, gradually made way for a new market ideology. The Turkish development strategy entered its privatization phase. This will be examined in Chapter 10. But first a political economy assessment of the Kemalist national development ideology is in order.

Contradictions of a monocentric system

The Kemalist national development ideology, exemplified by etatism did not fail; it outlasted its original usefulness. It was originally an enlightened, if authoritarian, corporatist ideology shaped by historical and actual circumstances of the young Turkish Republic (Tachau 1984). For a decade or two it performed well, providing the Turkish nation with essential infrastructure and an opportunity of indigenous development by learning. Although its social costs were high, it put the Turkish Republic on the road to economic development (Rostow 1963: 38).

Subsequently, however, the national development ideology became dysfunctional. The Turkish economy could not graduate from the take-off stage of development into a self-sustaining phase. Etatism legitimized a self-serving, monocentric system (Heper 1979–80). In the institutionalization of the monocentric system, the authoritarian Ottoman mind-set re-emerged. Economic policy was cornered by the monocentric elites who, while preaching Kemalist ideology, skewed income distribution in their favour at the expense of disadvantaged groups such as the *koylu* and the *gecekondu* folk. This elite mismanagement, facilitated through state corporatism, functioned for so long because of the centralist. nature of the 'centre–periphery' tradition in the Ottoman–Islam heritage (Mardin 1973). The nationalism of the Kemalist ideology merely replaced the traditional Ottoman–Islamic *kapikulu* mentality of gratitude for state paternalism. It justified and entrenched an authoritarian system with inadequate accountability of the elite to the grass roots. Significantly, this accountability problem, traceable to the same Islamic values of gratitude and obedience, are vividly evident in the failure of Malaysian national development strategy (see Chapter 7). At the same time, however, these deep-seated cultural values validate the Islamic social contract; in particular they shape a strong popular demand for social justice in the ruled–ruler relationship, as discussed in Chapter 3.

The accountability problem

Waste and mismanagement in the etatist economy lasted so long for two reasons. First and foremost, the centrist elites at the top lacked full accountability to the grass roots. It widened the 'elite–villager gap' by failing to develop an organic relationship with the peasantry (Cohn 1970: chap. 3). On the other hand, as a result of the one-party rule and frequent military interventions, the grass roots did not have the opportunity to prevent self-perpetuating elitism at the centre. Second, the mystique of Kemalism tended to legitimize etatism as a taboo, not only among the masses, but, even more importantly, among the military top brass. Thus, the entire system of etatism, and the elitism which it institutionalized, lacked adequate checks and balances.

This, of course, was quite contrary to Kemalism. The Turkish War of Independence was won by the peasant population of Anatolia, and to them the new, free Republic was dedicated. Ataturk wanted Turkey to be prosperous and the peasantry – the real masters of the nation – to share in this prosperity. He declared:

> Let our country be prosperous. Let our people live in plenty. Let them be rich! . . . This country of ours is one that is not only fit, but most suitable to be made into a paradise for our children and grandchildren.
>
> (Kinross 1964: 447–8)

Kemalist ideology was popularized by means of the Six Arrows, which referred to Republicanism, Secularism, Populism, Nationalism, Etatism and Reformism (Fisher 1979: 426–33). The last arrow was the dynamic element in Kemalism. By this Ataturk hoped to ensure that policies were always in tune with the National Will. By Reformism, he meant:

opposition to blind conservatism and a rigid adherence to the status quo. He did not believe in change for change's sake, but he knew all too well how reformers grow old and conservative, especially when they hold responsible government posts. Kemal wanted his revolution to evolve and expand, *as a continuing process*.

(Fisher 1979: 432, italics added)

As shown above, the spirit of continuing reformism died with Kemal. It was replaced by an authoritarian monocentric system pushing etatism partly due to inertia, but primarily for reasons of personal gain. This result is remarkably similar to the Malaysian experience under NEP trusteeship.

Is the National Will really supreme?

Along with secularism and populism, central to Kemalist ideology was the doctrine of the supremacy of National Will (*Ulusal Egemenlik*). A major problem with the Kemalist doctrine of the National Will is that how and precisely by whom it is supposed to be expressed was not clearly defined. Unlike the western experience, Turkish democracy did not emerge from the 'bottom-up'; it was imposed from above. Ataturk's own experiments in multi-party politics in 1925 and 1930, reflecting his wish 'to create a liberal Republic', were terminated as premature (Kinross 1964: 450). The Grand National Assembly, the Turkish Parliament, acts as the ultimate organ for the expression of the National Will, but until 1950 the country was a one-party system, and on three occasions (in 1960, 1971 and 1980) parliamentary democracy was terminated by the military invoking its custodian role to 'save the nation'. Ataturk himself had 'personality splitting' tendencies of dichotomizing individuals as 'good' or 'bad' (Volkan and Itzkowitz 1986: chap. 21), tendencies which, at the hands of subsequent Kemalist elites, became structured intolerance of dissent and political opposition. The inherent risks of democracy by learning, justified by the Kemalist axiom that sovereignty belonged to the nation, disappeared in favour of a centralist, all-powerful state.

Yet, these risks of democracy are small compared to the social costs of elite mismanagement sheltered by inadequate accountability. In the top-down, monocentric approach to nation-building the social and economic distance between the centrist ruling elite and the large peasantry did not decrease, it actually widened. On the few occasions when the peasantry could freely express its voice, the results surprised the centrist leadership. Thus, when Inonu was defeated in the 1950 election he was so shocked by this unexpected result that he is reported to have remarked in anger: 'I never expected so much ingratitude' (Rustow 1987: 130). Similarly, the success of the Motherland Party in the 1983 general election was a great surprise to the military (Feroz Ahmad in MERIP 1984).

Income distribution and mass poverty

The reverse side of the quasi-rents and high social costs of etatism was an increasingly unequal distribution of income. By 1973, the last year of official income distribution statistics, the income share of the botom 40 per cent continually fell in the post-war period. Turkey emerged as one of the worst countries in terms of income distribution (Mehmet 1983: Table 4; Celasun 1986: Table 7). These widening inequalities coincided with the highest growth performance in the etatist restoration phase after the 1960 coup. During the First Plan period (1963–7) GDP grew by 6.4 per cent per annum, and by 6.7 per cent annually during the Second Plan (1968–72), reaching 7 per cent per annum for the 1970–5 period. Rising income inequality hit especially the agricultural and industrial workers. During 1968–79 the former's share declined from 32.4 per cent to 20.7 per cent, and the latter's from 19.7 per cent to 16.8 per cent. On the other hand, salaried civil servants virtually held their income share constant at about 10 per cent, while the big gainers were the non-agricultural, non-wage earners, especially those in services whose share registered a remarkable increase from 27.4 per cent to 44.6 per cent (cited in Mehmet 1983: Table 5).

The majority of Turks in 1980 – the peasantry and the working poor in *gecekondus* – had little cause to be proud about the achievements of national economic development after long years of patience and sacrifice. By 1980, half the Turkish population lived in urban centres of more than 10,000 inhabitants, and more than one-quarter of the urban population lived in *gecekondus* in unhealthy and substandard conditions subject to constant fear of eviction (Weiker 1981: 65–6). For the masses, secularism and etatism, like western capitalism, appeared only as a path to mass poverty, alienation and social injustice. The Islamic option, by comparison, seemed correspondingly more attractive.

Social policy achievements

On the other hand, the national development strategy has undoubtedly achieved some major achievements. One undisputable success of the Kemalist national strategy has been international peace compared with the Ottomans' tendency to rely on war for conflict resolution. This had the effect of expanding the Turkish population. Instead of wasting themselves in wars, generations of Turks lived normal lives. Furthermore, starting in the 1940s, there was a sharp reduction in infant mortality rates and life expectancy at birth began to rise steadily. In 1923, Turkey had a population of 13 million; by 1985 it had reached 52 million. Now, at last, the Turkish nation could attain a sense of demographic and cultural security which they lacked in the Ottoman days. But this sense of security produced fears of overpopulation. Turkey, however, is not a small country and can comfortably accommodate a large population, provided that economic growth is efficient and sustained.

The second major social policy success under Kemalist national strategy was in the field of education. In 1927, less than one of every five Turks over six years of age was literate. In fact, only 17.6 per cent of males and only 4.8 per cent of females were literate. Almost all schools were in urban areas. By 1975, about four of every five males and one of every two females were able to read and write (Weiker 1981: 153–4). Secular schooling based on the Latin alphabet and emancipation of women were the major Kemalist reforms that contributed to this progress in literacy. The position of Turkish women, in particular, compares very favourably with the position of women in other Islamic countries.

Improved literacy resulted in an impressive growth and expansion in related sectors, especially in mass media and communications. Newspapers, books, radio and television revolutionized the attitudes and customs of the Turks, and a thriving Turkish literature and culture emerged. These improvements, in turn, contributed to increased political awareness, social pluralism and national integration. A modern, more confident sense of Turkish identity began to take shape.

In fact it is the direct benefits of secularized social policy achievements that stand out as the true lasting gains of Kemalist national strategy of nation-building. To their credit, etatist elites at the centre maintained their commitment to these secular social policies, although, of course, wasted resources in the SEEs could have been better utilized for the sake of even greater social progress through investments in low-cost housing, education and village development. In the end, it was secular schooling and social progress that opened the 'eyes and minds' of the Turks and slowly but surely contributed to a new and more confident sense of Turkish national identity, strong enough to take a critical look at Kemalism itself, to weigh the relative benefits of westernization, and to attempt a synthesis with its Ottoman–Islamic past.

The threat of Islamic fundamentalism

Coming to terms with the Ottoman–Islamic past is not without risks. One major risk is Islamic resurgence. While Islamic parties score less than 10 per cent in Turkish general elections, it is complacent to take this figure as the upper limit of Islamic sentiment among the Turkish population. Poverty and alienation operate as powerful social forces fuelling Islamic fundamentalism in Turkey as elsewhere, especially against the backdrop of events in Iran and the Middle East.

In the last half-century, the mass of the Turkish population has patiently waited for the promised benefits of secular development. Instead of affluence, the bottom 60 per cent have witnessed poverty. This unequal distribution of income was not created by the invisible hand of market forces; it was created by etatist elites at the top. In the process, nationalism, so effectively mobilized by Kemal Ataturk at the start of his Revolution, has lost some ground to Islamic ideals, or, to put it another way, Turkish nationalism has attained a more organic balance with Islam.

Now etatism is giving way to market ideology and privatization. While the new market ideology can be justified in terms of a more balanced mix of public and private sectors in the Turkish economy, it also poses brand new challenges, in particular because these sectors augment the power of private monopolies and oligopolies. They therefore need to be regulated by means of appropriate public policies to prevent fraud and other unfair trade practices, but also to protect the public interest and sustain growth with social justice. That is the surest way of checking Islamic extremism. These issues will be discussed in greater detail in Part IV.

No amount of economic regulation through appropriate public policy, however, could solve the Turkish yearning for a synthesis with its Ottoman–Islamic past. Such synthesis would require a bold concession to the spiritual dimension in the Turkish identity. This spirituality, causally linked to the universality of Islam, is a bond that binds the Turk, a citizen of the Turkish Republic, at once to God and all other Muslims everywhere, and it is as real a manifestation of self-identity as his citizenship. This bond, lost since 1924 when the Caliphate was abolished, could now be revived, if the Turkish state would take a historic step to undo the 1924 decision. Such a step, which would be quite popular in Turkey and even more so in the Islamic world at large, would have to be done in such a way that it could not be interpreted as anti-Ataturk. Thus, two conditions would seem to be essential: first, the Caliphate would be under the rule of law, not under *sheri'at*; and second, it would function as a symbol of unity and co-operation among Islamic nation-states. Such a bold act by Turkey would be an act of self-confidence and reconciling her achievements in nation-building with her Islamic heritage. At the same time, coinciding with her efforts to gain European integration, it would be an act of confirmation of her role as an economic and spiritual bridge between the east and west.

Chapter seven

Malaysian development by trusteeship
The broken trust

The Malaysian economy is structurally different from Turkey's: colonialism has burdened it with a racially mixed society. It still remains a dualistic, plantation economy. As such it is extremely open and vulnerable: the export/GDP ratio is about 50 per cent. While trade and ethnic pluralism have contributed to Malaysian prosperity, the same factors are also causes of external dependence and domestic disharmony. Thus, Malaysia is a victim of boom— bust fluctuations in the prices of primary products such as rubber, palm oil and tin. In turn, this vulnerability effectively subordinates domestic development to external conditions beyond the control of Malaysia. Racial harmony between the three major races – Malays (50 per cent), Chinese (35 per cent) and Indians (10 per cent) – rises and falls with the commodity cycles.

Malay nationalism which gave birth to the United Malays National Organization (UMNO) was the major force leading to *Merdeka* (Independence) in 1957. But, unlike the Kemalist ideology in Turkey, UMNO nationalism did not immediately lead to drastic national reconstruction in post-independence Malaysia. On the contrary, the colonial economic structures and policies remained intact. Post-independence policies to diversify the economy via industrialization have not reduced the degree of external dependence; neither have they altered the colonial legacy of inequitable distribution of income. Urbanization has increased the Malay presence in cities and towns, but the Chinese pre-eminence in the modern private sector has changed little. Most significantly, the large volume of Malay poverty has remained unresolved and is a major cause of rising Islamic fundamentalism in both the urban and rural areas of the country.

Despite its multiracial character, Malaysia is officially an Islamic federal country. It is made up of states each ruled by a sultan who is a hereditary ruler in the classical Islamic tradition. He is the head of Islam within his state, in charge of a form of *shari'ah* which varies from state to state, and enjoying considerable feudal authority ruling over the devoutly religious *rakyat*, the Malay *Bumiputera* (Syed Husin Ali 1984). Theoretically the sultans own the land within the boundary of their state. A political tradition originating from the golden days of the Malacca Sultanate represents a kind of Islamic social contract whereby the sultans get unquestioned loyalty from the *rakyat* in return for 'protection' (Chandra 1979). In modern constitutional terms, this 'protection' has been defined in the form of 'special Malay rights' and has been the basis of the New Economic Policy.

Federal secularism

Despite the official status of Islam as a state religion, national development policy at the federal level has been highly secular, i.e. based on western criteria. Responsibility for policy formulation and implementation has rested with civilian political and bureaucratic elites, not the sultans. Secular policies are particularly evident at the federal level thanks to an ethnic political partnership legitimized by a relatively successful application of pluralistic or communalistic form of democracy (Vasil 1971; Gale 1987). The source of Malaysian secular development policy is the fact that the post-independence ruling political partnership has continued to rely on the colonial economic tools of dualistic development and resource exploitation in a trade-oriented environment highly dependent upon foreign investment and technology transfers.

Thus Malaysia is bedevilled by two fundamental tensions: an inter-racial tension stemming from its racially mixed demographic character, and an intra-Malay tension centred on secularism, represented by elected political authority, and Islamic authority imbedded in a feudal system of values and institutions culminating in hereditary sultanates. Prosperity through rapid economic growth is the traditional medicine for both of these potential problems. When the economy booms, there is inter-racial harmony and, there is a pragmatic, moderating influence on the Malay views about Islam and secularism. In recent years, however, there has been a growing realization among the *Bumiputera* that secularist policies managed by the nationalist leadership in control of UMNO are inherently inappropriate for Malaysia's inequality and poverty problems. As a result, Islam has become an increasing force in federal politics (Sundaram and Cheek 1988).

The accountability problem

The overall purpose of this chapter is to show that the failure of the UMNO nationalist strategy to solve Malay poverty stems from elite management of the economy; post-colonial leaders merely replaced the colonial administrators and maintained the *de facto* colonial structure of the economy.

Elite management in Malaysia, as in the Turkish case, discloses a fundamental accountability problem: policy-making and implementation has been too 'top-down', concealing inadequate accountability of the leaders to the followers. Accountability here is used in a public policy sense, referring to the answerability of those in charge of policies and programmes. At the time of *Merdeka* colonial rule was transferred to a multiracial coalition which chose the same old colonial policy tools, including cheap-labour policy on plantations, to manage the economy. As a result, the economic benefits have enriched a small ruling class at the top – just as in colonial times. In British Malaya, these colonial policies were manipulated to produce a budget surplus and a positive trade balance for the benefit of the expatriate class and the colonial interests. After *Merdeka* in 1957, the dualistic economy based on cheap-labour policy was maintained both in the plantation economy as well as in the new industrial estates and export processing zones to promote industrialization. Despite rapid annual growth of GNP in excess of 7 per cent per annum, the cheap-labour and forced-saving policies prevented growth with equity. The benefits of this rapid growth have enriched the ruling elites who sacrificed poverty redressing in the pursuit of state-sponsored Malay capitalism – i.e. the idea of creating, by political selection, a class of Malay capitalists to parallel the Chinese. In short, the successor ruling elite extracted the surplus of the country, as in colonial times, for self-enrichment while paying lip-service to poverty eradication with suitable nationalistic and/or religious slogans in a manner comparable to the centrist control of Turkish etatism.

The NEP trusteeship

The chief instrument of state sponsorship for the creation of Malay capitalists was the New Economic Policy (NEP) 'trusteeship' (Mehmet 1986). Adopted in the aftermath of the bloody race riots in May 1969, the NEP is a twenty-year socio-economic restructuring plan favouring the Malays through state subsidies, scholarships, job quotas, licensing regulations and a wide range of other preferences. These rewards, however, are not available equally to each and every Malay; they are provided preferentially through patronage and sponsorship which ensure continuation of elite control and management of the economy and the political system.

The Malaysian strategy of NEP trusteeship, like the Turkish etatism, is a highly centralized, top-down system concentrating decision-making over budget allocations and development priorities in the hands of the centrist elites. Trusteeship reflects a fundamental lack of trust by the centrist leaders in the followers, i.e. the masses. Under the Malaysian NEP trusteeship all decisions about budget allocations and investment priorities are made non-competitively by rules and procedures set by trustees, and control over resources is separated from their ownership and vested in the trustees. In theory, the masses are the owners, and the trustees are supposed to act on behalf of the masses. Effective separation of control from ownership, however, ensures that the trustees bear no accountability to the masses, neither in a managerial nor in a legal sense. Even political accountability is frustrated by the 'money politics' of sponsorship, patronage and institutionalized corruption.

The emergence of the NEP trusteeship strategy

What are the historical roots of the NEP trusteeship? Although it was adopted in the aftermath of the May 1969 race riots, it is a strategy with long historical roots. A proper appreciation of these historical roots is necessary to understand why the NEP trusteeship came about at all, and to evaluate its impact objectively.

In Malaysia, economic activity has traditionally been identified with race. This is the direct consequence of colonialism. The colonial interests controlled the plantations, banking, finance and, of course, public administration. The Chinese and Indians, originally imported as cheap labour for tin mines and plantations, gradually emerged as the dominant groups in the modern sectors. The indigenous Malay inhabitants, Muslim *Bumiputeras*, were left dependent on subsistence peasant agriculture, consisting of wetland rice and fishing. As a result of this colonial experience, the Malaysian economy has been burdened with a legacy of fragmented organization, inter-racial inequality of wealth and a large incidence of *Bumiputera* poverty. Although Malaysia gained political independence in 1957, these historical imbalances and inequalities remained unchallenged. In fact, the Alliance Government of Tunku Abdul Rahman relied on the old colonial system of administration giving higher priority to inter-racial peace than to structural changes to redress poverty and inter-racial inequality. His failure to respond to Malay needs resulted in the May 1969 riots and the emergence of the New Economic Policy, a Malay national development strategy, a kind of *affirmative action programme*. The need for such a strategy to uplift and modernize the Malay was a hotly debated subject in the 1960s.

Under the NEP trusteeship a small group of top political and bureaucratic leaders, inspired by Tun Razak, then Deputy Prime Minister, simply assumed the role of trustees (i.e. guardians) of the Malay community. The overall objective of NEP was to give effect to the constitutional special rights and privileges of the Malays through a two-pronged approach: the eradication of poverty, especially amongst the rural peasantry; and the restructuring of corporate assets ownership and employment structure in the country in accordance with the target of 30−40−30, i.e. 30 per cent Malay share, 40 per cent for other Malaysians and 30 per cent for foreigners. Designed as a twenty-year perspective plan, the objectives of NEP were to be achieved by 1990.

The NEP trusteeship was a bold and innovative strategy, quite appropriate and justifiable in its intent. Historically the Malays were at a great economic disadvantage in relation to the other racial groups who were brought into the country by colonial rulers and had prospered thanks, in a large measure, to the preferential and 'divide and rule' colonial policies. Tun Razak and the political trustees, as guardians of the Malays as a whole, were nationalists with good intentions and motivated by a desire to eradicate poverty and uplift the Malays. In this sense, their ideology was very similar to the Kemalist one of the 1920s and 1930s which guided Turkish development strategy. In fact, as was shown in Chapter 5, Kemalism had a major influence on Malay nationalism at the time, and in particular it contributed to the emergence of UMNO as a secular, national 'Turkish-style' party.

The NEP as an innovative development strategy

The original NEP trustees were men of vision; their central objective was the creation of a new middle class of Malays. To accomplish this they selected some highly innovative policy instruments. They selected two major sets of policy instruments: subsidies and special purpose financial institutions. To cure rural Malay poverty they relied on the traditional state subsidy formula. Thus, a great variety of subsidy programmes were offered in aid of the Malays. These included subsidies intended for Malay artisanal fishermen, paddy farmers and small-scale rubber holders; scholarships for Malay students; licensing and trade concessions for Malay

businessmen; and large-scale plantation development and settlement schemes to give poor Malay peasants a new start. For
purposes of employment restructuring the NEP trustees relied
upon job quotas in a comparatively successful industrialization
strategy designed to attract foreign investment and technology
transfers.

Anti-poverty subsidy programmes, on the whole, have been a
failure (Mehmet 1986: chaps. 2 and 3). There are several reasons
for this, but the basic explanation is the selection of non-
competitive delivery techniques. The NEP trustees rejected the
market ideology of competition and efficiency, and relied on
political or bureaucratic middlemen, who not only lacked business
experience, but, even more importantly, were primarily interested
in self-enrichment. The net result of this approach was 'money
politics' which politicized the *rakyat* by nepotism and favouritism
in exchange for party loyalty (Shamsul 1986).

The second major policy tool which the NEP guardians relied
upon was even more bold and innovative. To achieve the 30 per
cent Malay ownership of corporate assets by 1990 (relative to a
mere 2.6 per cent in 1971), the guardians created a new concept of
financial institution: *Bumiputera* trust agencies. These were to be
set up as special-purpose financial institutions acquiring equity in
the name and on behalf of the Malay community as a whole. All
existing companies in Malaysia were to be restructured to change
their equity base in line with the 30−40−30 policy. These
Bumiputera trust agencies were authorized to acquire the new
assets and manage the portfolios on behalf of the Malay community. They were financed by the government from general
revenues.

The missing link in these *Bumiputera* trust agencies was accountability, especially management accountability. For reasons of
either naïvety or ulterior motive, the NEP trustees separated
ownership and control. Nominally, ownership belonged to the
rakyat, the entire Malay community. This was no more than
artificial ownership, however, since control rested with the trustees
who enjoyed full independence of management decision-making,
including portfolio decisions, with no effective accountability to
the nominal owners. As a result of this fundamental omission, the
equity restructuring under NEP emerged, subsequently, as a grand
opportunity for self-enrichment at the top benefiting the trustees
and their associates. It also had a corrupting influence on Malay
politics which speedily evolved as the politics of sponsorship and
favouritism extended from the top of the trusteeship down to the
rakyat at the village level (Shamsul 1986: chap. 5).

Industrialization strategy

One area in which the NEP trustees were particularly innovative and quantitatively successful was trade-oriented industrialization designed to attract foreign investment and technology. Manufacturing was identified as the leading sector and it outperformed the economy by a wide margin. During 1971–80, it grew at an annual growth rate of 11.4 per cent compared with a GDP growth of 7.8 per cent (in constant 1970 prices). The share of the manufacturing sector rose during this period from 13.5 per cent to 18.6 per cent. By the early 1980s Malaysia had become the world's largest exporter of semiconductors, with an annual export value of M$2 billion.

The key to Malaysian industrialization was the ability of the NEP trustees to learn from Japan and South Korea. It adopted a 'Look East' policy of imitating the success of such countries as South Korea and Taiwan which had made such a big success with export-led development. As in the Gang of Four countries, Malaysian NEP trustees saw to it that the country was covered with specially built industrial estates and free trade zones offering serviced industrial land and factories to foreign companies. The Malaysian Industrial Development Authority (MIDA) offered tax holidays, accelerated depreciation allowances and many other kinds of investment incentives to attract foreign investors. The State Economic Development Corporations (SEDCs) were designated as responsible for land acquisition for industrial estates, while the Malaysian Industrial Estates Limited (MIEL) coordinated the construction of ready-made factories. Even local financing was offered to foreign investors by agencies such as the Malaysian Industrial Development Finance (MIDF).

MIDA, SEDCS, MIEL, MIDF and numerous other special-purpose agencies contributed towards the emergence of export-oriented Malaysian industrialization. The NEP deserves credit for this achievement. At the same time, the numerous agencies afforded opportunities for self-enrichment through rent-seeking behaviour. The top-heavy bureaucratic procedures provided the ideal environment for corruption. Influence-peddling by those with access to privileged information or contacts could realize huge personal profits. Middlemen could earn handsome fees for arranging contracts and securing permits. Speculation in land and real estate became big business. Joint-ventures with multinationals and foreign investors provided profitable opportunities not only for local businessmen, but to those who could secure government subsidies to go into business.

The NEP trustees saw to it that employment in industries provided only low-wage employment. This was essential for two reasons. First, low wages acted as inducement for foreign investors. For the same reason, the trustees ensured labour supply stability by labour laws restricting workers' rights. Second, the trustees wished to maximize job opportunities in order to to employ as many *kampong* job-seekers as possible. These jobs were preferentially allocated, on the basis of a pro-Malay quota system. Most significantly, this cheap-labour policy had the effect of transferring rural poverty into the industrial sector. For these reasons, industrialization failed to contribute, as originally expected, towards the poverty reduction goal of the NEP.

Wealth concentration under NEP

Unlike poverty reduction targets of the NEP, equity restructuring has been highly successful. By 1983, *Bumiputera* share capital ownership had risen to 18.7 per cent, most of it held by *Bumiputera* trust agencies. Significantly, this official figure underestimates the actual *Bumiputera* share, which is closer to the target of 30 per cent by 1990, due to important omissions. For example, 'nominee companies' – secret holding companies set up by rich stockholders – are excluded from the *Bumiputera* share, even though a high proportion of such companies are owned by *Bumiputera* interests.

Unfortunately, equity restructuring has been, at best, a qualified success. It has resulted in a tremendous concentration of wealth via asset ownership at the top, thereby creating a new and widening inequality within the Malay community. Wealth acquisition betrayed the original intent of the NEP. Those in places of trust, power and influence, particularly the aristocratic, military, political, bureaucratic and even religious elites, enriched themselves while poverty among the *rakyat* persisted (Mehmet 1986: chap. 5).

The growing intra-Malay inequality is so serious that it threatens to destroy the traditional unity among Malays. It is a major cause of the rise of Islamic fundamentalism in the country. How did this division and inequality come about? To answer this question, let us look in some detail, at two important *Bumiputera* trust agencies: the National Equity Corporation (Permodalan Nasional Berhard – PNB), which operates, among other things, the National Unit Trust Scheme (Amanah Saham Nasional – ASN), and Tabung Hajji, originally an Islamic saving association for the purpose of facilitating pilgrimage to Mecca, which took advantage of the equity acquisition opportunities created under the NEP trusteeship system to become one of the country's largest corporate conglomerates.

PNB and ASN

The PNB is a wholly-owned subsidiary of the Bumiputera Equity Foundation, created in January 1978 for the specific purpose of acquiring stocks and equity in restructured companies as required under the NEP regulations. By the end of 1983, PNB had become the largest single stockowner listed on the Kuala Lumpur Stock Exchange. Its portfolio included fifteen listed companies and plantations, such as Guthrie's and Harrisons, bought with public funds from British interests through expensive raids on the London Stock Exchange.

The ASN is a large-scale unit trust scheme. Each unit is priced at M$1, available in M$100 denominations or more, and each unit holder can purchase up to a maximum of M$50,000. It was launched in 1981, with a lot of fanfare, as a significant vehicle for implementing the transfer of corporate assets to the *rakyat*. Participation in the ASN is restricted to Malays aged 18 years or over. Some non-Malays who are employees of certain organizations are entitled to purchase ASN units, but these are numerically insignificant.

The ASN is in reality no more than a large-scale system of mobilizing Malay savings to provide liquidity for stock acquisitions by the PNB. This is because of the restrictions governing participation in the scheme. Participation in the ASN is based on ability to pay, not on ethnic membership, notwithstanding the nominal ownership criterion so basic to the NEP trusteeship. Since most of the Malays are poor, the ASN scheme has been designed with affordability in mind. Thus, low-cost loans and payroll deduction plans are available to encourage purchases of ASN units. In fact, employers and workers are coaxed into investing in ASN. Despite all these encouragements, ability to pay has restricted the participation rate of Malays. By January 1984, only 31.9 per cent of the eligible *Bumiputera* population had actually participated in the ASN.

The ASN contains several other weaknesses. Lack of accountability is a fundamental limitation. In practical terms, corporate control and portfolio management are separated from equity ownership. Unit holders do not have the right to appoint or change the managers. The management team is appointed by the PNB and the Bumiputera Investment Foundation. In theory, unit holders can remove any manager by calling a special meeting, provided that two conditions are met: first, that such a request is made by no less than fifty unit holders or 10 per cent of the total number of unit holders, whichever is less, and second, that a motion to remove any manager must be approved by no less than 75 per cent of the voting power vested in registered unit holders.

Another serious weakness of the ASN scheme stems from restrictions placed on capital gains. Under the ASN regulations, unit holders can only resell their units back to the fund at the original part value of M$1. They cannot sell it for capital gains. This restriction, in force until 1990, has been justified as allowing ASN to build a strong equity base. In fact, during the equity boom lasting until 1987, ASN funds have done quite well, realizing huge capital gains. Only a fraction of these have been paid back to the unit holders as annual dividends. While these dividends and the stock splits have been quite attractive, the restrictions which prevent unit holders from realizing capital gains until 1990 are unfair. Who bears the capital losses resulting from the market crash like the one in October 1987? Also, if all unit holders patiently wait until 1990 and then rush to sell their units, it is almost certain that such a rush would so depress the resale market as to wipe out any prospect of capital gains. These speculative risks make the ASN more like a gambling or a lottery system than a safe investment in Malay development or an Islamic way of distributing wealth among the *rakyat*.

Tabung Hajji

ASN is not the only method by which the NEP trustees have taken advantage of the Islamic feelings of the *rakyat*. These trustees have turned the recent resurgence of Islam into highly profitable opportunities. Islamic banks and saving institutions have been set up, ostensibly in conformity with Islamic principles, but in reality to mobilize funds for speculative equity acquisitions by the trustees. One such successful organization is the Tabung Hajji, the Pilgrims' Management and Fund Board (LUTH), set up in the mid-1960s for the purpose of collecting deposits from devout Muslims who wish to accumulate savings to finance their pilgrimage to Mecca. Over the years, these savings have grown into a large amount, and when the equity restructuring opportunities of the NEP regulations were set up, the LUTH management decided to assume a capitalist role. It invested these Islamic savings in stock acquisitions, taking advantage of its privileged status as a *Bumiputera* trust agency. As a result, it acquired a highly diversified corporate portfolio and has become one of the largest holding companies in Malaysia. It controls a large network of interlocking directorships through its majority and controlling stockholding interests in manufacturing, plantation and real estate sectors.

LUTH's performance as a capitalist organization is quite impressive. Its investment policy has been in the hands of a committee of professional bankers and financial experts. By the end of 1983, LUTH had equity interests in no less than twenty-seven public companies listed on the Kuala Lumpur Stock Exchange. During the financial year 1983, LUTH's net profit was M$33.1 million, from which M$2.7 million was paid as *zakat*, M$17.4 million was paid out as bonus to its depositors – at the rate of 8.5 per cent, virtually identical to the interest on one-year fixed-term deposits in non-Islamic banks – and the remaining M$13 million, or 39.2 per cent, was put into the reserve fund to finance further investment and stock acquisitions. In the course of 1983, a total of M$75.1 million was utilized from the reserve fund for equity and real estate investments.

Despite its Islamic character, LUTH has not shied away from taking full advantage of profitable opportunities made available under the NEP trusteeship to become a capitalist holding company. It has not been deterred by the inherent risks and the un-Islamic nature of speculative stock market transactions. In a bullish market, these transactions are highly profitable. LUTH's lack of accountability towards its simple, Islamic savers might then be overlooked. However, in a bearish market, or worse still in a stock market crash, it would be difficult to explain the large financial losses inflicted on the *rakyat*.

Quasi-rents, speculation and corruption

What is most disturbing about the speculative investment habits of the LUTH organization is that it is not an isolated case. It is, in fact, a typical example of the basic inequity of the NEP trusteeship system: the fact that it has institutionalized a post-colonial upper class living off quasi-rents, speculation and corruption. These quasi-rents are derived as unearned bonuses for multiple company directorships, 'consultation fees' and numerous kinds of personal gains through influence-peddling by privileged persons with access to confidential information about government contracts and spending plans. The LUTH trustees are a component of the larger NEP trusteeship obsessed with corporate growth and self-enrichment.

An intrinsic feature of economic trusteeship is that income shares are not determined competitively according to merit and performance. Income distribution is, instead, biased by collusion and influence-peddling. Thus, the fundamental weakness of the NEP trusteeship was the fact that it institutionalized a non-competitive system of economic rewards based, not on efficiency and merit, but on nepotism and favouritism. Organizationally, the NEP trustees created what Mancur Olson (1982) has called 'distributional coalitions'. These are small, cartel-like networks seeking rewards through collusion, transaction costs and other privileged bargains. Special interest groups and lobbies are visible examples of distributional coalitions. Their paramount logic is to strike mutually enriching deals for their members through exchange of vital information about contracts, investment opportunities, capital gains, etc. Access to such information is a closely guarded secret, monopolized by members of the cartel-like networks. It is the product of official or privileged status enjoyed by the members.

The NEP trusteeship provided ideal opportunities for the formation of several of these distributional coalitions. The military top brass, for example, have utilized the pension fund of the rank and file to make fortunes through equity acquisitions under the favourable conditions of the NEP trusteeship. The aristocratic elites, families of the sultans and Malay royalty, have similarly taken advantage of their privilege and status. Politicians and political parties have acquired businesses often with interlocking corporate interests. The typical NEP trustee would have multiple directorships on the boards of several interlocking companies and a portfolio of equity interests.

Details of the rent-seeking techniques of these distributional coalitions have been provided elsewhere (Mehmet 1986: chap. 6). What is remarkable is that these rents have been expropriated, under the guise of national development strategy, without any rules to prevent conflict of interest and to ensure proper accountability and abuse of power for corrupt practices. In the process, national surpluses realized from rapid economic growth have been diverted into highly speculative stock or real estate deals in and outside Malaysia, in many cases resulting in huge amounts of financial losses. Accordingly, the NEP objective of Malay poverty eradication has been ill-served, while privileged elites at the top broke the national trust.

The BMF scandal

One notorious case of broken trust is the Bank Bumiputera Finance (BMF) scandal, involving the loss of some M$3 billion public funds in speculative real estate dealings in Hong Kong. The BMF is a subsidiary of the largest Malaysian bank, Bank Bumiputera, which is wholly owned by the government. Despite extensive and independent investigations by a committee of inquiry headed by the former Auditor-General of Malaysia, accountability for this case has never been adequately explained. Many questions have remained unanswered. Why were such large sums of public funds exported from capital-importing Malaysia for speculation abroad? Why was this done by government-controlled *Bumiputera* trust agencies? What is known is that these losses were absorbed only at the expense of national wealth from hard-earned commodity exports of the country. In September 1984 PETRONAS, the national oil company, was obliged to take over the Bank Bumiputera in a M$2.4 billion 'rescue operation' to save the bank from financial hardship. Thus, the bad debts resulting from speculation and corruption had to be written off at public expense.

Bad debts and losses by the NEP trustees are real social costs. They represent valuable resources which could help to eradicate poverty among the disadvantaged groups of Malaysia. Furthermore, these are resources largely generated through forced savings by compressing consumption and living standards of the working poor on plantations as well as in factories. In both sectors, the NEP trustees have maintained the colonial policies of cheap labour, ostensibly in order to protect Malaysia's relative productivity and comparative advantage in world markets. In fact, however, these policies sacrifice the well-being of the peasants and workers in order to generate the savings entrusted to the NEP trustees.

Sources of impoverishment

Persistent poverty in the period of NEP trusteeship is primarily policy-induced poverty. A great volume of Malay rural poverty has simply been converted into urban poverty in slums and shanty towns. Many traditional fishermen and paddy farmers have been resettled in new rubber and oil palm plantations under new conditions of indebtedness and shared poverty. The poverty-generating policies do not significantly differ from exploitative colonial policies such as forced savings and cheap labour.

Forced savings

Saving mobilization was a central objective of the NEP trustees and it was promoted with considerable success. During the 1970–80 period, the aggregate savings jumped from 21.6 per cent of GNP to 27.2 per cent in 1980. This was partly due to forced savings through statutory payroll deductions (such as the Employees Provident Fund, and other various pension funds) or through participation in schemes like the ASN or LUTH. But the single most important form of forced savings was the cheap labour policy which the NEP trustees inherited from the colonial rulers.

Cheap-labour policy

This well-known colonial policy was employed by the NEP trustees in the plantation economy, and it was employed in the modern industrial sector. It had the effect of depressing current consumption for the sake of greater surplus value extraction by the ruling elites who then diverted such surpluses for stock acquisitions and corporate growth. The cheap-labour policy is manifested in the rural and in the manufacturing sectors.

The emergence of the Federal Land Development Authority (FELDA) as a diversified conglomerate is a case in point. When FELDA was originally set up in mid-1950s its primary mission was rural modernization. Its mandate was to settle poor Malay paddy (rice) farmers and fishermen on brand new plantations. By the end of 1981 FELDA had developed a total of 308 schemes and had settled 70,563 settler families. It had emerged as one of the largest plantation enterprises in the world. Its economic management has been extremely efficient and FELDA takes considerable pride in the fact that it passes the conventional cash flow profitability test with relative ease.

Unfortunately, however, this financial success is largely due to a cheap-labour policy which exploits the FELDA settlers. In theory, these settlers are expected to become owners enjoying the rights of private ownership. In practice, this is rarely feasible under the financial management system employed by FELDA. The Authority acts as the central paymaster for the settlers from its headquarters in Kuala Lumpur. The revenues earned from the sale of rubber, oil palm and other plantation crops are collected in the first instance by FELDA which charges all the development and infrastructural costs to the settlers. These are treated as fixed costs and collected in equal instalments from the settlers. The balance is then divided among the settlers. However, since commodity prices fluctuate widely and regularly, the effect of fixed cost deductions is to pass on the full impact of these fluctuations to the settlers. To prevent excessive month-to-month fluctuations in settler net incomes, FELDA has instituted a repayable credit system under which settlers can take out cash loans against their future net incomes. These credits accumulate as arrears and are deducted from settlers' monthly incomes. Consequently, the typical FELDA settler family is seriously in debt and has no practical hope of acquiring title to his land. With growing families, many FELDA schemes now face a serious 'second generation' problem of excess labour. Yet, many FELDA schemes are faced with labour shortage problems simply because, as a protest against FELDA policies, the settlers go on strike or refuse to perform the essential tasks. As a result, FELDA has increasingly been relying on imported cheap Indonesian workers, most of whom enter Malaysia illegally and who are recruited by labour contractors retained by FELDA. While these workers are paid exploitation wages, the labour contractors and FELDA derive large profits from their productivity (Mehmet 1986: chap. 3).

Despite settler indebtedness, FELDA is a highly profitable enterprise thanks, in a large measure, to its cheap labour policy. It generates large net profits and surplus revenues. What happens to these? They are utilized for corporate expansion and diversification of the company. Some of this is justifiable on the usual criteria of backward and forward linkage involving marketing and processing of main crops. Thus, in recent years, FELDA has entered into several joint ventures with Japanese, Dutch and Swiss multi-nationals (such as Nestlé). It also acquired a major interest in Boustead Holding Bhd., a previously British-owned plantation company, and has invested in a large number of other companies in banking, real estate and manufacturing sectors. These equity interests have provided the trustees in charge of FELDA with an expanding network of company directorships and opportunities for personal enrichment.

With corporate growth and diversification, FELDA's character and original mission underwent significant transformation. This has been at the expense of the welfare of settlers and, even more significantly, at the expense of the poverty eradication objective which was the original driving force behind FELDA. Profitability has made the trustees in charge of FELDA less concerned about social justice, and more concerned with corporate growth and personal enrichment. Not surprisingly, most recently FELDA management has expressed a desire to join the current fashion in Malaysia of becoming 'privatized' which may signal the end of any remaining pretence that FELDA is playing any 'modernizing' or anti-poverty role.

The cheap-labour policy has also been a major aspect of the managed industrialization pursued by the NEP trustee. As a result, rural poverty has been transformed into urban poverty in urban slums. Malaysia acquired a secondary labour market with a growing population of working poor. At the same time, however, the trustees must be given credit for launching a competitive, export-oriented industrial strategy. Their failure lies in the fact that they did not promote social justice in the industrial labour market by protecting real wages with appropriate social policies such as low-cost housing and adequate industrial training.

Under the NEP trusteeship, industrialization, as we saw above, was the chosen leading sector of development. The trustees' declared objective was to modernize and urbanize the Malays. In policy terms, this was called socio-economic restructuring 'to reduce and eventually eliminate the identification of race with economic function' (Malaysia 1976: 7). To achieve this, the NEP trustees adopted a 'Look East' policy (Malaysia 1985: 25) and attempted to imitate the experience of South Korea and Japan (Eddy Lee 1981). They designed and managed an industrial strategy which emphasized low-wage, labour-intensive, export industries in order to attract branch plants of Japanese, American and European multinational corporations. They established industrial estates and export processing zones to set up modern assembly lines and factories by using generous tax credits, no-strike labour laws and many investment incentives offered to these foreign investors. The result was the creation of many 'footloose' low-wage electronics, textiles and garment industries. While Malaysia emerged as one of the world's biggest producers of electronic parts and components, and while large-scale job opportunities were indeed created, these were largely low-wage, unskilled jobs on the assembly line. The trustees relied on pro-Malay job quotas to award most of these low-wage jobs to rural Malays, especially *kampong* female workers.

The cheap-labour policy undermined the declared objective of the NEP trusteeship to modernize and uplift the Malays. As in the plantation sector, this policy perpetuated the age-old poverty problem by merely shifting its incidence from rural to urban centres. Why did the trustees do it? Why did they assume a modernizing role in the first place and then undermine it with a cheap-labour policy? Part of the answer lies in the dynamics of trade policy and international investment. Malaysia, as a developing country, feels the force of competition for investment and foreign technology; in order to attract these, it must offer foreign investors attractive incentives to entice them into Malaysia rather than Taiwan, Thailand or somewhere else. This, however, is a weak argument, because it subordinates national interest (and the declared policy objective of modernizing and uplifting the Malays) to the requirements of international trade and investment.

A more powerful explanation for the cheap-labour policy is the lack of concern on the part of the NEP trustees, managing the industrial policy at the top, for the welfare of workers at the bottom. For example, labour laws enacted by the trustees prevent the workers from organizing themselves into effective unions to counteract the monopolistic powers of their employers (Wendy

Smith in Jomo 1983). In their zeal to attract foreign investment and technology, the trustees have found it more profitable to collaborate with foreign interests, than to pursue policies to maximize the interest of the workers. Yet the experience of such countries as Singapore and Japan is the opposite. These countries have always adopted policies which first and foremost protected the national interest. They followed cheap-labour policies in periods of severe unemployment (for example in the case of Singapore from 1964 until 1974), but at the same time enhanced labour productivity through massive investments in manpower training, and protected real wages through low-cost housing, public transit and other social policies. As a result, they successfully pursued growth with social justice (Peter Chen 1983).

Islamic resurgence, money politics and the breaking up of UMNO

Low-wage industrialization contributed to Islamic resurgence for two main reasons. First, it gave rise to uneven capitalist development which promoted a rural exodus into urban slums where it bred alienation, which, in turn, led to spiritual awakening (Chandra 1987). Second, it threatened the traditional Islamic values and family ties. While wage employment, in theory, afforded economic liberation, wages were substandard and the assembly lines alienating, especially for migrant female workers (Jamillah Ariffin in Aziz and Hoong 1984). In the hostile, urban slums the recent migrants and the working poor began to turn to Islamic voluntary and charitable organizations, partly out of economic desperation attracted by promise of assistance, and partly out of an identity crisis caused by the dehumanizing consequences of industrial employment (see Chapter 2).

The NEP trusteeship contributed to Islamic resurgence in Malaysia in yet another way. It gave rise to money politics which has divided Malays at the national as well as the village level (Shamsul 1986). The greatest threat to UMNO nationalists came from Islamists. The response was UMNO's own Islamization policy (Sundaram and Cheek 1988). In the process, Islam, which generally had been conspicuous in federal politics by its absence since 1957, began to make new inroads, causing increasing concern amongst the non-Malays as well as the foreign investors.

Privatization, discussed in Chapter 10, has worsened the atmosphere of Malay politics as a result of more and bigger charges of influence-peddling in the awarding of large contracts such as the North–South Highway project. These divisions finally erupted into the public domain at the occasion of the May 1987 UMNO

Supreme Council Meeting at which time Mahathir's leadership was openly challenged by a motley group of Malay politicians. This marked the end of UMNO and monolithic Malay nationalism at the federal level. The end of UMNO may signal the beginning of a more competitive Malay politics in place of the old UMNO style in which racial solidarity was regarded as a mark of Malay nationalism. In future, Malay politics may be more open, competitive and more responsive to the economic and social needs of the *rakyat*. Malay religious groups may emerge, similar to the Turkish case, as factions in bigger political coalitions concerned more with 'bread and butter issues' than with Islamic fundamentalism. But this may well be a highly risky prospect; given the multiracial nature of Malaysia, it runs the risk of undermining the dominant position of the Malays in the country. At least in the shorter term Malaysian politics is likely to experience increasing authoritarianism as the Mahathir administration attempts to cope with perceived threats to its survival. Already many dissidents have been detained under the notorious Internal Security Act and the judiciary, in the past known for its independence, has been politicized. As risks of political instability are heightened, the scheduled termination of the New Economic Policy in 1990 is approaching. What to do after 1990 is a crucial question for Malaysia. Fortunately, there are encouraging signs of an economic recovery in the making with strong upward trends in all commodity prices (save oil). Healthy export earnings and an induced investment boom may well be the most significant prescription for economic and political stability as well as harmonious race relations in Malaysia after 1990.

Part four

Development in the Islamic Periphery: the modern state and the privatization challenge

Why did capitalism triumph in modern Europe and not in Muslim countries (among others)?

Islam has not in the past sought to mobilise the masses for economic ends.

Maxine Rodinson (1973: 3, 224)

The major conclusion of Part III is that nationalism *per se* is not a sufficient condition for development. A national development policy is not enough to guarantee rapid economic growth with social justice. Development policy not only needs to be secular, but it should also contain adequate checks and balances to ensure that socially sound policies are designed and implemented. This is especially necessary as the development process is shifting from a nationalist towards an increasingly privatized (i.e. market-oriented) phase. Privatization runs the risk of replacing public monopolies with private monopolies. Unless the private profit-motive is effectively regulated in the larger public interest, inflation, inequalities and higher living costs may drive the Muslim masses into the fold of extremists and militants.

In the past, as Rodinson has argued, Islam has failed to mobilize the masses for economic development. Although Rodinson argued from a Marxist perspective, his judgement cannot easily be dismissed on ideological grounds. Weber and Marx alike shared the view that capitalism is the characteristic form of modernity, and, as regards Islam and capitalism, despite their ideological differences, they both had unfavourable opinions. Marx placed Islam within the abstract category of the Asiatic Mode of Production, a conceptualization devoid of any historical content. Weber's references to Islam suggest that the dominant Islamic ethic, whether warrior or anti-hedonistic, was such as to discourage capitalist development (Binder 1988: chap. 6). Turner (1974) has attributed Islamic backwardness to the authoritarianism of medieval rulers.

More to the point, however, is the anti-scripturalism position taken by Geertz. Scripturalism is a reactionary and rigid world-view perpetuated by the *ulama*: 'scholastic, legalistic, and doctrinal' (Geertz 1968: 62). Traditional merchants, too, bear part of the blame because they acted as satisficiers, not as maximizers; they would rather earn a middleman's margin than undertake an investor's risk. They would rather stay small than accumulate, reinvest, innovate and expand.

Thus, the traditional Islamic world-view of economic and market relations has been shaped by rigid scripturalism. Monopolies and unfair trade practices have simply been declared 'unlawful' and banned, instead of the more realistic approach, adopted in western societies, of regulation. Banning, moreover, seldom works. It has not eliminated 'unlawful' transactions: it has merely pushed them into underground economies encouraging black markets, smuggling and other illicit operations. In political and administrative terms, banning has been coercive and often brutal. At the plane of theory, it has precluded the evolution of an Islamic theory of imperfect competition which is essential to guide regulatory legislation. This omission is particularly serious in the contemporary world economy which is dominated by oligopolies and cartels and where privatization has emerged as a key challenge of development policy.

The overall aim of Part IV is to focus on the transition of development policy in Turkey and Malaysia from its national to the latest phase of privatization. What are the transition problems? How can they be dealt with? It will be argued that the transition from the national to the privatized phase of development represents an evolution of public policy from the domain of public monopolies to private monopolies and oligopolies. The thrust of public policy in this new environment must be how best to regulate private firms in the social interest. This policy approach needs to be based on the economics of imperfect competition. The traditional Islamic doctrine of banning monopolies, cartels and unfair trade practices needs to be updated with the modern policy instrument of regulation in the public interest. Accordingly, Chapter 8 begins with an examination of Islam, the modern state and imperfect competition, and then attention shifts, in Chapters 9 and 10, to the Turkish and Malaysian experiences of privatized development.

Chapter eight

Islam, the modern state and imperfect competition
To ban or to regulate?

Islamic economics requires a theory of imperfect competition. For this is the dominant form of industrial organization in the modern world. As shown in Part II, Islamic scholars in the past failed to proceed beyond the ideal of perfect competition. This intellectual failure does not, of course, alter the fact that coping with imperfect competition is a challenge facing the modern state.

But what exactly is a 'modern state'? What is its proper role? Formulation of appropriate public policies to regulate monopolies, oligopolies and unfair trade practices requires not only criteria derived from the theory of imperfect competition, but also an understanding of the changing role of the state in the modern world. This world is rapidly changing, as a result of new computer-based communications and information technologies, and also fundamental structural changes in the world economy, triggered by the emergence of newly industrializing countries and the opening up of China and the USSR. In brief, the world is fast emerging, in Marshall McLuhan's phrase, as a Global Village. But international trade in this new Village is still dominated by powerful cartels, oligopolies and multinational corporations; the traditional state is very much 'at bay' (Vernon 1985). This chapter begins with a brief survey of the contemporary theories of the state as a prelude to the main subject under discussion: Islam and imperfect competition.

Theories of the modern state

Theories of the state are constantly changing. Beginning in the nineteenth century the dominant theory has been the instrument-alist view whereby the *raison d'être* of the state is public service by harnessing science and knowledge to improve the human condition. The utilitarian philosophers and Fabians in England, and the continental social scientists like Weber and Comte, all shared the

173

same liberal belief that the state was an instrument of the public good; they differed only in terms of modalities of policy design and implementation.

The Industrial Revolution and trade expansion provided the means for the emergence of the welfare state. But what gave the major impetus to the welfare state was Keynesian fiscalism. Under the influence of Keynes, western market economies, first in the United States, began to assume direct responsibility for the creation of an elaborate system of social safety net built on full employment. Thereafter, the state accepted responsibility for every able-bodied citizen being entitled to a job earning a decent income. The maintenance of full employment was to be the deliberate objective of fiscal and monetary policies. Whenever the state could not live up to its full employment responsibility, the social safety net was there to help the jobless and the disadvantaged. Thus, social security, unemployment insurance and other welfare programmes were designed and implemented. The classical *laissez-faire* policy of non-interference was no more. An unprecedented liberalization of world trade after 1945 had ensured continued economic supremacy of western market economies. The Third World, then undergoing a wave of decolonization, played its part in this process with a new strategy of import substitution industrialization which facilitated the emergence of the multinational corporation.

Now the welfare state is under attack. Surprisingly, this attack is coming from all ideological sides. Thus, neo-conservatives as well as neo-Marxists all seem united in their criticism of the state. In the current debate it is useful to distinguish three alternative schools of thought: the predatory state; the private property theory; and public choice theory.

The predatory state

This theory, pioneered by the economic historian Douglas North (1981), at first seems very close to the neo-Marxist class analysis. North regards the state as an organization with a comparative advantage in violence (North 1981: 21). Thanks to this comparative advantage the state can trade service (for example protection, justice) for revenue. In particular, it can specify and enforce property rights. The ruler is a wealth-maximizer who derives revenue from these property rights in the form of rents, taxes and transaction costs.

The wealth-maximization objective of the ruler is limited by the threat of potential rivals to his rule and by the 'free-rider' problem whereby some of his subjects may avoid payments while still enjoying the service provided by the state, thus raising the cost of tax collection. The result is inefficient property rights, potential loss of tax revenue and, over time, instability of the state organization. Thus, the wealth-maximizing ruler must, for his own interest and survival, be efficiency-driven. He must be an innovator and encourage institutional reform in order to maximize social efficiency to ensure that the output of society is highest which alone would ensure his own wealth-maximization. At the same time, the ruler must formulate a 'successful ideology' to 'overcome the free-rider problem' (North 1981: 53).

Conversely, failure on the ruler's part to innovate and induce institutional progress may lead to his downfall. Social inefficiency, measured in terms of rising rents and cost burdens, erodes the revenue base of the ruler; it contributes to inflation and undermines loyalties. In due course, social inefficiency makes the ruler a parasitical (i.e. predatory) entity and his downfall an inevitable event.

It has been shown by Deepak Lal (1984) that predatory behaviour can be utilized to explain the fall of several empires in the Indian subcontinent such as the Moghuls, Hindus and the British Raj. Similarly, sociologists specializing in the history of bureaucracies have explained the rise of feudal-like riverine kingdoms and chiefdoms in South-east Asia, before the advent of European colonizers, in terms of their predatory taxation imposed on regional trade which enabled them to finance standing armies or mercenaries (Evers 1987).

Private property school

Ruttan and Hayami (1984) have extended North's work to present a general-equilibrium model of induced institutional change. They argue that economic development occurs when the state enacts laws which encourage and regulate private property rights. Their survey of the economic history of several countries leads them to conclude that where land reform based on private ownership was successfully implemented (for example seventeenth-century England or South Korea and Taiwan shortly after the Second World War), the result was increased agricultural productivity and output generating conditions for industrial take-off.

Private property rights are not limited to land ownership. Industrial inventions also represent private property. In the western market economies industrialization was encouraged and facilitated by the legal protection of inventions through copyrights and patent laws, which guaranteed the inventors pioneer profits. These profits

175

acted as incentives stimulating research and development. In the same manner, authors and other literary creators could rely on legal protection of their creative works.

Now in the age of computer technology, the fastest-growing private property is intellectual property. World trade in services, based on informatics, is the fastest expanding form of trade. Micro-chip technology is expanding the horizons of information acquisition, storage and retrieval by leaps and bounds. This new form of private property represents only the latest form of man's creativity made possible by the incentive system sustained by the regulatory role of a supportive state enacting laws intended to reward the pioneer and the inventor.

The public choice theory: lobbies and rent-seeking

Public choice theory, pioneered by J.M. Buchanan (Buchanan *et al.* 1980), regards the political process as a complex competitive game with different actors pursuing conflicting interests. Thus, special interests (for example tobacco, steel, consumer groups) fund organizations staffed by professionals who specialize in lobbying legislators and bureaucrats on behalf of their clients. Tariff-seeking special interests, tariff evading and premium seeking for specific import licenses are examples of activities that influence the political and legislative processes and shift income. The winners are the organized, the influential and those with skills at lobbying and fund-raising, while the losers are the unorganized and poor. Confronted with special interests, the bureaucrat and the policy-maker are no longer the disinterested, neutral agents of public service. Instead, they are themselves 'actors' in the public policy arena with self-serving objectives and own agendas. For example, Niskanen (1971) has developed a variant of public choice theory to explain bureaucratic behaviour in terms of budget maximizing, whereby the larger are bureaucrats' operating budgets the greater is their 'empire' and the quicker is their promotion to positions of greater power.

Mancur Olson (1982) has gone furthest among the public choice theorists to explain the dynamics of special interest groups by means of the concept of 'distributional coalitions'. These are cartel-like networks which, while rational from a private viewpoint, are often socially wasteful. Their inner logic is the pursuit of unproductive 'rent-seeking' (Krueger 1974b) by subordinating public interest to the material advantage of the members of 'distributional coalitions'. The techniques by which rents are sought in the public policy and political arenas include collusion and influence-peddling, thereby shifting income distribution in favour of particular special interests. In a macro sense, these unproductive rents increase 'transaction costs' and fuel inflation; ultimately, they can generate economic decline.

The policy recommendations of the public choice school favour a new role for the state; not a return to *laissez-faire* economics, but a new, regulatory role. Buchanan, Olson and others in this school argue for public policies that maximize information and regulation in the public interest. The public's freedom to know is essential to curtail the powers of cartel-like networks, while conflict-of-interest rules and disclosure regulations are seen as means of safeguarding the public interest. Thus, competition policies are essential components of modern public policy.

Islam and imperfect competition

In Islam, on the other hand, where secularism has generally been shunned, a theory (any theory) of state has been conspicuous by its absence. As a result there has been a failure to accumulate a tradition of public policy. Even in such a relatively secularized Muslim country as Turkey, public administration reform to introduce adaptability and innovation remains one of the most difficult areas of institutional reform (Cohn 1970: 85–99; Heper in Evin *et al.* 1984). In more general terms, Muslim countries, now shifting from a nationalist to a market ideology, are exceedingly deficient in coping with the complex world of imperfect competition. In a large measure this stems from inadequate interaction between the intellectual elites and their political and bureaucratic counterparts. The tradition of expert witnesses and consultants providing input into public policy-making in Islamic countries is virtually absent.

In Chapter 4 it was shown that Islamic economics has not evolved beyond the ideal of perfect competition. Thus, Islamic countries traditionally have been unable to deal with monopolies, oligopolies, cartels and other forms of imperfect competition. The *ulama* have denounced these practices as dishonest and contrary to Islam. The proper conduct for a Muslim entrepreneur is explained by Khurshid Ahmad as follows:

> Dishonesty, fraud and deception, coercive practices, and gamblesome or usurious dealings are prohibited. He should not do anything injurious to others. This rules out hoarding, speculation and collusion among producers and traders against the interests of consumers. Monopoly is also regarded as injurious to

the interests of society. He is charged with justice and truthfulness in all his dealings.

(Kurshid Ahmad 1976: 207)

Maududi considers the following to be unlawful in Islam:

misappropriation, bribery, usurpation, embezzlement of public funds (from *Bait-al-Mal*), felony, spurious weights and measures, business which promotes immorality, such as prostitution, manufacture and trade of wine and other intoxicants, usury, gambling, speculation and all forms of sale under false pretences or duress, or which give rise to dispute or friction or which are derogatory to equity or public interests. Islam curbs these by force of law. Besides, it bans hoarding and prevents the formation of such monopolies as deprive the common public from availing of wealth and the means of its production without reasonable cause.

(Maududi 1984: 88)

These quotations contain many vague terms on which different *ulama* have conflicting opinions. Thus, Kurshid Ahmad's denunciation of monopoly is more sweeping than Maududi's, although both fail to give a definition of the term. From the perspective of public policy, they merely ban what they consider to be unlawful or unfair trade practice. But are there not more appropriate or more effective alternative means of regulating the evils of monopoly?

To ban or regulate?

Since the *ulama* failed to formulate a tradition of public policy to administer economic and trade relations, their prescriptions on these matters are primitive. Banning unlawful or unfair trade practices does not exempt Muslim societies from the exploitative consequences of monopolies, oligopolies and cartels. It did not prevent colonial exploitation in the past, and it does not now stop multinational corporations from extracting monopoly profits. Banning a product or trade practice prevents neither its existence nor its damaging effects: the ban merely pushes it into some underground or hidden economy. It encourages deception, dishonesty and corrupt practices.

What is the alternative to bans? Regulation and enforcement are more efficient instruments of controlling unlawful and unfair trade practices than outright bans. But regulation and enforcement must be based on laws which are clearly written and objectively enforced in a court of law. This type of rule-making requires a theory of monopolistic competition to articulate the forms and characteristics thereof as a basis of modern trade and competition policy.

The world economy is now dominated by large monopolistic corporations. A new form of global competition is emerging based on large economic blocks, centred in Europe, North America and Japan. To adjust and cope, western capitalist economies are now adopting new trade and competition policies in their national interest. They are privatizing public enterprises, passing new laws to protect intellectual property, and encouraging research and development in order to remain competitive at home and abroad. But they are also passing consumer protection laws, health and safety regulations and environmental controls in order to regulate unfair and ecologically unsound trade practices.

Structural adjustment and privatization are also fashionable in the Third World in a large measure owing to the debt crisis. What is happening in Islamic countries? Most do not have coherent policies. Often there is an *ad hoc* mixture of subsidy programmes, inefficiently administered, which perpetuate artificially low prices that, while cushioning urban consumers against the high cost of living, discourage domestic production. In countries with a more secular policy tradition, such as Turkey and Malaysia, privatization and structural adjustment are being implemented against a backdrop of inadequate public policy. In particular, there is a lack of proper legal-institutional regulatory machinery to counterbalance the interests of winners and losers. Consumer interests are not being protected when prices are deregulated. Public monopolies are turned into private monopolies. Jobs are being terminated without providing alternative employment opportunities. Overall, social justice is being sacrificed for structural adjustment and foreign debt servicing.

Alternative forms of imperfect competition

Formulation of a public policy to deal with imperfect competition requires, first and foremost, information about the forms of monopoly and unfair trade practices. In the following pages, a brief survey presents some of the principal examples of these practices encountered in the capitalist economy. These include marketing and advertising, market-sharing arrangements (such as cartelization and franchising), pricing techniques (such as price discrimination, predatory pricing, transfer pricing) and zero-sum bargaining.

Marketing and advertising

In contemporary capitalism marketing and advertising occupy a central place. Successful marketing ensures corporate survival. Advertising is an example of non-price competition intended to create consumer loyalty through product differentiation (Koutsoyannis 1982). Profit-maximizing firms regard expenditures on advertising, public relations and other forms of marketing as essential investment in future profits through expansion of market shares at the expense of actual or potential competitors. Highly-paid advertising and public relations experts utilize all manner of tricks and gimmicks, sometimes borrowing military tactics, in developing marketing strategies in their single-minded pursuit of selling for profit – the so-called 'bottom-line' approach. That these marketing techniques are highly successful is almost self-evident as demonstrated by the most casual observation of Americanization of many Third World cultures (Barnet and Mueller 1974).

In Muslim countries, strictly speaking, marketing and advertising are regarded as un-Islamic. Such practices are seen as deceptive and corrupting, and they are therefore generally discouraged and sometimes suppressed. Undoubtedly advertising and marketing can be carried to excessive limits. That is why protective laws are necessary to prevent such excess. But not all marketing is socially undesirable. Social marketing, concerned with the promotion of socially beneficial ideas and causes, can provide useful services to society (Fox and Kostler 1980). Take, for example, the problem of dangerous driving on public highways. Remedy may be sought through legal, coercive or persuasive approaches. The legal approach would be to pass a law raising the age limit for drivers. The coercive approach would be to force car dealers and manufacturers to go out of business. The persuasive approach, relying on social marketing, would be to use advertising and information campaigns which draw the attention of the public to the negative effects of dangerous driving and offer practical preventive remedies. Other forms of social marketing inform the public about the useful activities of non-profit organizations.

In general, advertising, properly regulated, informs potential customers of the range of products and services available and contributes to product quality improvements. As such, it promotes a more informed public, enhances customer choice and can help minimize price discrimination and unfair trade practices. Socially responsible marketing could be made compatible with the Islamic code of conduct.

Market sharing arrangements

Capitalist economy is dominated by oligopolies and cartels. Giant multinational corporations (MNCs) are the most visible examples. These corporations are the corporate descendents of mercantilism, created as monopolies by royal charters such as the East India Company, the Hudson Bay Company, the Dutch East Indies Company, etc. They grew and expanded in the age of European colonialism which carved out the global economy into exclusive economic zones of exploitation in the interest of the Mother Country (Stavrianos 1981). The policy instruments used to this end included cheap-labour policies for large-scale movement of indentured labour; free trade in raw materials and primaiy products destined for the factories of the industrialized countries; and suppression of indigenous manufacturing industries to create markets for the imports from the Mother Country. Clearly, the dominant motive was the converging economic interest of these companies and the colonial powers.

The idea of exclusive economic zone is carried on in all facets of the present-day capitalist economy, not just by MNCs, but even by small- and medium-size companies. Sub-contracting, production licensing and franchising are standard techniques of market sharing. Such practices are sometimes carried out to extreme limits through collusion, monopolization and cartelization to create excessive profits at the expense of customers. Such unfair trade practices are illegal and carry heavy penalties under anti-combines and anti-trust laws. The effect of such preventive laws is to protect the consumer while encouraging competition and entrepreneurial spirit through innovation and dynamic growth.

Market-sharing arrangements can also have important advantages. It is a risk-aversion technique which minimizes potential business losses and failures resulting from cut-throat competition and over-production. In addition, by protecting future markets, it encourages innovation through research and development. Thus, firms holding copyrights and patents can invest in new product designs and developments secure in the knowledge that they will derive pioneer profits from future sales in secure markets. This, of course, is the purpose and rationale behind copyrights and patent laws. Lack of such laws in Islamic countries is one of the major impediments to development through innovation and creativity. Similarly, the lack of standardization laws regulating fair-trade standards and practices in Islamic societies is a serious gap, placing customers at the mercy of unscrupulous sellers, foreign and local, who choose to ignore Islamic ethical norms of righteousness and truthfulness in market transactions. Public health and safety in trade, industry and services compel the adoption of such laws and regulations.

Monopolistic pricing

There is a wide range of pricing policies adopted by monopolistic firms to exercise their market domination for the sake of maximizing profits. Multi-branch firms operating in different markets, physically separated from one another and each reflecting differing patterns of consumer tastes, can practice price discrimination. Thus, exactly the same product or service would be sold at different prices in different markets; the less the degree of competition from substitutes, the higher the price charged. Price discrimination is not illegal because there is nothing sinister about it. It may even be fully justified by transportation costs. It is in the open so that it can be checked by existing or potential competitors of the multi-branch firm, or by others who wish to buy in lower-price markets and resell in the higher.

Some monopolistic pricing techniques are conspiratorial and, therefore, illegal. Such is the case with predatory pricing, a deliberate corporate strategy which may be used by existing firms to drive smaller competitors out of the industry, or to prevent new ones from entering it. Thus, an existing firm, typically a large leader firm, may initiate a 'price war', i.e. lower its price to a level that its competitors are unable to match, so that ultimately they are obliged to shut down. Thereafter the leader firm, left alone to monopolize the industry, may hike up its price sufficiently to recoup any short-term losses incurred during the 'price war'. Predatory pricing is illegal because it is in restraint of competition and fair trading, yet it is practised (by multinational oil companies, for example, through their retail outlets) owing to difficulties of detection.

In the case of large multi-product, multi-branch firms, transfer pricing is a highly profitable pricing strategy generating large profits. It is used extensively by multinational corporations, especially those in pharmaceutical, extractive and parts-and-components manufacturing industries, precisely because these corporations are vertically and horizontally integrated oligopolies with many product lines and subsidiary plants all over the world. They therefore have ample opportunities for transfer pricing in their global intra-corporate transactions. In essence, transfer pricing is over-invoicing purchases by and under-invoicing sales from subsidiaries so as to under-report the corporate income of the subsidiaries to evade local tax and royalty obligations; in the process, incomes and profits are shifted to the parent company in the home country at the expense of the host country. For years prior to 1973, the seven large multinational oil corporations were regularly shifting huge sums of incomes and profits out of Iran, Iraq, Saudi Arabia, etc. by means of artificially low well-head prices in oil-producing countries, while charging considerably higher retail prices at the gas pumps in consuming countries. They got away with it for so long because oil-producing countries had no public policies in the national interest. More recently, multinational companies have taken advantage of poor patent laws and public safety regulations to realize huge profits in many Third World countries through transfer pricing and sometimes they have even been dumping unsafe drugs and medicines, simply because these countries have no laws to prevent such abuses (Vaitsos 1976). In Bangladesh, to cite one example of an Islamic country, the availability of unsafe drugs is notorious because there is a total lack of health and safety standards. In the absence of rules and regulations, drug companies have virtually unlimited market powers pushing unsafe drugs for profits.

The clear message again is that Islamic societies need public policies which prevent transfer pricing, protect health and safety and promote the national interest. Relying on religious norms of righteousness and truthfulness are simply inadequate to deal with the complexities of modern economic and international realities.

Zero−sum negotiation: bilateral monopoly

In Islam, negotiations to resolve conflicts are approached from the perspective of justice and righteousness, pure and simple. In market economies, the approach is based on self-interest. In this clash of perspectives, self-interest dominates because appeal to justice is passionate and subjective, whereas self-interest is more pragmatic and pecuniary.

The pecuniary self-interest approach to negotiation is not only more pragmatic; it is also more specific and confrontational because self-interest is pursued within a game-theoretic framework. The gain of one side may be exactly matched by the loss of the other as in the case of a 'zero−sum game', or it may be balanced as in a 'win−win game' in which reciprocity ensures that both parties gain equally. This game-theoretic approach is true of collective bargaining between capital and labour; it is true of international tariff and trade negotiations. The analytical basis of these negotiations is perhaps best described as 'bilateral monopoly'.

Under bilateral monopoly the two parties, say labour represented by the union (A) and capital represented by the employer (B), enter negotiations to reach a well-defined settlement (package of wage and working conditions). A and B explicitly recognize the conflicting nature of their pecuniary interests, even though in some respects these interests are mutual. Each party enters and conducts negotiations to maximize its own self-interest at the expense of the other. Any show of altruism or concession is jealously safeguarded by reciprocity. The opening strategies of A and B are deliberately over-targeted since both know that the final outcome of the 'game' is a mutually acceptable 'compromise'. Thus if the union is prepared to settle for a minimum of a 10 per cent wage increase, would like to get 15 per cent, and would be delighted to get anything more than 15 per cent, it would open negotiations claiming, say, 30 per cent. Similarly, the employer would adopt a counter negotiating strategy.

The final outcome of bilateral monopoly negotiation is determined by the interplay of rational self-interests, previously articulated, in great detail, by A and B. When one party fails to articulate its own self-interest, while the other party has done its homework, or if one party blindly trusts in the goodwill of the other, the outcome may well be 0−1, as in a zero−sum situation with one party getting all the winnings rather than the balanced result of a 50−50 win−win situation.

What holds in collective bargaining between labour and capital, also holds in other spheres of economic relations, interpersonal, domestic or international. Dispassionate analysis of pecuniary self-interest, the basic driving motivation of the 'economic man', provides the essential rod to guide public policy aimed at regulating economic relations in the modern world. The pecuniary self-interest has been most sharply defined in the case of the private sector where, for example, it has been articulated in terms of profit-maximization. The market ideology of privatization gives vent to pecuniary self-interest, but it also creates several new challenges for public policy and the regulatory role of the state.

The privatization issue: a theoretical survey

Privatization is now the fashionable development strategy with a growing literature on its definition, objectives, techniques and impacts (Jones 1982; Asian Development Bank 1985: OECD 1988). In the discussion below the narrow definition of privatization as denationalization (i.e. sale of public enterprises to private interests) will be rejected in favour of the broader concept of privatizing the development ideology itself (i.e. relying on the private sector as the engine of growth).

Privatization as the new development ideology marks a landmark in the Third World. It represents the end of state capitalism based on direct government intervention in the economy and its replacement by the ideology of the market place based on efficiency and competition. The market ideology presumes that bureaucracy is top-heavy and over-sized, public enterprises uncompetitive and badly managed, and that the private sector is stifled by over-regulation. These social costs add up to huge public deficits. With advice and support from such bodies as the World Bank, developing countries are following the lead of Great Britain, Canada and other industrialized countries and are now selling off public enterprises to private interests, contracting out services, deregulating and cutting red-tape, liberalizing their economy, actively inviting foreign investors and turning to the private sector as the new engine of growth. All this reflects confidence in neo-classical economics: that market forces of competition and profit-driven private entrepreneurship do a more efficient job of allocating scarce development resources than politicians and bureaucrats. In short, the Market Model is superior to the Bureaucratic Model (Aylen 1987). But the road to privatization is not easy, especially in developing countries lacking an effective system of checks and balances and an efficient public policy tradition.

We can identify five theoretical challenges facing policy-makers in the Third World on the road to privatization. These challenges are the issues of: (1) conflicting objectives; (2) regulating a natural monopoly; (3) pricing policy; (4) safeguarding consumer interests; and (5) controlling rent-seeking behaviour.

Conflicting objectives

One of the major problems that have bedevilled public enterprises in developing countries is the fact that they have been burdened with multiple objectives. Most often these objectives have included promotion of competition, efficiency, employment generation and some kind of equity usually in the provision of 'essential services'. The practical reality is that these are often conflicting objectives. For example, employment generation, justified on grounds of social policy aims, has often resulted in 'featherbedding' which harms managerial and allocative efficiency.

Another serious problem of conflicting objectives concerns the question of which public enterprises should be privatized. If the policy objective is to reduce the budget deficit, then clearly the best candidates for sale are loss-making public enterprises, but, naturally, it is difficult to find potential buyers for these unless public subsidies 'sweeten' the deal. On the other hand, it is difficult to justify selling profitable public enterprises. It may be argued that such sales raise revenue for the public budget, but this is valid only in the short term, i.e. the year when the sale occurs. In subsequent years there is potential loss of public revenue and this is a burden on the taxpayers. Furthermore, unless the disinvestment exercise includes specific safeguards for widely-held stock ownership to benefit the smaller investors, the sale of stocks may actually result in further concentration of portfolio assets.

Regulating a natural monopoly

Public enterprises are what economists call 'natural monopolies'. Who owns them does not alter their intrinsic character. They require substantial start-up capital expenditures and are subject to rapidly declining unit costs due to the operation of the economies of scale. As a result, entry of potential competitors into these industries is virtually impossible.

Given lack of competition, the natural monopolist enjoys market power and can exploit this power to pursue monopoly profits. This, of course, would be at the expense of consumers. Thus, in view of the inherent conflict of interest between the natural monopolist and the consumers, natural monopoly industries have traditionally been regulated by governments. The overall objective of such regulation is that it is 'in the public interest'. Normally, this regulation takes the form of limiting the pricing power of the natural monopolist by means of a 'rate review' tribunal or a political process with the active participation of consumer groups, the industry and the government (Bradley and Price 1988).

When public enterprises are privatized the necessity of regulation is generally acknowledged, though not always implemented. But regulating privatization sounds like a contradiction in terms. If the aim of privatization is to promote competition, then the necessity of regulation in the public interest places a limit on this competition. Unfettered market competition may ultimately be self-defeating: for example, through mergers and acquisitions it may encourage monopolization in a given industry. Therefore, regulatory measures are necessary to monitor private monopolies.

The pricing policy

When competition is limited by regulation, the critical question that arises is: what should the pricing policy of the privatized enterprises be?

Economic theory offers three options: the rate-of-return (yield) method; marginal cost pricing; and average-cost pricing. Each of these methods involves elaborate computations and detailed information, and they all have their relative merits and demerits. This is not the place to go into methodological details. Suffice to say that average-cost pricing is the most appropriate pricing policy, assuming that prices do reflect costs. Marginal cost pricing, which would be the most suitable given competitive markets, in this case would most likely result in excessive monopoly profits. On the other hand, the rate of return method is likely to encourage excessive capital intensive production (Averch and Johnson 1962).

The important point to make here is that, in the final analysis, the socially optimal pricing policy appropriate for privatized public enterprises is not purely an economic exercise. It is as much a political act of compromise requiring balancing of the conflicting interests of consumers and stockholders on the one hand, and the requirement, on the other, of at least a break-even condition essential for managerial and economic efficiency of the enterprise. This balancing act – what the constitutional lawyers call 'checks and balances' – is an essential precondition of any privatization strategy and it reflects the fact that privatization is much more than simply selling public enterprises to private interests.

Safeguarding consumer interests

Privatization leads to higher prices for consumers. This is almost invariably true, and, in fact, often justifiable since usually public enterprises are characterized by low administered prices which are offset by subsidies. In fact, it may be more efficient to pay the full market price than the indirect burden of subsidy.

Privatization, however, introduces a conflict among four sets of interest groups: consumers, entrepreneurs, stockholders and employees. Of these, the weakest and the least organized are the consumers. The entrepreneurs are profit-driven and have market power, the stockholders are rich and powerful and the employees are organized by unions. Consumers, at best, have the protection of politicians, but waiting for the next election to throw them out may be a long and futile solution. Consumers, especially those in rural communities, hit with higher toll charges, utility rates and higher user fees, often have no remedy. What is required is a system of legally enforceable checks and balances to protect the public interest, i.e. consumer protection laws, rate-review tribunals, competition policies such as anti-monopolies and unfair trade practices rules, etc.

In developed market economies, public and consumer interests are protected, albeit less than perfectly, by an institutionalized system of checks and balances. Thus, regulated industries are often required to seek approval for rate increases from special tribunals which include participation by consumer groups, environmentalists, etc. There are also rules and regulations ensuring public hearings on such issues as the licensing of radio and television, construction of airports, and pollution controls. In fact, consumer groups are often paid from public funds in order to prepare and submit their briefs at these hearings and rate review tribunals. Trade, commerce and marketing are extensively regulated in the public interest to ensure fair trade practice, and there are anti-monopolies and anti-trust laws to prevent fraud and other economic crimes. These laws and regulations may work imperfectly, but at least they provide a legal safety net against systemic abuse and corruption. Public policy in Islamic countries is severely deficient in the regulation of economic and market relations in the public interest. Attempting to privatize in this environment may be an invitation to social conflict and political instability. For available evidence clearly demonstrates that privatization, without adequate safeguards, generates inflation, worsens income distribution and increases foreign control of the economy (Shirley 1983).

Controlling rent-seeking behaviour

Privatization creates new opportunities for windfall gains and personal wealth. When governments sell the stock of public enterprises, they virtually guarantee, for obvious political reasons, that this will be profitable for new investors. Windfall capital gains generate rents for investors, dealers and middlemen with funds, power and privileged information. Since ordinarily these rents would accrue to the rich and powerful, often privatization exercises in industrialized countries provide for conditions stipulating wide distribution of privatized stocks (for example the BP case in England). In the end, however, most of the stock ends up in the hands of large corporate interests.

How to control rents is an important question to ensure fair play and equitable distribution of income from rapid growth stimulated by private initiative. A partial solution is a capital gains tax, but this by itself does not prevent rent-seeking behaviour. There is need for rules against conflict of interest, insider trading and collusive action among those with access to privileged information. Specifically, the need is for safeguarding the public interest by means of conflict-of-interest rules and arms-length regulations. Privatization must not be allowed to institutionalize rent-seeking behaviour. Unfortunately, the Malaysian and Turkish evidence to date is not very encouraging as the next two chapters will demonstrate.

Chapter nine

Privatizing the Malaysian economy
Transition from a national to a market
ideology

Malaysia has been one of the most active adherents of the new
development strategy of privatization, especially under the prime
ministership of Dr Mohammad Mahathir who assumed power in
1981. Privatization, which is essentially a market ideology, stands
in sharp contrast to the nationalist ideology of NEP trusteeship
discussed in Chapter 7. In an important sense, however, it represents the latest phase of Malaysian development by state nurturing
aimed at the creation of a viable Malay middle class within the
long-term goal of modernizing the Malays. As such, it finds itself,
in much the same way as the nationalist development ideology did,
under challenge from a resurgent Islam.

This chapter is organized in two sections. First, the Malaysian
privatization strategy is reviewed with particular attention focused
on the problems of transition from a nationalist to a market-driven
ideology of development. In the second part the prospects and
challenges of Malay modernization beyond 1990 are discussed
against the background of increasing Islamization.

From NEP trusteeship to privatization

In the Malaysian approach to privatization, it is possible to identify
two stages. In the first stage, from 1982 to 1985, the government
sought to introduce a new work ethic through such slogans as
'Privatization and Malaysia Incorporated' and through the 'Look
East' policy (Mahathir in Mahathir *et al*. 1984). The central
objective was to mobilize greater effort on the part of Malaysians,
including the private sector, in fulfilment of the restructuring
targets of the New Economic Policy (NEP). In Mahathir's words:

> The alternative to privatisation may be to stop improving or
> providing the needed facilities. This will result in increasingly

poor services and will stifle growth. Development will be retarded and the second prong of the NEP, poverty eradication, will not be accomplished.

(Mahathir in Mahathir *et al.* 1984: 5)

More to the point perhaps, privatization was meant to revitalize the economy. The Industrial Co-ordination Act of 1975 had discouraged foreign investment in Malaysia and the new Mahathir–Musa administration sought new ways and means of reversing this trend while also encouraging the collaboration of domestic investors in the private sector. In 1982 the Ministry of Trade and Commerce set up an Industrial Advisory Council to advise the Minister on a new growth strategy with greater private sector participation (Thillainathan 1986).

But the real impetus for Malaysian privatization came with the onset of the recession in 1984. Falling commodity prices, declining foreign exchange earnings coupled with rising public deficits forced the government to adopt economic austerity, impose a freeze on public sector hiring and curtail development expenditure. Public enterprises, and especially many *Bumiputera* statutory bodies set up under the NEP to promote Malay equity ownership and industrial development, had not performed as efficiently as expected; in fact, many, such as the SEDCs, had accumulated large deficits requiring increasing public subsidization (Mehmet 1986).

Privatization is an ideology in keeping with Mahathir's own concept of development as explicitly formulated in his book, *The Malay Dilemma* (1970) concerned with the root causes of traditional Malay underdevelopment. Although a Malay nationalist, Mahathir differed from the architects of the NEP strategy of development by state subsidy and nurturing. He was more market oriented, more interested in encouraging his fellow Malays to enter the business world and compete with the non-Malays. He saw the roots of Malay poverty in fatalistic attitudes and reliance on state protection (Mahathir 1970: chap. 6). Consequently, privatization was launched as a new drive as much directed against the 'subsidy mentality' and its replacement by a new 'Malaysia Inc.' work ethics, as at selling public enterprises to raise government revenue, or cut public deficits.

Malaysian privatization: aims and experience

How can privatization be assessed? What are the criteria for determining whether or not it is successful? Economic theory provides some answers, but privatization is more than purely an economic question of efficiency. It involves questions of distribution and equity. These are of particular relevance in Malaysia where, for historical reasons, equalization of incomes and economic opportunity are of fundamental importance.

The objectives of Malaysian privatization strategy have been stated in a policy document in 1985 (EPU 1985) as follows:

(1) relieving the financial burden of the government by reducing the size of the public deficit;
(2) promoting competition, efficiency and productivity by exposing public agencies to market forces;
(3) accelerating growth by encouraging the role of private sector in development through deregulation and liberalization;
(4) reducing the size of the public sector in the economy by gradual disengagement of the government from non-traditional areas of the economy; and
(5) providing new opportunities for *Bumiputera* entrepreneurs to expand their share of privatized services in line with the 30 per cent equity target of the New Economic Policy.

Several cases of major privatizations have occurred in Malaysia (Toh 1989). In 1983, a new commercial television channel, TV3, was given to private interests in the Fleet Group which is closely connected to UMNO, the ruling Malay party in power. In 1985 several highly profitable privatization cases were implemented: 50 per cent equity of the national airline, Malaysian Airline System (MAS), was sold on the stock market; Sports Toto was turned over to the BMB Enterprise and Makuwasa Securities Sdn Bhd; the North Klan Straits By-Pass was transferred to Shahpadu Holdings Sdn Bhd. In 1986, the container terminal at the country's leading port, Port Klang, was turned over to a joint-venture company involving P&O (Australia) and Kontena Nasional Sdn Bhd. The rural water supply was privatized by being turned over to Antah-Biwater, a joint venture between a British firm, Biwater PLC and Antah Holding Sdn Bhd, a publicly listed firm that is majority owned and controlled by the Negeri Sembilan royal family. Telecommunications was privatized in 1987, as was the North–South Highway in the following year, in both cases with significant foreign joint venture participation. We shall now examine these two cases of privatization to gain a better understanding of the specific issues involved.

Tolls or taxes: the North–South Highway

The planned North–South Highway (NSH) project raises some interesting questions about privatization including the relative efficiency of highway tolls in comparison with road taxes. It is estimated that over the thirty-year concession agreement period private interests will collect up to M$62 billion from toll charges (Lim Kit Siang 1987).

The first observation about the NSH project is: why privatize it? The Malaysian road system, already one of the best in Asia, has been well developed and maintained by the Ministry of Public Works and the Malaysian Highway Authority (MHA). In fact, the Ministry and the MHA have already constructed almost 40 per cent of the 904 km highway stretching from the Thai border in the north to Singapore in the south. The Malaysian road system has been financed out of the traditional general taxation method, including petroleum taxes and road licensing fees. Since 1982 the MHA has developed parts of the NSH relying on toll charges in line with the pay-as-you-drive philosophy popularized by the World Bank.

In February 1986 the Ministry of Public Works launched its tender exercise for privatizing the construction and operation of the remaining portion of the NSH project. Thus, this project is more a case of contracting out. The M$3.4 billion (now raised to M$4.5 billion) (New Straits Times 9 May 1988: 23), is to be built by private sector interests, who were not only extended generous financial guarantees by the government to underwrite the capital outlays, but were also authorized to recover development costs through revenues generated from tolls levied on users.

Completion is expected in 1995. Malaysians travelling on the NSH will be charged tolls. The toll rates are to be set high enough to recover capital costs and ensure profits to private interests. Currently, these toll rates are estimated at about M$0.075 per km. But in future who will set the toll rates? How often and by whom can they be increased? Will there be a toll review process? It is difficult to answer these questions at this time.

One of the central issues raised by the toll method of financing public highways is whether tolls are superior to taxes in terms of efficiency and equity. It may be argued that toll collection by private entrepreneurs is more efficient than general petroleum or highway taxes: that, for example, road maintenance may be superior under the toll system compared to maintenance provided by such government agencies as the Public Works. The danger with the user-cost system of financing highways through tolls is that at best only profitable segments will be serviced, leaving the less profitable roads (for example rural and secondary roads) in a general state of disrepair. Thus, in the Malaysian context, *kampong* roads will be ill-served by the toll system, while urban populations, who will be the primary users, will be relatively advantaged. Accordingly, these roads will continue to be financed through the traditional system of general taxes. The financial relief for the government due to the privatization of the North–South Highway will be relatively small.

Rural communities will be negatively impacted by the toll system for a second important reason: they will experience a significant extra cost of travel. The cost of travel from *kampong* to urban areas will be so prohibitive that either there will be increased isolation of the rural communities, or, more likely, the *rakyat* will have to be subsidized by the government to offset the higher travel cost.

Theoretically, the welfare effects of the highway toll can be measured by means of the consumer surplus theorem. On the basis of this theorem, it can be predicted that the lost consumer surplus will fall primarily on rural and low-income groups, whereas the economic benefits of revenue from tolls will acrue to profit-oriented entrepreneurs. To the degree that rural communities in Malaysia carry a lot of political weight, the social cost of consumer losses can be given a very high value.

The NSH project has also created widespread controversy owing to the preferential manner in which the contract has been awarded. The M$3.4 billion contract was awarded to United Engineers Malaysia (UEM) despite the fact that this company had had no experience at all in highway construction. Furthermore, its bid was significantly more costly than the bids submitted by other companies, such as Pilecon and Hasbuddin. In fact, there is clear evidence of conflict of interest implicating top politicians in the selection of the UEM contract. It turns out that UEM is controlled by a holding company, Hatibuti, which is a two dollar company set up by UMNO. It is hardly surprising, therefore, that the opposition parties have been asking whether Hatibuti is not, in reality, 'the investment arm' of the UMNO and the political leadership (Lim Kit Siang 1987: 7).

On balance, privatization of highways does not seem to be adequately justified on efficiency or equity grounds. And the implementation strategy adopted provides more questions than answers. There are more efficient and equitable alternatives such as relying on taxation instead of tolls, or, if tolls have to be collected, they could be collected by the Malaysian Highways Authority (MHA).

Reducing the public service: the case of STM

On 1 January 1987 the Malaysian government announced the formation of Syarikat Telekom Malaysia (STM), registered under the Companies Act 1965, to take over the operations of the Jabatan

Telekom Malaysia (JTM). Regulatory powers have been retained by the government. In particular, Section 3 of the enabling legislation provides for the protection of consumer interests, although the modalities of this are not spelled out. STM is at the present time 100 per cent government owned pending completion of a detailed capital valuation exercise to determine the value of the assets of the enterprise for eventual privatization through sale of stock to investors. This is expected to take several years.

As a result of the creation of STM, the 30,000-strong work-force of the JTM have been transferred out of the public sector and turned into private sector employees. Thus, by the stroke of the pen, the size of the Malaysian public service has been cut in a significant way. Is this a real or artificial reduction in the size of the public service? At least for the time being, STM is 100 per cent government owned, and the job security and pension rights of the JTM employees have been safeguarded under the legislation.

In the longer term, when the stock of STM is sold off to private interests, a significant reduction in the work-force can be expected to promote higher productivity and economic efficiency. It is therefore understandable that the unions are uneasy. It is apparent that the size of the JTM work-force was considerably in excess of the international norm (i.e. 28 employees versus 15 employees per 1,000 telephones). In comparison, Bell Canada's ratio is 5.5 employees per 1,000.

Privatization of public utilities such as telephone and telecommunications means subordinating worker rights to profit-maximization. Job security, a hallmark of public service, is a casualty of privatization. This is, of course, the main reason why the unions are opposed to privatization.

Will the Malaysian government permit STM, if and when it is finally privatized, to cut its work-force in line with the efficiency requirements? This remains to be seen. Putting limits on the STM management would conflict with the objective of cost-efficiency and high productivity; these are essential for improved service delivery to the customers. On the other hand, limiting managerial efficiency is essential on the grounds of the nature of the industry as a natural monopoly, especially in relation to pricing policy (see p. 187). Whether limits on STM work-force can be similarly imposed is, ultimately, a political decision. In the long run STM's employment cannot be sustained regardless of profitability. Its work-force and its personnel policy will have to be governed by the profit-and-loss situation of the company. Presumably, higher labour productivity in the long run will be achieved through normal attrition rather than massive layoffs.

Will a privatized communications industry run on commercial lines be socially beneficial for Malaysia? The answer to this question depends on three principal factors: demand for services such as telephones, quality of service, and price charged for the service.

The traditional method of supplying telephone and communications services through a special-purpose public utility has been bedevilled by the problems of poor service and excess demand. The root cause of these problems is low administered prices. The rates at which these regulated services have been supplied have been too low, even below the break-even condition. As a result, demand for service has typically far exceeded supply. Unmet demand means frustrated customers. Low prices mean not only inadequate revenues to finance expansion to eliminate excess demand, but also continuous dependency on subsidies to offset operating deficits.

Malaysians have had long waits for telephone connections, while the department has been unable to get sufficient budgetary resources from the public treasury for modernizing and expanding the system. Telecommunications is a field which is experiencing very rapid technological innovation. To take advantage of these technologies is extremely costly. The required capital expenditures to meet current and future demand are huge.

Recurrent resources at the disposal of the JTM have been limited as well. The size of its work-force grew too rapidly and too easily with little concern for efficiency. The result is an oversized work-force in relation to service provided. In addition to long waits for connections, repairs and maintenance, operations have been poor, while collections have tended to be in a chronic state of arrears.

Thus, unlike the North–South Highway project, there are some economic and technological reasons which tend to support privatization of the telephone and telecommunications in Malaysia. Nevertheless, there are potential problems which need to be kept in mind. In fact, some sort of regulatory role to prevent abuse is essential.

First, there is the matter of the pricing policy of STM. Is STM expected to run on an average-cost basis with a 'reasonable' profit margin? Second, as a natural monopoly, there is a need to regulate rate-setting in the public interest. This is recognized in the enabling legislation. But the procedures for safeguarding the public interest are not spelled out. Already the rates have been increased, but the basis of these increases is unclear. Furthermore, billing has been computerized and collections are now done on a monthly basis with unusual promptness. When its stock is sold to private and corporate investors, STM will be exposed to two conflicting economic pressures from its customers and stockholders. On the one hand, it will experience expanding demand for more and better services. It is virtually certain that Malaysians will pay higher prices for their telephones. To the extent that higher STM prices are commensurate with better quality service there is no need to worry. How to balance the conflicting interests of customers and stockholders within the context of economic efficiency depends ultimately on the nature of regulation imposed on the STM. Consumer participation in the rate-setting process is essential.

There are some several powerful reasons for the protection of consumer interests *vis-à-vis* STM. One is the need for disclosure of information about rates, quality of service and profit—loss situation of the company. The public has the right to adequate and timely information about these aspects to offset the built-in bias of the STM to maximize profits through higher prices. Evidence so far suggests that the Malaysian public has not been receiving improved quality of service despite the higher rates which STM has quickly begun to charge. Another reason for consumer protection is the fact that when JTM was in existence it was obliged to submit annual reports to the Minister even though as an off-budget agency it did not fall under the purview of the Auditor General. However, its actions were open to questioning in Parliament. Now, under the Companies Act, STM is only obliged to supply audited accounts, but no opportunity for additional public scrutiny exists.

A further area of concern is STM's increased dependency on foreign technology. Malaysia lacks modern telecommunications technology. To modernize this important sector means importing foreign research, technology and management skills, typically under joint ventures, turnkey projects and technology contracts. Thus, privatization of Malaysian telecommunications runs the risk of increased foreign exchange costs as well as greater foreign control. Additionally, imports of modern equipment and inputs may displace some domestic production and cause some unemployment. All these factors entail higher social costs, including higher balance-of-payments burden.

But, perhaps the greatest potential risk associated with the privatization of the telecommunications industry is the stimulus it may give to rent-seeking behaviour. With the formation of STM, the country has been divided into four regions and each region has been allocated as a concession to a particular company. Thus, the north has been given to Sri Comm; the capital city of Kuala Lumpur and the Klang Valley to Uniphone; Selangor, Negeri Sembilan, Tregganu and Kelantan to Binafon; while Electroscon got the rest of the country. These companies have already entered into turnkey arrangements with foreign partners. The regional sub-division has been defended as a means of generating some competition, but in practice this is more likely to result in non-competitive award of contracts to service and equipment suppliers, sometimes at the expense of domestic firms (Malay Mail 19 December 1986). Non-competitive contracts always generate rents creating higher costs for the Malaysian consuming public at large. If STM encourages the pursuit of rent-seeking behaviour by cultivating influence-peddling or by relying on dummy service and equipment suppliers, then it will do so at the expense of efficiency and its long-term survival.

Conclusions

We can now briefly comment on the extent to which the five policy objectives of the Malaysian privatization exercise are being met:

(1) With regard to the first objective concerning the financial burden, the evidence suggests that this burden is not being reduced, in fact in some cases it is likely to have been exacerbated.

(2) The objective of increased competition is questionable on theoretical and practical grounds. Natural monopolies contradict the idea of market competition, and ownership does not change their inherent monopoly character. Therefore, regulation in the public interest is a necessary condition of privatization of natural monopolies like highways and telecommunications.

(3) The objective of accelerating growth via the private sector has yet to be achieved. Much remains to be done to boost investor confidence, both among domestic and foreign investors.

(4) The fourth objective of reducing the size of the public sector is partially being met, but as the STM case illustrates, this may be more an apparent than a real reduction.

(5) The fifth objective of expanding *Bumiputera* business opportunities contains a basic inconsistency between the efficiency-oriented objectives of privatization and the redistributive methods which have characterized the *Bumiputera* policy.

Overall, the evidence so far on Malaysian privatization is that its implementation is partial and incomplete. Privatization is more than simply transferring or selling public enterprises to private interests. If it is to promote the declared policy objectives of reduced public deficit, greater efficiency and competition, it is necessary to have rules and regulations to protect the public interest against private monopoly exploitation. There are legal and institutional reforms which are required: Malaysia needs competition policies to protect consumers against monopolies and unfair trade practices. Price setting and approval procedures are essential in privatized industries which are natural monopolies in order to protect the public interest against monopoly profits. There is also need of conflict-of-interest laws which prevent abuse of the public interest for private gain. Procedures for bidding and awarding contracts must be clarified and preferential treatment of non-competing groups avoided. This is essential for checking rent-seeking behaviour.

National versus market ideology

In the final analysis, Malaysian privatization strategy must be seen within the context of the NEP. It represents the latest manifestation of an 'official culture' – a culture of Malay modernization, imposed from above, intended to restructure and transform the Malay community from a peasant society into an urbanized, managerial and industrial one. There are strong historical reasons supporting this strategy. It is consistent with the need to create a Malay entrepreneurial class as a step towards the goal of national integration based on *rukunegara* (national unity). Privatization strategy seeks to consolidate the nascent Malay middle class and intends to transform it into an economically viable entity, able to meet the challenge of competition from the non-Malays and foreign firms.

Yet, privatization of the Malaysian economy represents a fundamental shift from the nationalist ideology of Malay development through state protection. This was the underlying ideology of NEP trusteeship which failed, largely, due to the rent-seeking behaviour of the trustees at the top. The most persuasive argument in favour of the new market ideology is the theoretical expectation that it puts greater emphasis on efficiency and merit than on favouritism and sponsorship.

Despite its social costs, the NEP trusteeship must be credited with having initiated the creation of a new Malay middle class and a new form of economic pluralism amongst the Malays. New economic interests inevitably take the place of traditional alliances and loyalties. Economic pluralism led to political pluralism. In this sense, pluralism amongst Malays is a healthy evolution, a progressive escape from monolithic structures based on the myth of racial solidarity which, as happened in the days of the NEP trusteeship, seemed only to enrich the trustees at the top. If this is correct, then in future Malay pluralism can be expected to be more open and competitive. Just as the Chinese firms compete with each other without destroying the Chinese ethnicity of Malaysia, so the Malay businesses and politicians in future may be expected to be more responsive to competing economic and political interests of the *Bumiputera* than on a single religious or party banner. More competitive Malay politics would mean greater efficiency and more effectiveness in public policies intended to modernize and develop the Malays. Under this competitive scenario subsidies and direct state nurturing in aid of Malay enterprises would be gradually phased out while, at the same time, the efficiency of poverty-redressal policies would be enhanced. This would require that growth-stimulating policies should be separated, as much as possible, from equity-promoting policies.

One way of promoting equity to solve the Malaysian poverty problem is to ensure that public expenditures for poverty redressal do reach the poor rather than enriching some middlemen. The most efficient way of doing this, is often simply putting cash in the pockets of the poor directly or providing them with low-cost housing, manpower training and similar productivity-enhancing benefits. While this would inevitably entail some wastage, it is likely to be considerably less than the wastage in bailing-out loss-making business ventures, not to mention speculative deals on stock exchanges or overseas real estate markets. In some cases, the low-income groups may be provided with business loans and/or entrepreneurial skill-development assistance in order to enable them to go into small-scale businesses. In some cases, aid may be in the form of social or welfare payments, for example in the case of handicapped people or abandoned women. These programmes are especially suitable policies to be entrusted to not-for-profit organizations, including Islamic charitable ones.

But competitive politics do not come risk-free, any more than competitive markets are fail-safe. In the Malaysian context, a competitive Malay political system runs a great danger of intra-Malay disintegration and conflict due, in particular, to Islamic fundamentalism. The increasing encroachment of Islamization at the federal level since 1982 is a potentially serious threat to prosperity and stability. Malaysian development policy, primarily a federal responsibility, has been run in the past on quite rational, secular lines. Planning by the Economic Planning Unit, fiscal policy by the Treasury, and monetary policy by Bank Negara, for example, have relied upon orthodox economic criteria. This has enabled rapid economic growth, in spite of the fact that the fruits of this growth have not been optimally distributed (Mehmet 1986).

Since 1982, however, Islamization has been gathering momentum. Initially, the creation of such institutions as the Islamic Bank, the International University, and the Department of Islamic Affairs could be justified as concessions towards an Islamic synthesis intended to balance material improvement and spiritual awakening among the *Bumiputera* in their adjustment to a modern, commercialized and urbanized world (Mauzy and Milne in Gale 1987). Since traditionally Muslim countries, and Malysia itself, have not clearly separated politics and religion (with the notable exceptions of Turkey and Indonesia), there is always a danger of sliding into Islamic extremism.

The introduction in 1988 of certain elements of the *shari'ah* law at the federal level, by amending Article 121 of the Malaysian Constitution and, furthermore, giving it precedence over civil law, constitutes a serious limitation of the traditional secularist role of the federal government in Malaysia. It represents a serious erosion of Mahathir's own prescription for Malay underdevelopment and his 'Ataturk-style' leadership (Milner 1986: 127). Instead of a 'Revolusi Mental' (Senu Abdul Rahman 1973), it subordinates secular public policy to *Kaum Tua* traditionalism and tends to encourage extremists wishing for the restoration of the *shari'ah* in Malaysia.

A careful balancing of the values of market ideology and of Islamic ethics is essential in order to respond to the preferences of the Malays. For the *rakyat* in particular, spiritual and religious needs are meaningful human needs which no Malay leadership could ignore. But in the domain of public policy, the more modernized Islamic countries such as Malaysia and Turkey must continue along the lines of their secularist development. They need effective, modern public policies to pave their transition from non-competitive nationalist development ideologies which have tended to promote rent-seeking behaviour towards more efficient and competitive markets. However, such transition should ignore neither the interests of consumers *vis-à-vis* private monopolies and oligopolies; nor, at the spiritual plane, the Islamic injunction in favour of social justice.

There is another potential opportunity for giving vent to the Islamic identity of the Malays, without sacrificing domestic policy secularism. In the international arena Malaysia could assume a greater role to promote unity, co-operation and solidarity among Islamic countries. Malaysia is a key member of the Organization of Islamic Countries, a body that has a great potential especially as the international system moves towards economic and political blocks. Promotion of Islamic unity might be achieved by, for example, a joint project between Turkey and Malaysia, aimed at the restoration of a modernized Caliphate, while closer inter-Islamic co-operation could be worked out in banking, investment, trade and tourism. These international acts of unity and co-operation would be extremely meaningful for the Malays, it would overcome their relative isolation in the Islamic periphery, and it would give substance to their sense of identity as members of the *umma*.

Chapter ten

Privatizing the Turkish economy

The year 1980 was a watershed in the evolution of the Turkish modernization movement. It marks the end of top-down etatism, reviewed in Chapter 6, and the launching of economic liberalization and privatization of the economy. It is a major turning point when the nationalist ideology gave way to the ideology of the market place; power shifted from bureaucratic elites to market-oriented political elites willing to forge new alliances with corporate interests. This chapter briefly examines the post-1980 economic reforms, their implications and the latest phase of the Turkish identity search.

The architect of Turkish economic liberalization is Turgut Ozal, the former prime minister, who was first the chief economic advisor to the Demirel government which was overthrown by the military in the *coup d'état* of September 1980. The military left Ozal as the economic tsar, but he was obliged to resign when his name was linked to the Kastelli business scandal. Subsequently he entered politics and, following his election victories in 1983 and 1987, economic liberalization emerged as an institutionalized fact of the Turkish economy. The chances of an etatist restoration are virtually non-existent.

Ozal is a pragmatic, neo-classicist in the tradition of Margaret Thatcher of the United Kingdom and Ronald Reagan of the United States. He believes in the incentive system of free enterprise and the individualism of the 'economic man'. He sees a direct causal link between economic liberalism and political freedom: 'Economic liberalism and political democracy are heterozygote twins. . . . An economic actor free from the strings of state is better placed to defend his individual political rights'. When the individual is the decision-maker this 'makes him more responsible, more motivated, and individually stronger' (Ozal 1987: 161).

But the single most important factor in Ozal's initial popularity was his 'charisma'. Although more popular among urban voters, he was able to communicate with the peasantry of Anatolia in a manner which past Turkish leaders had found either irrelevant or, at best, uncomfortable. This is, in part, due to the fact that Ozal, the rationalist technocrat, is also a devout Muslim, thus appealing to the religious feelings of the masses. Although in time Ozal's style became more imperial than populist, and his leadership increasingly authoritarian and anti-bureaucratic, at the beginning he was an impatient reformer whose passion was to implement a bold agenda.

Stabilization and structural adjustment

In 1979 the Turkish GNP registered a negative growth of −0.4 per cent, and in 1980 there was a futher negative growth of −1.1 per cent (Turkey 1988: 4). The current account deficit in that year was US$3.4 billion while merchandise exports earned only US$2.9 billion. The oil dependence, measured as the ratio of the oil import bill to total exports, was over 90 per cent. The country was financially bankrupt and had to rely on balance-of-payments assistance from the IMF and other sources. Domestically, the country was bleeding from strife amongst militant groups, and the economy was suffering from shortage of essential goods. Factories were working at less than half capacity owing to lack of fuel and imported inputs. Houses and offices were obliged to ration electricity and heating. The annual inflation rate was in excess of 120 per cent and rapidly rising in the face of speculative buying and stockpiling of essential goods.

Then came Ozal's economic liberalization programme after the military coup of September 1980. A major component of this programme was the adoption of a more realistic pricing policy in place of the highly inefficient regime of administered prices. In response, relative prices slowly began to allocate resources more efficiently in both the public and private sectors. In the money and credit markets, interest rates were partially deregulated and allowed to rise to positive levels in order to stimulate private savings. To liberalize trade, the Turkish lira was devalued and finally made convertible, and import restrictions were eased. The long period of import substitution industrialization finally ended. A strong boost was given to exporting by means of a wide range of additional export incentives. To eliminate budgetary deficits, prices of the SEEs were decontrolled and state subsidies phased out. The tax system was overhauled. To control inflationary monetary expansion, the public sector borrowing requirement was sharply reduced. In addition a freeze on public sector hiring was imposed.

To accelerate growth, foreign investment and technology imports were encouraged, and foreign borrowing resumed.

Overall, the response was dramatic. In the wake of economic liberalization, the short-term response of the economy was impressive. The GNP in 1981 registered a 4.1 per cent growth rate, and inflation plummeted to below 30 per cent, primarily as a result of the termination of the consumer stockpiling which had characterized the years of instability and violence in the previous decade. Positive interest rates generated steadily rising savings which rose from about 10 per cent in 1980 to 16 per cent in 1983 and to 24 per cent in 1987. The decontrolled SEEs began to raise their prices and report profits, and tax revenues showed a healthy increase as a result of tax reform and greater efficiency in fiscal administration (Kopits 1987).

By far the most impressive post-1980 response was in the export sector, partly because of export incentives and partly because of rapidly rising demand from Iran, Iraq and other Middle Eastern markets. These favourable circumstances enabled the Turkish entrepreneurs to gear the pre-1980 idle productive capacity for an unprecedented export boom. Between 1980 and 1985 exports more than tripled, the export/GNP ratio rising from 6 per cent to 17 per cent. In 1987, the total value of Turkish exports was US$10.1 billion (of which more than half were industrial goods) compared with US$2.9 billion in 1980. At the same time, imports also rose quite substantially, but the trade deficit in 1987 (US$3.2 billion) was less than what it had been in 1980 (US$4.8 billion). There was also, however, a sharp increase in foreign debt (US$29.6 billion in 1987) compared to US$15.9 billion in 1982), but, thanks to the export boom, Turkey's foreign debt service performance was one of the best in the world.

Nevertheless, there have been disappointing responses as well. One notable case is the rather sluggish response of private investment. The manufacturing sector, in particular, has failed to respond to new investment owing, in part, to the existence of unused capacity inherited from the pre-1980 era. The leading private investment activity was in service sectors such as tourism, education and health, which were stimulated by new privatization opportunities in these sectors. A limited investment boom occurred also in the construction of housing, stimulated by the establishment of the Housing Development Fund in 1982 to provide low-cost credit for co-operatives and municipalities as well as for private developers.

Inflation and monetary policy

Another source of serious concern and disappointment in the post-1980 period has been inflation. There are many factors contributing to inflation in the Turkish economy, some structural but many induced by inappropriate policies in the past. During the Second Republic, but especially from 1965 to 1980, there was undisciplined monetary expansion, largely on account of deficit financing and loss-making SEEs (Kopits 1987). The Turkish Central Bank was too weak, and lacked the necessary independence to conduct an autonomous monetary policy. Thus, in effect, money supply was a politically-determined variable. Even after 1980 this weakness persisted, and at least in one respect it was reinforced. Several extra-budget funds have been created, of which the Public Housing, Public Revenue Sharing Scheme and the Defence Support are the biggest (The Economist Intelligence Unit 1987: 14). In addition, a number of municipalities undertook major public works projects, such as the US$0.5 billion Izmir seafront sewer project. Several mega-projects, such as the South Anatolian Project and the F-16 fighter plane, also contributed to monetary expansion.

The single most important source of inflation after 1980 was the rapid devaluation of the lira and its impact on domestic prices (Ozmucur and Onis 1988). Decontrolled SEE pricing, while reducing operating losses of the SEEs and the corresponding requirement for state subsidies, also had an inflationary impact and, in particular, added to the cost of living of the lower-income masses. Realistically, however, this higher cost is, in a large measure, the lagged effect of historical price distortions in the Turkish economy caused by such factors as exceedingly low administered prices and overvalued Turkish lira. Deregulation of SEE prices in particular, and economic liberalization in general, are necessary and desirable to allow resource allocation in accordance with the market forces of supply and demand, provided real wages and incomes are adequately protected.

Wages, employment and income distribution

Labour market imbalance, in particular unemployment, remains a major challenge of the post-1980 stabilization and adjustment programme. According to the most recent data, real wages fell by almost 50 per cent between 1980 to 1984 (Celasun and Rodrik 1987). The share of profits rose and income distribution, already highly unequal prior to 1980, deteriorated further. On the other hand, however, job creation has more or less matched the growth of the labour force and, as a result, unemployment has been maintained steady at about 15 per cent of the labour force. A cheap-labour policy – one which puts greater priority on job creation – is appropriate so long as excess labour conditions prevail. This is a 'lesson' strongly suggested by the experience of the Gang of Four: South Korea, Taiwan, Hong Kong and Singapore. However, a cheap-labour policy needs to be complemented – as was done in these countries – with compensating social policies (such as low-cost public housing, public transportation and skill training) to protect real wages and ensure 'growth with equity' – something the Turkish authorities have failed to promote. A rising share of labour income can be expected to boost demand for housing and consumer durables thereby stimulating construction and manufacturing.

One major deficiency in the Turkish labour market is the highly restrictive nature of trade union laws which unnecessarily limit the workers' freedom of association and their rights for collective bargaining. This biases income distribution in favour of capital at the expense of labour in a manner which clearly damages social justice. Thus, evidence compiled by the Turkish labour union, TURK-IS, shows that since 1982 real wages have declined while the profit share of national income rose quite sharply. In addition an inordinate share of profits have been invested in high-interest-bearing government securities. This is a distorted overcrowding effect which stimulates public sector spending at the expense of private investment. Private investment is the key to accelerating job creation as well as to the production of consumer goods and services in order to ease inflationary pressures.

Privatization

A major cornerstone of the post-1980 economic liberalization strategy is privatization. As in Malaysia, many forms of privatizing the Turkish economy are being employed: selling shares of public utilities to private investors, subcontracting operations from public enterprise to profit-oriented private sub-contractors, introducing user fees (for example highway tolls), deregulating administered prices and, of course, stimulating private enterprise by means of economic incentives.

The Turkish privatization strategy is still in its infancy. It began in 1984 with the highly popular public offering of the shares in the Bosphorus Bridge. Since then extensive feasibility studies have been commissioned to prepare the sale of several public enterprises to private interests, but so far relatively little has actually been privatized. In 1988, part of the equity of the telephone company, Teletas, was sold to Turkish and foreign investors and the stock was listed on the new Istanbul Stock Exchange to encourage the development of a capital market for mobilizing private savings into the private sector. The Exchange is an innovation in Turkey, but precisely because it is an innovation, it is bound to be risky and may backfire especially if speculators try to corner the market because of its small size.

Privatizing public monopolies is a highly complex task. It requires, as demonstrated in the case of the giant Sumerbank (the oldest state economic enterprise in Turkey active in textiles and many other industries) which has been earmarked for privatization for a number of years now, long and careful financial and technical analyses before the terms of sale to private interests can be determined. For these reasons, it may be more feasible to implement privatization by means of deregulation intended to make the industry more competitive for new firms (for example the airline or the tobacco industries) or by introducing it in sectors especially dependent on modern technology (for example the telecommunications industry). This is what happened in the case of Teletas.

Transitional problems

Transition from an etatist to a competitive economy is not easy. In Turkey it requires not only dismantling a loss-making, oversized public enterprise sector; it also means eliminating an underground economy, built on the smuggling of banned imports and illegal transactions. Since many special interests derived huge profits from the underground economy, and these interests still have strong networks with influence and power, it is foolhardy to expect that the transition to a competitive, open economy will be plain sailing, accomplished overnight. A typical example of the kinds of transitional problems likely to be encountered on the way to a more competitive Turkish economy is the 'artificial exporting' scandals that have appeared in the Turkish press. These scandals refer to the fact that some exporters have faked their export documents in order to take advantage of export incentives offered under the liberalization programme.

There are, in addition, further complicating factors slowing down the pace of Turkish privatization. One is the need to write or amend the personnel laws to ensure equity and fairness for those employees whose job security is threatened by privatization. Chapter 6 described the serious problem of featherbedding in the Turkish SEEs. With economic reforms, the level of SEE salaried personnel has remained stationary, but there has been a large growth in the number of 'contract' employees (Basbakanlik 1988). Contract personnel cannot be dismissed without due legal process.

A particularly serious transitional problem created by privatization is the danger of further concentration of corporate assets due to the fact that new owners of privatized enterprises are likely to be already wealthy and powerful. Special measures intended for wide public sale of privatized assets may ensure widely held acquisition in the first round, but this cannot prevent subsequent asset concentration through resale acquisitions. This type of concentration would, in time, lead to private monopolization unless effective anti-monopoly and anti-trust laws are enacted and implemented. Similarly, decontrolled prices are likely to lead to inflation and excessive profiteering unless fair competition policies are in place to prevent private enterprises from abusing liberalized market conditions.

In Turkey, as in Malaysia, privatization is being introduced without adequate legal safeguards. Both countries urgently require consumer protection and anti-trust policies in order to prevent monopoly profit exploitation by profit-driven firms. Privatization does not mean abandoning public regulation; it means reducing direct government intervention in the economy. Part of the privatization strategy must be regulations in the public interest such as providing for public hearings at rate-setting tribunals, and appeal and remedy procedures for consumer complaints, setting minimum standards of public safety in hazardous situations, environmental and zoning controls, etc. The drafting of laws and regulations in these areas would require a careful look at international experience, especially the United States experience in the field of anti-trust laws and consumer protection and competition policies.

Consumer protection and fair competition policies

Privatizing the Turkish economy runs the risk of converting public monopolies into private monopolies. It opens the doors to excessive profit-driven pricing strategies by new, private owners. There is a need to protect consumers against unfair trade practices and to ensure that market competition is fair.

The current high rate of inflation places a heavy burden of the cost of living on the public. This is especially true for rural communities because the latest evidence points to a serious deterioration in the agricultural terms of trade (Celasun and Roderik 1987). Countervailing measures are necessary to protect consumers against profiteering and unfair trade practices. These countervailing measures entail new fair competition laws and better enforcement of trade regulations. Such new laws and regulations need to be based on extensive public hearings to solicit the widest possible input from consumer groups as well as unions and corporate interests. A strong public education and information programme should be undertaken as soon as these new laws are enacted. Government encouragement, even funding support, for consumer groups would be highly desirable to provide adequate consumer protection.

Adjusting to structural change will, no doubt, take some time and there will be some transitional difficulties. In the Turkish case examples of such difficulties include the problem of 'artificial exports' and the excessive private quasi-money creation through bad cheques and promissory notes. These transitional problems can best be checked by improving the government's inspection and monitoring capabilities with the enactment and implementation of new competition policies and unfair trade practices regulations.

Trade and foreign investment

Privatization requires foreign technology and capital. Foreign competition is essential for productivity and quality enhancement. On the other hand, foreign investment increases foreign ownership and control. In the Ottoman Empire foreign capital played a major role in the financial bankruptcy of the Empire and this disastrous consequence was a major factor in the emergence of the autarkic, etatist strategy in the early decades of the Turkish Republic. The post-1980 economic liberalization strategy is showing a new sense of national confidence in the ability of the Turkish Republic to collaborate with foreign capital in a mutually enriching manner. Thus, there has been significant streamlining of bureaucratic obstacles in the way of foreign investment. Joint ventures have been particularly encouraged through the innovative formula of build, operate and transfer (BOT) offered to foreign investors (*South* 1987: 46). This formula has attracted investments, in particular in the tourism and energy fields.

Taking a leaf from Malaysian experience, Turkey recently announced a policy of establishing Free Trade Zones (FTZs). The objective is to attract foreign investment and technology and to transform Turkey into a regional manufacturing base serving the rich Middle Eastern markets. The response of foreign investors, so far, has been rather disappointing. While this is due, in part, to the economic recession in the global economy, and the depressed oil prices in particular which have curbed demand in oil-producing

Middle Eastern markets, there are also some policy bottlenecks in the Turkish bureaucracy. For example, there is a perception among some potential investors that the foreign investment licensing procedures, despite recent streamlining, are still cumbersome and time-consuming. It seems clear that a truly one-stop foreign investment agency (as for example in Singapore or Malaysia) does not exist in Turkey since the investor has to apply to the Ministry of Commerce for a manufacturing licence, to the Customs for duty exemption and to the Ministry of Finance, the Central Bank, etc. for all the various permits. The truly one-stop agency would co-ordinate all these and obtain the necessary permits for the investor. There are two further shortcomings of the existing system. One is an apparent lack of a tax holiday incentive; the other is the administrative separation between the Directorate for Free Trade Zones and the Foreign Investment Directorate. A much closer co-ordination here might result in greater stimulation of FTZs.

Public investment and regional development

Despite economic liberalization since 1980, public investment accounts for a very high proportion of total Turkish investment. This is partly due to several infrastructural projects in the public sector such as the South Anatolian Project (started during the Demirel administration), and partly due to large-scale public-work projects initiated by municipalities following decentralization of fiscal policy after 1980. Public infrastructural expenditures tend to be inflationary, at least in the short run. On the other hand, such spending contributes towards a higher growth rate. The challenge facing Turkish macro-planners is to find a balance within an investment timetable which attempts to ensure dynamic equilibrium between additional supply of goods and services and inflation-prone public sector spending.

Etatist strategy was urban-biased, favouring the more developed Western Turkey. One of the major innovative aspects of post-1980 development strategy is the increasing importance attached to regional development, especially in the underdeveloped Eastern Anatolia. The largest on-going project in the country is the South Anatolian Project (GAP) which, when finally completed in the 1990s, will triple electricity production, increase irrigable land in Turkey by 50 per cent and enable Turkey to become the bread-basket of the Middle East. It can bring stability through prosperity to a region which has recently been the scene of ethnic and sectarian violence, and it can raise regional incomes and reduce rural migration into overcrowded urban centres in the west.

There are two major constraints on regional development in the poorer parts of the Turkish hinterland: lower economic returns on investment, and limited private sector participation. The fact that the rate of return on such projects as GAP is relatively low stems from its public infrastructural nature. However, it means that the region is being subsidized by the rest of the country, and, given the relatively long gestation period of the project and the large sums of public expenditure involved, it is a significant source of inflationary pressures in the economy. Short- and medium-term sacrifice would be justified if, and only if, long-term economic efficiency is indeed attained. Efficiency is also essential to stimulate greater private sector participation in the GAP region to promote spin-off effects through backward and forward linkages.

Turkish–EC connection: now or later?

For the Turkish political elites at the centre, the European Community (EC) application is a logical culmination of the 150-year-old westernization drive. But, would the EC membership, and all that it would entail, match the aspirations of the Turkish nation as a whole? This is not an idle or irrelevant question, given the fact that the nationalist leadership since 1923 has yet to develop a truly organic relationship between itself and the masses.

In strict economic terms, evaluation of the prospective Turkish membership raises serious problems both for Europe and Turkey. For the Europeans, the magnitude of potential Turkish labour mobility would be immense given the fact that the Turks, now numbering 55 million, are expected to become the second largest nation in Europe by the year 2000. The EC, which in recent years accepted three new relatively poor members (Greece, Portugal and Spain), will be hard pressed to absorb the cost of an even poorer and larger member. Tariff-free, cheaper Turkish manufactures, especially in such labour-intensive sectors as textiles, leather goods and processed food, would present serious competition to European industries and threaten jobs. On the other hand, many Turkish industries, especially capital- and technology-intensive ones such as automobiles and consumer durables, would be severely damaged. Huge increases in Turkish agricultural surpluses, once the South Anatolian Project enters production in the 1990s, would also conflict seriously with the common agricultural policy of the EC.

But the major Turkish loss would be foregone dynamic benefits. Turkey would now be bargaining from a position of economic weakness. An accession agreement hurriedly concluded now would run the great risk of converting Turkey into a labour reserve for a technologically superior Europe. In ten or twenty years, given sustained growth at the present rates, the Turkish income per capita would surpass that of Greece and Portugal. Since 1982 the Turkish economy has been growing at rates in excess of 5 per cent per annum, considerably faster than Greece and Portugal. At these rates of growth, Turkish income per capita can be expected to catch up with and surpass Greece and Portugal somewhere around 2010.

A prosperous Turkish economy would be a major economic power-house in the Middle East. If such projects as the GAP do, indeed, achieve the rates of return anticipated and enable the Turkish economy to emerge as the regional bread-basket and manufacturing base of the Middle East, Turkey would be in a far stronger position of bargaining not only with the EC, but with Middle Eastern and global trading partners. At the present time, 40 per cent of Turkish exports are delivered to Middle Eastern markets; and this is a fraction of the available potential for Turkey with its obvious comparative cost advantage to service these high-income markets. Unlike European markets, Turkish exporters and businessmen in the Middle East have relatively easy access with virtually no tariff and non-tariff barriers. While religion and culture are obvious barriers for a European integration, these same factors are very much an advantage in the Middle Eastern trade. The Ozal government's balanced Middle Eastern policies, including his readiness to join the Organization of Islamic Countries and visit Saudi Arabia, are examples of the profitable trade diversification policies which can be developed.

As far as trading in the world markets beyond are concerned, there are impressive potentials as well, both within and outside the framework of Islamic co-operation. This is, of course, contingent upon the ability of the Turkish entrepreneurs to offer price- and quality-competitive goods and services. Japan's successful industrialization (see chapter 11) is derived from such comparative advantage.

The end of totalitarianism in eastern Europe in the final months of 1989, coming at the heels of Gorbachev's glasnost and perestroika, has far-reaching implications for EC–Turkish relations as well as for east–west relations. The prospect of German reunification and the emergence of new trade and investment opportunities in central and eastern Europe are as significant as the creation of a Single European Market in 1992. It is almost certain that the economic map of Europe will be redrawn at the same time as the question of full membership for Turkey appears on the EC agenda. As a result, this question may now be subjected to a long delay. In the meantime, the EC will be under considerable pressure to divert its subsidies and investment resources to central and eastern Europe at the expense of not only Turkey but also such existing members as Greece. Multilateralism, rather than putting all the Turkish eggs in the EC basket, may emerge as the inevitable trading strategy for Turkey.

The new market ideology and the Turkish identity search

Some observers are pessimistic about the post-1980 economic strategy on the ground that abandoning the etatist nationalist ideology in favour of an internationalized market ideology would, once again, open the floodgates of foreign debt, domination and subordination in the new international division of labour (Shick and Tonak 1987: esp. chap. 12). They point to the record of foreign debt in Turkish history and argue that foreign domination occurred twice before, once in the nineteenth-century Ottoman days, and, again in the Menderes decade in the 1950s.

These dependency theorists understate the inherent inefficiencies of the nationalist ideology and overstate their own historical determinism. The chief lesson of the Ottoman debt crisis as well as the Menderes mismanagement is the imperative of efficiency in resource allocation. The Ottomans borrowed to finance wars (Pamuk 1987: 134); Menderes squandered Western aid on 'political factories' (Hale 1981: 92). The relative advantage of the market ideology, especially international market ideology, is the discipline of efficiency imposed by competition. This is how Japan and the Gang of Four, starting from no more advantageous conditions than Turkey, were able to achieve development in the post-war period (Mehmet 1989: chap. 2).

For the last 250 years the Turkish nation has undergone an identity crisis of tremendous proportions, longer and deeper than Japan's, for example, because Japan wisely resisted cultural restructuring, opting instead for blending western science and technology within a Japanese cultural mould. But the Japanese did not ignore efficiency and they did not shy away from market competition. On the contrary, they promoted these by the very nationalist ideology which the Kemalists attempted: state nurturing. The Turkish nationalists, however, gradually, and in the end (i.e. 1979–80) totally, abandoned the rules of efficiency and competition.

A Turkish scholar (Berkes 1965) captured the Turkish identity crisis very aptly in one of his titles: *Ikiyuz Yildir Neden Bocaliyoruz?* (Why Have We Been Waffling For the Last Two Hundred Years?). The surest path to regaining lost identity is the most efficient path. Whether the destination is west or east, a competitive and cost-efficient Turkish economy is unavoidable. The Europeans will not respect the Turks merely because of their westernization preference any more than the Ottomans won the Arabs' respect for becoming the sword of Islam. International respect for the Turks in the future, as the Japanese have most recently demonstrated, will be proportional to their economic clout. That means putting the Turkish economic house in order, first and foremost. The market ideology, based on efficiency and competition, with proper safeguards, is the way to define Turkey's place in the Middle East as well as in the rest of the world.

Part five

Conclusion

6

This concluding part pulls together the main threads of the study and highlights its principal conclusions. The study has utilized the Turkish and Malaysian top-down development experiences to demonstrate that nationalist ideology is not by itself a sufficient guarantee of growth with social justice.

The nationalist failure to promote growth with social justice has strengthened the hands of Islamic reactionaries, while obliging the centrist elites to shift gears, so to speak, and switch from nationalist to market ideology, i.e. from state capitalism towards a more privatized development strategy. But a profit-driven privatization strategy, without proper regulation, is less likely to promote social justice and can be expected to intensify socio-economic polarization and provide further ammunition for Islamic extremists and militants.

The great majority of Turks and Malays are rational, behaving as 'economic man' while also having an abiding faith in Islam. They have a strong preference for development, i.e. most simply stated, an expectation that the standard of living of one generation should be significantly better than that of the preceding generation. However, this expectation is qualified by an equally strong conviction that God's resources are gifts for all and meant for equitable distribution, not, as in unfettered capitalism, for the benefit of just a few. In other words, development must be responsible development based on a process of public policy designed and implemented in an organic relationship with the Islamic constituency. The concluding chapter will outline the features of responsible development.

Chapter eleven

Responsible development in the Islamic Periphery
Regulation, competition and public policy

Suppose it was the year 1950 and a fifty-year forecast was wanted of the development prospects of Turkey, Malaysia and Japan. How would these countries be ranked? Japan would most likely be in the last place in view of her war-damaged economy and occupation by the United States. Resource-rich Malaya (as it was called at the time) would be better placed, but the escalating communist insurgency would cast a serious doubt about her stability and prospects. On the other hand, Turkey, which came out of the Second World War intact thanks to her neutrality and enjoyed a healthy trade balance would appear quite impressive. In terms of income per capita, Japan was behind both Malaya and Turkey. In 1952 at the outset of the Korean War, the Japanese per capita annual income was $162 (Okita 1980: 108), the Turkish figure was $169 (Singer 1977: 444–5) and the Malayan figure, at about $250 'was the highest in the Far East'. (IBRD 1955: 13).

These three countries have one fundamental characteristic in common: they all relied upon imitative growth, imported from outside by a modernizing leadership that was highly motivated by a nationalist development ideology. Japan has been the most successful by far. It is illuminating to highlight the reasons why.

Japanese Miracle

Japan's successful integration of western technological knowledge with Japanese culture is a remarkable story of modernization representing at least 100 years of state nurturing and business-government partnership. Like Turkey and Malaysia, it was an elite-imposed process of top-down growth strategy justified by national ideology. In all three cases the social and economic costs of modernization were great. In the case of Japan this has been well put by a Japanese historian:

The cost was borne primarily by the masses in terms of the following: greater burdens imposed upon the peasantry, the dehumanizing practices that accompanied industrialization in the exploitation of factory and mine workers; and the brutalizing effects of modern militarism. Meiji leaders envisioned the object of modernization as the strengthening of the nation – the masses were the means for achieving this.

(Mikiso 1986: 1989–90)

The post-war Japanese Miracle rewarded the masses impressively for their past sacrifice and economic burdens. In 1986, the Japanese per capita income had risen to $12,840 compared with $1,830 for Malaysia and $1,110 for Turkey (World Bank 1988: Table 1). What emerges from the Japanese successful development by imitation is not that nationalist ideology is irrelevant or counter-productive, but, quite the contrary, that it can be an effective technique of mass mobilization for modernization so long as the modernizing leadership remains committed to the rules of efficiency in public policy.

The objective of development policy and organic growth

But development is not merely economic development aimed at income maximization. There are higher goals and objectives, such as social cohesion, cultural security and spiritual ends. Higher prosperity, generated by economic growth, provides the means to attain these higher ends. But the fulfilment of higher ends depends on organic growth, in other words the existence of a dynamic, symbiotic relationship between the rulers and followers that recognizes and respects followers as active participants in policy-making.

The Japanese Miracle was a case of organic growth because development policy was a successful blend of indigenous culture and growth-stimulating technology. Japan developed its own work ethics of which *nenko* (lifetime employment) is only the most celebrated example; it did not have to import the western system of confrontational trade unionism. Although education was utilized as an instrument of national culture, it was heavily vocationalized in order to raise the productivity of the masses and help equalize income distribution. Industrial strategy, designed and implemented under the leadership of the Ministry of International Trade and Industry (Johnson 1982), was interventionist, with generous state subsidies and protection to nurture industry, but state assistance was based on the conditionality of market efficiency and competitiveness. *Japan Incorporated* was a home-made development strategy based on active state–business partnership. This formula successfully harnessed the Japanese value system for industrialization. It took advantage of the *vertical* nature of the Japanese society (Nakane 1970) in which hierarchical relations govern family, kinship and organizational relations. The vertical nature of Japanese society, intimately connected to Shintoism, has been credited as the source of such virtues as loyalty, respect and discipline. Instead of destroying these values, the architects of the Japanese Miracle harnessed them. They designed and implemented a development strategy built on a symbiotic harmony with the indigenous values and institutions. Japan, of course, had a great relative advantage: it was an island kingdom with a remarkably homogeneous racial and linguistic composition (Rustow and Ward 1964: 438). The absence of this homogeneity may have great explanatory power for the relative retardation of the Malaysian and Turkish development experience.

The Japanese Miracle is significant in yet another respect. It differed from the western, profit-driven capitalism which was based on a classic confrontation between labour and capital. The modernizing Japanese state emphasized efficiency and competition. It encouraged competition by breaking up the traditional *zaibatsu* monopolies, but it also took responsibility for a full-employment policy even before John Maynard Keynes' *General Theory* was published (Allen 1962: 136). Thus, the Japanese development strategy demonstrated the existence of an alternative path of development via state nurturing, efficiently administered, leading to growth with full employment and social justice.

Profit-driven capitalist growth

The inner logic of capitalism is the profit motive. Psychologically, it is a system built on the assumption that more is better. Its ideology is freedom of choice (Friedman and Friedman 1981). The fundamental weakness of profit-driven capitalism is that it thrives on functional inequality. Unlimited freedom of choice of the capitalist leads naturally to excessive concentration of wealth at the top for the few and mass poverty for those at the bottom. Greed at the top of the pyramid is matched by functional poverty at its bottom.

Profit-driven capitalism makes poor ethics because it converts natural resources, such as water and air meant as public commons, into private property. It externalizes ecology and underprices externalities. Everything else becomes a commodity and is assigned a price tag. Forests, mines, oceans, machines and labour all become commodities to be exploited for a surplus value which is expropriated as profit by the capitalist as his reward for further exploitation. As profits accumulate in the form of wealth enjoyed by the privileged few, subsistence wages impoverish the masses generating social injustice. But subsistence wages are necessary for capitalist profits. Technology and machines are means at the disposal of the capitalist to enhance productivity, often through investment in labour-displacing new technology. As profits diminish in given national markets, the capitalist goes international, exploiting natural and manpower resources of the world at large in a ceaseless global search for profit.

The most effective remedy is regulation in the public interest. This is responsible development. For Muslim societies responsible development in the modern world means a development strategy, implemented by public policies based on an organic relationship with the masses, and implemented cost-effectively in response to human needs. The end result of such a development policy would be growth with equity ensuring rising standards of economic well-being and markedly improving the quality of human life.

Responsible development

Responsible development is an evolving process of public policy having the following four characteristics: (1) it promotes efficiency through competitive rules which reward merit and productivity; (2) it regulates unfair practices through legally enforceable standards and procedures; (3) it provides a social safety net for those who have earned it (for example pensioners) or for those who, for reasons beyond their control, are in need of social assistance (such as disabled people), and (4) it requires legal disclosure of adequate information to the public about public expenditures and private corporations to ensure proper and timely audit and evalutation of investment projects from the standpoint of public safety, environmental impact and social soundness.

Responsible development differs from unfettered profit-driven capitalism in which, as we saw above, few gain at the expense of the great majority. This unjust outcome results primarily because of the failure of public policy to restrain excessive wealth accumulation. The usual defensive argument is that capitalists need unlimited freedom; limiting their freedom is limiting their incentives.

This is a fallacious argument. There is no such thing as unlimited freedom: life itself is finite. Unlimited incentives maximize more than profits; they maximize greed and 'beggar-thy-neighbour' selfishness. The challenge of public policy in general, and of development policy in particular, is how to balance singly desirable, yet mutually conflicting, public objectives, for example how to balance freedom of choice with social justice. This is the task of responsible development policy.

Socially responsible regulation, which regulates unfair trade practices, offers the means for regulating excessive greed and selfishness. Responsible public policy encourages efficient resource allocation, very much as under capitalism, but it exercises a significant influence over income distribution in order to promote growth with social justice. National welfare is a collective good. Accordingly, national income is regarded not as an exclusive private property, but as a national dividend in which all citizens have a stake. This is in recognition of the mutuality of interests of all citizens who have shared entitlements to air, water and natural resources.

Inter-generational dimension of development

Responsible development has another important dimension: it is development that is also just to future generations. It is development which promotes social justice without destroying the environment. Thus, in responsible development, the full costs of ecological capital utilized along with other factors of production are properly accounted. Thus a component of the surplus generated by growth is channelled for reinvestment in sustainable development in aid of future generations. For example, forest and other renewable resources which are depleted as a result of economic growth are replaced through new investment in the replenishment of those resources. In the case of non-renewable resources there is reinvestment in new research to discover new technologies. Similarly, to safeguard against pollution or health hazards created by mega-projects (e.g. dams), part of the surplus is channelled into preventive programmes to control such damaging consequences.

Sustainable development

The idea of 'sustainable development' is central to *Our Common Future*, the report of a World Commission set up by the UN General Assembly (World Commission 1987). By 'sustainable development' is meant policies which maintain and expand the environmental resource base so that future generations of mankind can enjoy equal or better standards of living. Sustainable development is thus solidly based on the principles of global interdependence, co-operation and social justice to ensure survival.

The new paradigm of sustainable development is highly compatible with the Islamic concept of responsible development. Both sustainable and responsible development require integrating environmental and economic planning and subordinating technology and wealth to service human needs in order to solve poverty while simultaneously expanding the resource base for the benefit of future generations.

The transition to responsible development

The key lies in the adoption and implementation of a public policy that is in a dynamic organic relationship with the society it is serving. This requires two essential conditions: first, a responsive political leadership which is accountable to its 'political masters', i.e. the citizens; and second, a social consensus about development goals derived from the ethical values of the society. The interplay of these two conditions should guarantee state laws and public policy which promote efficient growth of national income while also expressly spelling out the criteria for the reward system to be applied in the distribution of that income.

We have seen in Part IV that development in Turkey and Malaysia is becoming privatized. This is a global trend marking the end of government-led development. Privatization has the potential advantage of encouraging self-employment, creativity and initiative in place of a culture of state paternalism or welfare dependence. Unfortunately, if not checked by proper laws, it may also mean more monopolistic power, more user fees, higher cost of living, greater foreign investment and greater prospects of unfair trade practices. These risks and dangers can best be avoided by encouraging the formation of consumer and other interest groups to act as countervailing forces in society and by means of regulation through appropriate public policies for legal protection of the public interest.

Pluralism

One of the manifest results of progress and modernization is socioeconomic pluralism. This pluralism must lead to growth and development of special interest groups to play an active part in the formulation of public policy by representing special interests and by providing information about particular issues such as consumer protection, environmental concerns, disadvantaged groups, etc. Thus pluralism can strengthen the bonds of organic development by facilitating the maintenance of checks and balances in society. Different interest groups, such as trade unions, employer federations, professional and consumer associations, etc. act as countervailing forces leading to the formation of social consensus through the balancing of competing interests ultimately influencing the content and the process of politics and public policy formation.

Islamic revival, no doubt, is an expression of human rights. Denial of religious freedom by militant secularism bottles up citizens and societies. Intolerance does not silence extremists, it drives them underground. On the other hand, it can become a tool of extremism, fanaticism and even violence. These risks cannot be eliminated by such state law as internal security legislation, however punitive it may be in scope or application. Oppressive methods are not only contrary to basic human freedoms; in more practical terms they merely push extremism and violence underground, thereby aggravating rather than resolving conflict. The most effective methods of dealing with extremism and violence are by exposing these movements and their leaders in the press and other news media and relying on the common sense of the body politic. A few may be fanatical, but the vast majority are bound to be reasonable.

There is good empirical evidence of such reasonableness. As we saw in Chapter 2, although there has been a mushrooming of religious sects in recent years, an even more remarkable trend is their readiness to enter the secular political process and seek alliances with major parties in pursuit of not only spiritual but material aims. Their main activities have been in social and welfare fields, providing charitable and voluntary assistance, typically for victims of economic growth, left helpless by a remote and, apparently, uncaring state machinery.

Islamic charity and voluntarism

Social justice is the corner-stone of Islam, but its implementation remains the least developed aspect. *Zakat*, *waqfs* and other forms of Islamic charity are essential instruments of wealth redistribution. They can be utilized to build a modern Islamic social safety net based on voluntarism to complement the social and welfare policies of the state. Social and welfare services represent a huge area which is big enough to accommodate both state agencies and non-governmental organizations working in a complementary manner. For example, family law is properly the domain of the state, but many children's aid functions such as foster parents and services for women victimized by rape or violence, can be provided by voluntary organizations financed by private donations. Another important potential field of action for Islamic voluntary organizations is community service, especially adult education, arts and crafts, and recreational activities.

In some countries, Islamic voluntary organizations are already in existence and they provide an excellent service. In Malaysia there are organizations like ABIM and PERKIM, which we discussed in Chapter 2, operating a large and well-organized network of social and charitable services. In Bangladesh, where there is a widespread problem of abandoned and destitute women caused by polygamy and economic distress, many non-governmental organizations have been set up to provide support, shelter and training for these destitute women and their children. Another significant innovation from Bangladesh is the Grameen Bank which provides unsecured loans to the rural poor, typically landless and assetless women (Yunus 1988). In Indonesia Islamic voluntary organizations provide an impressive range of educational, welfare and charitable services for the benefit of various target groups such as unemployed city youth and micro-entrepreneurs in the informal sector (Mehden 1986: 94).

Islamic charitable and voluntary organizations need to be duly registered under state law. This provides for the rule of law, and avoids the potential dangers of subversive political action. In most countries there are laws providing for the registration and administration of not-for-profit organizations. Typically, they require that such voluntary organizations have a constitution setting out their aims, their board of directors and executive officers, and their liability. As a condition of registration, voluntary organizations undertake to report to the appropriate state authority, in particular to file a tax return, and they submit to audit inspection.

Funding of Islamic voluntary organizations raises some interesting questions. Should *zakat* be paid to the state or to Islamic voluntary organizations? What is the optimal administration of *waqfs*? The important point here is not that there should be a universal, uniform system, but rather that these Islamic formulae should be tapped and channelled efficiently to respond to human needs and raise the quality of life. It is conceivable that in some cases *zakat* can be collected, as a tax surcharge, by the state treasury and utilized for designated Islamic charitable projects (for example low-cost housing), or it could be collected by an autonomous agency, set up under state law, to operate a not-for-profit Islamic foundation. Such a foundation could undertake a range of Islamic social and charitable works. As for the regulation of *waqfs*, this would require a modern law regulating wills and estates in a manner deliberately intended to maximize the social welfare benefits of legacies and bequests in accordance with the wishes of the donor. Many foundations (for example in education providing scholarships) and special-purpose institutions can be set up to implement *waqfs*. The Malaysian Tabung Hajji, discussed in Chapter 7, is an example of a special-purpose Islamic organization which provides a multiplicity of services, including a travel agency, for Muslims intending to go to Mecca to perform the Hajj.

Ibadah and muamalat

The fundamental distinction between *ibadah* and *muamalat* is still relevant today: it provides a boundary between the individual's subjective relations, including prayer, to God, and the more objective, inter-personal relations in society at large. The former, *ibadah*, relates to man's duty to God and to fulfil his spirituality; the latter, *muamalat*, determines his ethical obligations as a member of the social community.

How an individual performs *ibadah* is a matter of conscience, a fundamental human right, i.e. freedom of belief. It may be practised as a member of a congregation or as a group of like-minded persons united in an association by virtue of another fundamental human right, i.e. freedom of association. All these associations and groups need to be registered under appropriate state law, not for purposes of censorship, but for legal protection under the rule of law. State law should not only protect, but safeguard, through due process, these fundamental human rights. Inevitably, there will be cases of abuses of these religious freedoms, but it would be unreasonable to equate every case of fanaticism and extremism as a political conspiracy justifying total suppression of religious freedoms.

In the domain of social and inter-personal relations, there is much in *muamalat* that is as rigid and ritualistic as a Japanese tea ceremony. Often obligations of *muamalat* may be overstated and respect for elders, obedience to parents and loyalty to rulers carried to archaic, feudal proportions. But, as with the Japanese tea ceremony, the positive aspects of *muamalat* can be harnessed via public policy for worthy social purposes to preserve and enhance cultural heritage, (for example through traditional festivals organized by community groups), and to promote social cohesion and such desirable moral qualities as responsibility, integrity and reasonable behaviour.

Legislation and public hearings

How can *muamalat* be harmonized with state law and public policy? One very meaningful way would be through public hearings at the legislation stage. In the Turkish Grand National Assembly, for example, although there are elaborate Commission structures for purposes of reviewing legislation, 'outsiders' are specifically excluded from Commission deliberations (Kalaycioglu in Ozbudun *et al.* 1988: 177). The Malaysian Parliament has similarly closed procedures. American-style public hearings enrich the work of legislators. They provide valuable input, in the form of views and information, to ensure that laws are socially sound. These imputs from below provide the legislators with alternative perspectives on social problems and human needs; they provide special interest groups with a say in the rule-making process. In this way, public awareness of, and respect for, state law is considerably enhanced.

Public hearings at the legislation state can be organized most conveniently by inviting expert witnesses, technical personnel as well as specialists in Islamic ethics to provide inputs for the consideration and possible use of the legislators. A good portion of such input may be useless, and some may even be unreasonable, but the advantages of openness and due process would far outweigh the social cost. Most significantly, the laws enacted and public policy implemented would have a more organic relationship with the society at large than any autocratic, top-down system or rule-making by edicts.

Public decision-making can be conducted in two principal ways. In a closed, secretive way, or in an open, consultative manner. In the former case, public policy is essentially a cartel-like decision-making, monopolized by a small, privileged and powerful group; this approach invites corruption, nepotism and favouritism. In the case of the open, consultative approach, there are checks and balances which provide alternative perspectives on public policy. In effect, public policy emerges as an ongoing process of conflict resolution in the open, where conficting interests and groups balance their objectives with the government playing the role of an independent umpire. The specific role of government in this context is to enact laws and set standards for the benefit of the citizens, including, of course, the protection of basic human rights, such as the freedoms of association, belief and expression of ideas in speech or written form. Some groups and individuals may attempt to abuse these rights by extremism, fanaticism or even violence. In such cases, due process as provided under state law should apply.

Public policy and corruption

No amount of legislative measures and formal state machinery can ever ensure a perfectly clean and efficient system of public policy. In Islam, scripturalism and formal legalism have, if anything, been excessive. Ultimately, the quality of public policy depends on the quality of the human character, and moral failure is a universal problem. A common symptom of moral failure is corruption, i.e. self-enrichment by officials who put self-interest before public interest (Alatas 1980). Appealing to high moral values, while necessary, is not a sufficient guarantee of corruption-free public policy. Such values need to be complemented by a system of checks and balances for an open, consultative public policy as discussed above, and reinforced by due legal process under state law.

One thing which merits emphasis is the fact that the risk of corrupt practice in the public policy domain is positively correlated with secrecy in cartel-like decision-making. The greater the degree of secrecy in how public decisions are made, the greater the risk of corruption. The reason is quite self-evident: secrecy can be expected to insulate corruption and public accountability. The quality of public accountability is a function of socio-economic pluralism, and the existence of legal and political rights guaranteeing freedom of access to information as well as freedom of expression, of association, and of the press.

Checks and balances in the modern state consist of formal special purpose agencies, such as the Auditor-General and Ombudsman, or special interest groups and not-for-profit associations. The latter, of course, must be legal entities, duly registered under relevant state law. In modern societies they can contribute significantly towards improvements in public policies, specifically in terms of social relevance and public accountability. Their actions, like the investigative reporting provided by a well-informed press, provide essential public information without which no open, consultative public policy would be feasible.

Islamic empiricism R&D and policy evaluation

One of the major deficiencies in Islamic scholarship is the lack of empiricism. This stems from the traditional disdain of secularist, pragmatic knowledge by the *ulama* in favour of theological and speculative knowledge. An efficient, responsive and accountable modern state requires empirical knowledge to formulate socially appropriate policies, to inform the public and to ensure effectiveness in policy performance. This is where and how such modern management techniques of cost-benefit evaluation, cost-effectiveness analysis, and budgeting and planning by objectives can be utilized to full public advantage.

The key to socio-economic development is technological innovation. Research and development (R&D) capability is not the result of some accident. As the western and Japanese experiences amply demonstrate, it is the result of state nurturing by strategic grants and public investments in 'learning by doing' and by supportive legislation (such as patent and copyright laws) encouraging and rewarding innovations. New technologies are created in universities, laboratories and research centres in industry. They require large and risky expenditures, highly paid scientists and professional experts, sophisticated equipment and support staff. These incentives, however, represent part of the necessary conditions for the generation of innovative technologies. Equally important, there must be intellectual freedom to enable researchers to carry out their experiments in a totally secular environment. Religious or ideological restrictions are incompatible with innovative technology generation. Thus, in the final analysis, the success of an R&D policy rests on the degree to which legislation guarantees basic human rights and freedoms.

Empirical approach to public policy formulation should not rest exclusively on legislators, political leaders and bureaucrats. Socioeconomic pluralism can, and should, be encouraged to the maximum degree, to assume an empirical direction. For example, special interest groups such as consumer protection groups can prepare factual briefs documenting specific cases of unfair trade practice or bureaucratic inefficiency; environmentalists may undertake social impact studies of land zoning regulations; or women's associations may provide facts and figures on daycare and child aid programmes.

However, the single most important group contribution towards the goal of empirically-based public policy in Muslim societies must come from the intellectual elite. This is the modern successor of the traditional *ulama*. As a group, it can shift its energies towards applied research focused on societal concerns of current relevance, and do better than the dysfunctional *ulama* class which has served the Muslim societies so poorly for so long. Such a research agenda requires policy-relevant contributions from many disciplines. In the social sciences, economists need to formulate an adapted version of the theory of imperfect competition to guide the formulation of fair trade rules in an Islamic society undergoing privatization; from political science, contributions can show the way for operational-izing public hearings in the legislative process; sociologists and anthropologists can similarly research the attitudes and aspirations of the masses to facilitate the evolution of an instrumentalist public policy truly responsive to human needs.

A 'Third Way'?

All this should not be regarded as a 'Third Way' to achieve Islamic development in the contemporary world outside capitalism or socialism. Third Way would amount to homogenizing the world of Islam, negating its rich cultural diversity and social relativity. What this study has attempted to demonstrate is that, despite the universality of Islam, its interpretation and application vary greatly with geography and historical experience, and that variations in human needs as well as constraints require specific public policies reflecting national priorities and aspirations.

Identity in the modern and fast-changing world is not a static trait to be written in stone in an exact and final form as a monopoly of wisdom possessed only by one or a few. Neither a single ruler nor a political elite can claim to possess such a monopoly. Identity is not being eastern or western; nor is it simply membership of a religion. These are outward symbols and labels. Identity is fulfilment of indi-viduality. It is a sense of confidence regained and sustained in a process of development, both human and national; a process in which the greater number of active participants the more fulfilling the assertion of identity.

But in the end, once all participants have had their say, develop-ment policy must be formulated and implemented on rational and secular criteria to ensure maximum effectiveness. Turkey and Malaysia, although differing in several respects, have both achieved, thanks to rational and secular policies in the post-independence era, a considerable degree of progress towards a modern development policy. In both cases, the rate of development would have been faster if the modernization debate between the nationalists and traditionalists had been less heated and if develop-ment policies were more efficient. The road ahead in both cases should be paved by secular and rational development policy, but the road should be open to all.

Conclusion

The Caliphate

At the outset this study posed the contemporary Islamic dilemma in terms of the following question: how can the universality of Islam be reconciled with the reality of the nation-state? This question can now be given a definitive, albeit a bold answer, bearing in mind the history reviewed in the preceding chapters.

The Islamic world needs a unifying institution. This can be achieved by recreating a modern version of the old Caliphate. Turkey and Malaysia are ideally placed to play a leading role in this venture. Turkey was the last trustee of this ancient office, and it unilaterally took the decision to abolish it in 1924. This created a vacuum that has fragmented the world of Islam. Now Turkey has achieved a significant measure of development and self-confidence and has made major strides towards coming to terms with her rich Ottoman and Islamic past. It is a functioning democracy under the rule of law which must respect not only political dissent but also religious beliefs. These conditions did not exist in 1924, when the young Republic faced many dangers and threats, including those from regressive Islamic extremists scheming to abort Kemalist secularism. Externally, Turkey has good relations with all its Arab and Middle Eastern neighbours and is a key member of the Organization of Islamic Countries (OIC).

Thus, Turkey is in the unique position of being able to play a role which no other Muslim country could possibly play: at the OIC it can sponsor the establishment of a modern version of the Caliphate, dedicated to the unity of the Islamic world – comparable, for example, to the Roman Catholic Pope in Rome. Elected, as the pope for life, by a conference of the leading *ulama*, appointed by the OIC, it would be logical to locate the Caliphate in Istanbul, on terms acceptable to the Turkish government as well as to the other Islamic countries. Istanbul already is the seat of the Greek Orthodox Patriarch, and this fact alone would seem to justify the choice of Istanbul for the location of the Caliphate without damaging Turkish secularism. Clearly no Turkish government could endorse a Khomeini-style imam, nor accept restoration of *Sheri'at*, but a formula based on the separability of public policy (the proper domain of the state) and a symbolic head of Islam, could be a feasible solution. Ataturk himself favoured such a formula.

Malaysia, at the other end of the Islamic world, would be well suited to second the Caliphate motion. The former Prime Minister Tunku Abdul Rahman, for one, has, in the past, lent his support to moves in this direction, and Malaysia has remained a staunch supporter of Pan-Islamic solidarity. Other countries, such as Pakistan, can be expected to lend their support to the Caliphate proposal. The moral as well as financial support of the countries of the Arab Core to the idea could be secured in particular by nominating as the first holder of the office a qualified *alim* from these countries.

Perceived purely as a symbol of Islamic unity and solidarity, the modern Caliphate can be expected to lend spiritual support to inter-Islamic co-operation. The world is rapidly moving towards major blocs: the Pacific Rim Basin, the North American free trade area and the European Community are obvious examples. The Soviet Union under Gorbachev's glasnost and perestroika, is currently reforming its economy and loosening its totalitarian system. The Cold War regime is fast disintegrating in central and eastern Europe where multi-party systems and market economies are emerging. These trends will have far-reaching implications for the future of the EC, NATO and east—west relations. Some observers are predicting the 'end of history' (Fukuyama 1989) while others the end of the Soviet Empire. What is the place of the Islamic countries in this new world of blocs? Co-operation in economic and international affairs is the key to strength and survival. Common Islamic bonds, enshrined in the doctrines of *tawhid* and the *Umma*, are solid foundations, symbolized by a modern Caliph reconciled to the reality of nation-state, on which to build the necessary elements of modern Islamic identity.

Islamic unity and co-operation in an age of emerging blocs could be an instrument of international peace and understanding. Since the time of the Crusades, Islam and Christianity have been involved in an 'historic confrontation' (Vatikiotis 1987). It is time that this Crusade mentality ended. Europe is surrounded by an oil-rich Islamic Crescent stretching from Gibraltar to Baku and the rational choice is to link the Christian and Muslim worlds in co-operation. As the Global Village dawns, the era of confrontation must be replaced by a new era of mutual respect and understanding. The Islamic Periphery can play a vital role in this process. In particular, Turkey, with her plan to join the EC counterbalanced by the Turkish—Malay proposal for a modernized version of the Caliphate, could indeed become the economic bridge and the moral voice linking east and west.

Glossary

adat (or *adet*) custom
adl justice
ayatollah title of high-ranking Shi'a religious leader
bayt al-mal public welfare fund
Bumiputera sons of the soil
dakwah 'Call to Islam' cause; more broadly, Islamic welfare
and missionary activities
caliph (*khalif*) representative or successor of the Prophet
ezan call to prayer
fetva formal legal opinion or decision of a *mufti*
ferman classical Ottoman imperial edict replaced in the
nineteenth century by *irade*
gecekondu shanty town
hadith recorded sayings and actions of the Prophet
Hajj pilgrimage to Mecca
halal lawful
halk folk
haram unlawful
ibadah (*ibadet*) prayer
irade nineteenth-century Ottoman edict
imam prayer leader
hatip deliverer of Friday mosque sermon
ilm knowledge
ijma' consensus
ijtihad independent analysis
irtica Islamic reaction
kampong Malay village
Kaum Muda New Order
Kaum Tua Old Order
jahiliyya period of mass ignorance, pre- (or un-Islamic)
ignorance
jihad holy war

kadi   Muslim judge
kanun   secular law issued by the Ottoman sultan
kapikulu   slaves of the Ottoman sultan
kavm   race or ethnic community
laiklik   secularism promoted by Kemalists
medrese   religious school
Merdeka   Malaysian Independence
millet   religious community
muamalat (muamele)   inter-personal relations
muballighs   missionaries
mudarabah   a risk- and profit-sharing contract or business
    partnership
mujtahid   one who is entitled to exercise itjihad
mufti   juriconsultant, interpreter of Islamic law
mullah   local religious leader
nass   a religious decision based on a 'clear text'
namaz   devotional worship
Nusantara   greater Indonesia
Orang Asli   indigenous people of Malaysia
rakyat   Malay subjects
Raja Rum   Ottoman sultan
riba   usury
Rumi Turks   Western or Ottoman Turks
rukunegara   national unity
sanjak   Ottoman province
sharakah   a profit-and-loss sharing business partnership
shari'ah (sheri'at)   Islamic law
sheyk   head of a *sufi* order
sufi   a follower of mystic orders
tablig   preaching
tarikat   religious orders, usually underground or militant
taqlid   uncritical acceptance of authority or learning by blind
    imitation
tawhid   unity of God or universality
tekke   convent
tughra   Sultan's seal
Umma (ummet)   Islamic community
ulama (ulema) (sing. alim)   religious scholars or clergy
vicdan   conscience
waqf (vakf)   religious endowment
yasa   pre-Islamic Turkish written law
zakat   2.5 per cent annual wealth tax

References

Abadan-Unat, Nermin (1985) 'Identity crisis of Turkish migrants' in Ilhan Basgoz and Norman Furniss (eds) *Turkish Workers in Europe, An Interdisciplinary Study*, Bloomington: Indiana University.
—— (1986) *Women in the Developing World*, Denver, Colorado: University of Denver.
Ahmad, Feroz (1977) *The Turkish Experiment in Democracy, 1950–1975*, Boulder: Westview.
—— (1988) 'Islamic reassertion in Turkey', *Third World Quarterly*, April.
Ahmad, Khurshid (1976) *Studies in Islamic Economics*, Mecca: King Abdul Aziz University.
——, and Ansari, Zafar Ishaq (eds) (1979) *Islamic Perspectives, Studies in Honour of Sayyid Abdul A'la Mawdudi*, Leicester: The Islamic Foundation.
Ahmad, Z. *et al.* (1979) *Money and Banking in Islam*, Jeddah: Institute of Policy Studies.
Akural, S.M. (1987) *Turkic Culture, Continuity and Change*, Bloomington: Indiana University.
Alatas, Syed Hussein (1977a) *The Myth of the Lazy Native*, London: Frank Cass.
—— (1977b) *Intellectuals in Developing Societies*, London: Cass.
—— (1980) *The Sociology of Corruption*, Singapore: Times Book International.
Alavi, H. (1982) 'Structure of peripheral capitalism' in H. Alavi and T. Shanin (eds) *Introduction to the Sociology of Developing Societies*, New York: Monthly Review Press.
——, and Shanin, T. (eds) (1982) *Introduction to the Sociology of Developing Societies*, New York: Monthly Review Press.
Albayrak, Sadik (1984) *Turkiyede Din Kavgasi*, 4th edn, Istanbul: Samil Yayinevi.
Alexander, A.P. (1961) 'Turkey' in A. Pepelasis *et al.* (eds) *Economic Development, Analysis and Case Studies*, New York: Harper and Row.
Algar, Hamid (1979) 'Said Nursi and the *Risala-i Nur*: an aspect of Islam in contemporary Turkey' in K. Ahmad and Z. Ansari (eds) (1979)

Islamic Perspectives, Studies in Honour of Sayyid Abdul A'la Mawdudi, Leicester: The Islamic Foundation.

Ali, Syed Husin (1975) *Malay Peasant Society and Leadership*, Kuala Lumpur: Oxford University Press.

—— (1984) *The Malays, Their Problems and Future*, Kuala Lumpur: Heinemann.

Al-i Ahmad, Jalal (1984) *Occidentosis: A Plague From the West*, Berkeley: Mizan Press.

Allen, G.C. (1962) *A Short History of Modern Japan*, London: Unwin.

Amin, S. (1977) *Imperialism and Unequal Development*, New York: Monthly Review Press.

—— (1978) *The Arab Nation: Nationalism and Class Struggle*, London: Zed Press.

Antonius, G. (1938) *Arab Awakening: The Story of the Arab Movement*, New York: Hamilton.

Ariffin, Jamillah (1984) 'Impact of modern technology on women workers in Malaysia: some selected findings from the Hawa Project' in Aziz and Hoong (eds) *Technology, Culture and Development*, Kuala Lumpur, IPT, University of Malaya.

Asian Development Bank (1985) *Privatization, Policies, Methods and Procedures*, Manila: ADB.

Al-Attas, Syed Muhammad Al-Naquib (1978) *Islam and Secularism*, Kuala Lumpur: ABIM.

Averch, H., and Johnson, L. (1962) 'Behaviour of the firm under regulatory constraint', *American Economic Review* vol. 52.

Aydemir, Sevket S. (1966) *Ikinci Adam, Ismet Inonu*, Istanbul: Remzi.

Aylen, Jonathan (1987) 'Privatization in developing countries', *Lloyds Bank Review* January.

Ayubi, Nazih N.M. (1980) 'The political revival of Islam: the case of Egypt', *International Journal of Middle Eastern Studies* vol. 12, December.

Aziz, Ungku A., and Hoong, Y.Y. (eds) (1984) *Technology, Culture and Development*, Kuala Lumpur: IPT, University of Malaya.

Barnes, John R. (1987) *An Introduction to Religious Foundations in the Ottoman Empire*, Lieden: Brill.

Barnet, R.J., and Mueller, R.E. (1974) *Global Reach, The Power of Multinational Corporations*, New York: Simon and Schuster.

Basbakanlik (1988) *1986 Kamu Iktisadi Tesebbusleri Genel Raporu*, Ankara: Yuksek Denetleme Kurulu.

Basgoz, I. and N. Furniss (eds) (1985) *Turkish Workers in Europe, An Interdisciplinary Study*, Bloomington: Indiana University.

Bauer, P.T. (1948) *The Rubber Industry*, London: Longmans.

Berberoglu, Berch (1982) *Turkey in Crisis*, London: Zed Press.

Berkes, Niyazi (1959) *Turkish Nationalism and Western Civilization*, New York: Columbia University Press.

—— (1965) *Iki Yuz Yildir Neden Bocaliyoruz?* Istanbul: Yon Yayinlari No. 1.

Blaisdell, D.C. (1966) *European Financial Control in The Ottoman Empire*, New York: AMS Press Inc.

References

Binder, Leonard (1988) *Islamic Liberalism, A Critique of Development Ideologues*, Chicago: University of Chicago Press.

Boratov, Korkut (1974) *Turkiyede Devletcilik*, Istanbul: Gercek.

Boulakia, J.D.C. (1971) 'Ibn Khaldun: a fourteenth-century economist', *Journal of Political Economy* September–October.

Bradley, I., and Price, C. (1988) 'The economic regulation of private industries by price competition', *Journal of Industrial Economics* September.

Brockelmann, Carl (1948) *History of the Islamic Peoples*, London: Routledge & Kegan Paul.

Buchanan, J.M., Tollison, R.D., and Tullock, G. (eds) (1980) *Toward a Theory of Rent-Seeking Society*, College Station: Texas A&M University.

Caroe, Olaf (1967) *Soviet Empire, Turks of Central Asia and Stalinism*, New York: St Martins Press.

Celasun, Merih (1986) 'Income distribution and domestic terms of trade in Turkey, 1978–1983', *METU Studies in Development* vol. 13, nos. 1–2.

——, and Rodrik, D. (1987) *Debt, Adjustment and Growth: Turkey*, New York: National Bureau of Economic Research.

Cetinkaya, H. (1986) *Kubilay Olayi ve Tarikat Kamplari*, Istanbul: Boyut.

Chandra, Muzaffar (1979) *The Protector? An analysis of the concept and practice of loyalty in leader-led relationships within Malay society*, Penang: Aliran.

—— (1987) *Islamic Resurgence in Malaysia*, Petaling Jaya, Selangor: Penerbit Fajar Bakti Sdn. Bhd.

Chapra, M. Umer (1985) *Toward a Just Monetary System*, Leicester: The Islamic Foundation.

Chen, Peter (ed.) (1983) *Singapore Development Policies and Trends*, Singapore: Oxford University Press.

Choudhury, M.A. (1986) *Contributions to Islamic Economic Theory*, London: Macmillan.

Cohn, E.J. (1970) *Turkish Economic, Social, and Political Change*, New York: Praeger.

Crone, Patricia (1980) *Slaves on Horses, The Evolution of the Islamic Polity*, Cambridge: Cambridge University Press.

Czaplika, M.A. (1918) *The Turks of Central Asia*, Oxford: Clarendon Press.

Dahlan, H.M. (ed.) (1986) *The Nascent Malaysian Society*, 2nd edn, Bangi: Universiti Kebangsaan Malaysia.

Davey, Richard (1907) *The Sultan and His Subjects*, London: Chatto & Windus.

Dawood, N.J. (ed.) (1981) *Ibn Khaldun The Muqaddimah, An Introduction to History*, Princeton University Press.

Dumont, P. (1987) 'Islam as a factor of change and revival in modern Turkey' in Akural (ed.) *Turkic Culture, Continuity and Change*, Bloomington: Indiana University.

Earle, Edward M. (1966) *Turkey, the Great Powers and the Baghdad Railway*, New York: Russell and Russell.

Economic Planning Unit (EPU) (1985) *Guidelines on Privatization*, Kuala Lumpur: Prime Minister's Department.

Economic Intelligence Unit, The (1987) *Turkey* no. 2.

Eisenstadt, S.N. (1973) *Tradition, Change and Modernity*, New York: Wiley.

—— (1987) *Patterns of Modernity*, London: Pinter.

Emerson, Rupert (1964) *Malaysia, A Study in Direct and Indirect Rule*, Kuala Lumpur: University of Malaya Press.

Emin, Ahmed (1914) *The Development of Modern Turkey as measured by its Press*, New York: Columbia University.

Esman, Milton (1972) *Administration and Development in Malaysia: Institution Building and Reform in a Plural Society*, Ithaca: Cornell University Press.

Esposito, John L. (1984) *Islam and Politics* [2nd edn, 1987] Syracuse: Syracuse University Press.

—— (1988) *Islam, The Straight Path*, New York: Oxford University Press.

Evers, Hans Deiter (1987) 'The bureaucratisation of Southeast Asia', *Comparative Studies in Society and History* vol. 29, no. 4, October.

Evin, Ahmet *et al.* (1984) *Modern Turkey: Continuity and Change*, Opladen: Leske.

Fanon, Franz (1965) *The Wretched of the Earth*, London: MacGibbon and Kee.

Farouki, Ismail (1987) *Islam*, Istanbul: Risale.

Faris, Hani A. (ed.) (1987) *Arab Nationalism and the Future of the Arab World*, Belmont, Mass.: Association of Arab-American University Graduates, Inc.

Fatimi, S.Q. (1963) *Islam Comes to Malaysia*, Singapore: Malaysian Sociological Research Institute.

Feyzioglu, Turhan (1987) *Ataturk ve Milliyetcilik*, Ankara: Turk Tarih Kurumu Basimevi.

Fisher, Sydney N. (1979) *The Middle East, A History*, New York: Knopf.

Fleischer, C. (1984) 'Royal authority, dynastic cyclism and "Ibn Khaldunism" in sixteenth century Ottoman letters' in B.B. Lawrence (ed.) *Ibn Khaldun and Islamic Ideology*, Leiden: Brill.

Fox, K., and Kostler, P. (1980) 'The marketing of social causes: the first 10 years', *Journal of Marketing* Fall.

Frank, A.G. (1966) 'The development of underdevelopment', *Monthly Review* September.

Friedman, Milton and Rose Friedman (1981) *Free To Choose*, New York: Avon.

Fukuyama, F. (1989) 'The end of history?', *The National Interest*, Summer.

Gale, Bruce (ed.) (1987) *Readings in Malaysian Politics*, Peraling Jaya: Pelanduk Publications.

Geertz, Clifford (1963) *Peddlers and Princes*, Chicago: University of Chicago Press.

—— (1968) *Islam Observed: Religious Development in Morocco and Indonesia*, New Haven: Yale University Press.

References

Gellner, Ernest (1981) *Muslim Society*, Cambridge: Cambridge University Press.

Ghayasuddin, M. (ed.) (1987) *The Impact of Nationalism on the Muslim World*, London: Open Press.

Gil, Moshe (1974) 'The constitution of Medina: a reconsideration' *Israel Oriental Studies*.

Giritli, Ismet (1988) *Ataturkculuk Ideolojisi*, Ankara: Turk Tarih Kurumu Basimevi.

Grant, G. (1969) *Technology and Empire*, Toronto: Anansi.

Grunebaum, Gustave E. von (1953) *Medieval Islam*, Chicago: University of Chicago Press.

Guillaume, A. (1956) *Islam*, Harmondsworth: Penguin.

Gungor, Erol (1987) *Islamin Bugunku Meseleleri*, Istanbul: Otuken.

Gutierrez, Gustavo (1973) *Theology of Liberation, History, Politics and Salvation*, Maryknoll, New York: Orbis Books.

Haddad, William W., and Ochsenwald, William (1977) *Nationalism in a Non-National State, the Dissolution of the Ottoman Empire*, Columbus: Ohio State University Press.

Hairi, Abdullah, and Dahlan, H.M. (eds) (1982) *Peasantry and Modernization*, Bangi, Selangor: Universiti Kebangsaan Malaysia.

Hale, William (1981) *The Political and Economic Development of Modern Turkey*, London: Croom Helm.

Harper, R.W.E., and Miller, Harry (1984) *Singapore Mutiny*, Singapore: Oxford University Press.

Hashim, Wan (1983) *Race Relations in Malaysia*, Petaling Jaya: Heinemann.

Heper, Metin (1979–80) 'Recent instability in Turkish politics: end of a monocentrist policy?', *International Journal of Turkish Studies* vol. 1, no. 1, Winter.

—— (1984) 'Bureaucrats, politicians and officers in Turkey: dilemmas of a new political paradigm' in Evin *et al. Modern Turkey: Continuity and Change*, Opladen: Leske.

Hirschman, O. Albert (1977) *The Passions and the Interests, Political Arguments for Capitalism Before its Triumph*, Princeton: Princeton University Press.

Hodgson, Marshall G.S. (1974) *The Venture of Islam* (3 vols), Chicago: University of Chicago Press.

Hooker, M.B. (ed.) (1970) *Readings in Malay Adat Laws*, Singapore: Singapore University Press.

Hourani, Albert (1970) *Arabic Thought in the Liberal Age: 1798–1939*, London: Oxford University Press.

—— (1981) *The Emergence of the Modern Middle East*, London: Macmillan.

IBRD (1951) *The Economy of Turkey*, Baltimore: The Johns Hopkins Press.

—— (1955) *The Economic Development of Malaya*, Baltimore: The Johns Hopkins Press.

Ibn Khaldun (1967) *The Muqaddimah, An Introduction to History*, edited and abridged by N.J. Dawood, Princeton: Princeton University Press.

Issawi, Charles (ed.) (1966) *The Economic History of the Middle East, 1800–1914*, Chicago: Chicago University Press.

—— (1982) *An Economic History of the Middle East and North Africa*, New York: Columbia University Press.

Jones, Leroy (ed.) (1982) *Public Enterprises in the Less Developed Countries*, Cambridge: Cambridge University Press.

Johnson, C. (1982) *MITI and the Japanese Miracle, The Growth of Industrial Policy*, Stanford: Stanford University Press.

Jomo, K.S. (ed.) (1983) *The Sun Also Sets: Lessons in Looking East*, Kuala Lumpur: Insan.

Kahf, Monzer (1978) *The Islamic Economy: Analytical Study of the Functioning of the Islamic Economic System*, Plainfield, Ind.

Kalaycioglu (1988) in Ergun Ozbudun *et al. Perspectives on Democracy in Turkey*, Ankara: Turkish Political Science Association.

Kamal Salih *et al.* (1978) *Transformation and Regional Underdevelopment: The Case of Malaysia*, Nagoya, Japan: UN Centre for Regional Development.

Karpat, Kemal (1959) *Turkey's Politics, The Transition to a Multi-Party System*, Princeton: Princeton University Press.

—— (1976) *The Gecekondu: Rural Migration and Urbanization*, London: Cambridge University Press.

—— (1981) 'Turkish democracy at impasse: ideology, party politics and the Third Military Intervention', *International Journal of Turkish Studies* Spring–Summer.

Kasaba, Resat (1988) *The Ottoman Empire and the World Economy, the Nineteenth Century*, Albany: State University of New York Press.

Keddie, N.R. (1972) *Sayyid Jamal al-Din al-Afgani: A Political Biography*, Berkeley: University of California Press.

Kedourie, Elie (1971) *Nationalism*, London: Hutchinson.

Kemal, Yashar (1984) *Memed, My Hawk*, London: Fontana.

Kepenek, Yakup (1987) *Turkiye Ekonomisi*, Ankara: Teori.

Keyder, Caglar (1987) *State & Class in Turkey, A Study in Capitalist Development*, London: Verso.

Kinross, Lord (1964) *Ataturk, The Rebirth of a Nation*, London: Weidenfeld and Nicolson.

Kiray, M. (1982) *Toplumbilim Yazilari*, Ankara: Gazi Universitesi Iktisadi ve Idari Bilimler Yayini no. 7.

Kopits, G. (1987) *Structural Reform, Stabilization, and Growth in Turkey*, Washington, D.C.: International Monetary Fund, May.

Koutsoyannis, A. (1982) *Non-Price Decisions, The Firm in a Modern Context*, London: Macmillan.

Krueger, A. (1972) 'Rates of return to Turkish education', *Journal of Human Resources* Fall.

—— (1974a) *Foreign Trade Regimes and Economic Development: Turkey*, New York: National Bureau of Economic Research.

—— (1974b) 'The political economy of rent seeking society', *American Economic Review* June.

Kuran, T. (1989) 'Economic justice in contemporary Islamic thought', *International Journal of the Middle East*, May.

241

References

Lal, D. (1984) *The Political Economy of the Predatory State*, Washington, D.C.: World Bank Discussion Paper DRD 105.

Landau, J.M. (1981) 'Islamism and secularism: the Turkish case', *Studies in Judaism and Islam*, Jerusalem: The Magness Press.

Lawrence, B.B. (1984) *Ibn Khaldun and Islamic Ideology*, Leiden: Brill.

Lee, Eddy (ed.) (1981) *Export-Led Industrialization and Development*, Geneva: ILO-ARTEP.

Lee, Susan (1984) 'Industrialization and the squatter phenomenon in the Kelang Valley: case studies of migrant Malay factory workers' living conditions' in Aziz and Hoong (eds) *Technology, Culture and Development*, Kuala Lumpur: IPT, University of Malaya.

Lerner, Daniel (1958) *The Passing of Traditional Society*, Toronto: Collier-Macmillan.

Lewis, Bernard (1968) *The Emergence of Modern Turkey*, 2nd edn, London: Oxford University Press.

———— (ed.) (1987) *Islam, From the Prophet Muhammad to the Capture of Constantinople*, New York (2 vols): Oxford University Press.

Lim, D. (ed.) (1975) *Readings in Malaysian Economic Development*, Kuala Lumpur: Oxford University Press.

Lim Kit Siang (1987) *North South Highway Scandal*, Pataling Jaya: DAP.

Lipton, M. (1977) *Why Poor People Stay Poor*, London: Temple Smith.

Lybyer, A.H. (1913) *The Government of the Ottoman Empire at the Time of Suleiman the Magnificent*, Cambridge, Mass: Harvard University Press.

Mahathir, Mohamad (1970) *The Malay Dilemma*, Petaling Jaya: Federal Publications.

———— *et al.* (1984) *Malaysia Incorporated and Privatization*, Kuala Lumpur: Pelanduk Publications October.

Malay Mail (1986) '800 hit by cables imports', 19 December, Kuala Lumpur.

Malaysia (1976) *Third Malaysia Plan 1976–1980*, Kuala Lumpur: Government Printer.

———— (1985) *Mid-Term Review of the Fourth Malaysia Plan*, Kuala Lumpur: Government Printer.

Malaysian Business (1987) 'Roads: a costly drive', 1 July, Kuala Lumpur.

Mardin, S. (1973) 'Center–periphery relations: a key to Turkish politics', *Daedulus* Winter.

———— (1982) 'Turkey: Islam and westernization' in Carlo Caldarola (ed.) *Religions and Societies: Asia and the Middle East*, Berlin: Mouton.

Margulies, R., and Yildizoglu, E. (1988) 'The political uses of Islam in Turkey', *Middle East Report* July–August.

Maududi, Syed Abdul A'ala (1984) *Economic System of Islam*, Lahore: Islamic Publications.

Mauzy, D.K., and Milne, R.S. (1986) 'The Mahathir administration: discipline through Islam' in Bruce Gale (ed.) *Readings in Malaysian Politics*, Petaling Jaya: Pelanduk Publications.

Mazrui, Ali (1988) 'African Islam and competitive religion: between revivalism and expansion', *Third World Quarterly* April.

Mehden, F.R. von (1986) *Religion and Modernization in Southeast Asia*, Syracuse: Syracuse University Press.

Mehmet, Ozay (1978) *Economic Planning and Social Justice in Developing Countries*, London: Croom Helm.

—— (1983) 'Turkey in crisis: some contradictions in the Kemalist development strategy', *International Journal of Middle East Studies* vol. 15.

—— (1986) *Development in Malaysia: Poverty, Wealth and Trusteeship*, London: Croom Helm.

—— (1989) *Human Resource Development in the Third World: Cases of Success and Failure*, Kingston: Frye.

MERIP Reports (1984) March/April.

Middle East Report (1988) July–August.

Mikiso Hane (1986) *Modern Japan, A Historical Survey*, New York: Scribner's.

Milner, A.C. (1986) 'The impact of the Turkish revolution on Malaya', *Archipel 31*, Paris.

Mumcu, Ugur (1987) *Rabita* (2nd edn), Istanbul: Tekin Yayinevi.

Nagata, J. (1984) *The Reflowering of Malaysian Islam: Modern Religious Radicals and their Roots*, Vancouver: University of British Columbia Press.

—— (1986) 'Islamic revival and the problem of legitimacy among rural religious elites in Malaysia' in Bruce Gale (ed.) *Readings in Malaysian Politics*, Petaling Jaya: Pelanduk Publications.

Nakane, C. (1970) *Japanese Society*, Berkeley: University of California Press.

Naqvi, Syed N.H. (1981) *Ethics and Economics, An Islamic Synthesis*, Leicester: The Islamic Foundation.

New Straits Times (1988) 'United Engineers to get listing soon', Kuala Lumpur, 9 May.

Niskanen, W.A. (1971) *Bureaucracy and Representative Government*, New York: Aldine.

North, D.C. (1981) *Structure and Change in Economic History*, New Haven: Norton.

OECD (1988) *Toward a Better Balance Between the Public and Private Sectors in Developing Countries*, Paris: Development Centre, May.

Oke, M.K. (1988) *The Armenian Question 1914–1923*, Oxford: K. Rustem & Brother.

Okita, S. (1980) *The Developing Economies and Japan, Lessons in Growth*, Tokyo: University of Tokyo Press.

Okun, A. (1975) *Equality and Efficiency, The Big Tradeoff*, Washington, D.C.: The Brookings Institution.

Olson, M. (1982) *The Rise and Decline of Nations*, New Haven, Conn: Yale University Press.

——, and Landsberg, H.H. (eds) (1973) *The No-Growth Society*, New York: Norton.

Ostrorog, Count Leon (1927) *The Angora Reform*, London: University of London Press.

References

Ozal, Turgut (1987) 'Turkey's path to freedom and prosperity', *The Washington Quarterly* Autumn.

Ozbudun, Ergun (1984) 'Antecedents of Kemalist secularism' in Evin (ed.) *Modern Turkey: Continuity and Change*, Opladen: Leske.

Ozbudun, Ergun *et al.* (1988) *Perspectives on Democracy in Turkey*, Ankara: Turkish Political Science Association.

Ozmucur, S., and Onis, Z. (1988) 'Exchange rates, inflation and money supply: testing the vicious circle hypothesis by vector autoregressive and traditional methods', Istanbul: Bogazici Universitisi (ISS/E 88-05) (mimeog.).

Pamuk, Sevket (1987) *The Ottoman Empire and European Capitalism, 1820–1913*, Cambridge: Cambridge University Press.

Parkinson, Brien K. (1975) 'Non economic factors in the economic retardation of rural Malays' in D. Lim (ed.) *Readings in Malaysian Economic Development*, Kuala Lumpur: Oxford University Press.

Pepelasis, I. *et al.* (eds) (1961) *Economic Development, Analysis and Case Studies*, New York: Harper and Row.

Piscatori, James P. (1986) *Islam in a World of Nation-States*, Cambridge: Cambridge University Press.

Qureshi, A.N. (1974) *Islam and the Theory of Interest*, Lahore: M. Ashraf.

Qutb, S. (1970) *Social Justice in Islam* (trans. John B. Hardie), New York: Octagon Press.

Rahman, Fazlur (1982) *Islam and Modernity, Transformation of an Intellectual Tradition*, Chicago: University of Chicago Press.

Reid, Anthony (1967) 'Nineteenth Century Pan-Islam in Indonesia and Malaysia', *Journal of Asian Studies* vol. XXVI, no. 2.

—— (1969a) 'Indonesian diplomacy: a documentary study of Atjehnese foreign policy in the reign of Sultan Mahmud, 1870–4'. *Journal of the Malay Branch of the Royal Asiatic Society (JAMBRAS)* vol. 42, part 2.

—— (1969b) *The Contest for North Sumatra, Atjeh, The Netherlands and Britain, 1858–1898*, Kuala Lumpur: University of Malaya Press.

Rodinson, M. (1973) *Islam and Capitalism*, New York: Pantheon.

Roff, William R. (1967) *The Origins of Malay Nationalism*, Kuala Lumpur: University of Malaya Press.

Rosenthal, F. (1984) 'Ibn Khaldun in his Time' in B. Lawrence (ed.) *Ibn Khaldun and Islamic Ideology*, Leiden: Brill.

Rostow, W.W. (1963) *Stages of Economic Growth, A Non-Communist Manifesto*, Cambridge: Cambridge University Press.

Rustow, D.A. (1987) *Turkey, America's Forgotten Ally*, New York: Council on Foreign Relations.

——, and Ward, R.E. (eds) (1964) *Political Modernization in Japan and Turkey*, New Jersey.

Ruttan, V.W., and Hayami, Y. (1984) 'Toward a theory of induced institutional innovation', *Journal of Development Studies* July.

Sadiq, Mohammad (1986) 'The *Kadro* Movement in Turkey', *International Studies* vol. 23, no. 4 (New Delhi).

Said, Edward (1979) *Orientalism*, New York: Vintage Books.

Samin, Ahmet (1981) 'The tragedy of the Turkish Left', *New Left Review* March–April.

Sardar, Z. (1987) *The Future of Muslim Civilization*, London: Mansell.

Saribay, Ali Yasar (1985) *Turkiye 'de Modernlesme Din ve Parti Politikasi, MSP Ornek Olayi*, Istanbul: Alan Yayincilik.

Saylan, Gencay (1987) *Islamiyet ve Siyaset, Turkiye Ornegi*, Ankara: Verso.

Schick, I.C., and Tonak, E.A. (1987) *Turkey in Transition: New Perspectives*, New York: Oxford University Press.

Schumacher, E.F. (1973) *Small is Beautiful*, London: Blond Briggs.

Scitovsky, Tibor (1976) *The Joyless Economy*, London: Oxford University Press.

Senu Abdul Rahman (ed.) (1973) *Revolusi Mental*, Kuala Lumpur: Utusan Melayu.

Serjeant, R.B. (1964) 'The Constitution of Medina', *Islamic Quarterly*.

Shamsul, A.B. (1986) *From British to Bumiputera Rule*, Singapore: Institute of Southeast Asian Studies.

Shari'ati, Ali (1986) *What is To be Done, The Enlightened Thinkers and an Islamic Renaissance*, Houston: The Institute for Research and Islamic Studies.

Shaw, R.P. (1983) *Mobilizing Human Resources in the Arab World*, London: Kegan Paul International.

Shaw, Stanford J. (1976) *History of the Ottoman Empire and Modern Turkey, Vol. I*, Cambridge: Cambridge University Press.

Shaw, Stanford J., and Shaw, Ezel Kural (1977) *History of the Ottoman Empire and Modern Turkey, Vol. II*, Cambridge: Cambridge University Press.

Shepard, W.E. (1987) 'Islam and Ideology: Toward a typology', *International Journal of Middle East Studies* August.

Shirley, Mary (1983) *Managing State-Owned Enterprises*, Washington, D.C.: World Bank Staff Working Papers no. 577.

Siddiqi, Muhammad N. (1981) *Muslim Economic Thinking, A Survey of Contemporary Literature*, Leicester: The Islamic Foundation.

Siddiqui, K. (1981) 'Nation states as obstacles to the total transformation of the *Ummah*' in M. Ghayasuddin (ed.) *The Impact of Nationalism on the Muslim World*, London: Open Press.

Simsir, Bilal N. (1989) 'The Turks of Bulgaria, 1878–1985', *Turkish Review Quarterly Digest* Spring.

Singer, Morris (1977) *The Economic Advance of Turkey, 1938–1960*, Ankara: Ayyildiz.

Slimming, John (1969) *Malaysia: Death of a Democracy*, London: Murray.

Smith, Wendy (1983) 'Japanese factory – Malaysian workers' in K.S. Jomo (ed.) *The Sun Also Sets: Lessons in Looking East*, Kuala Lumpur: Insan.

Snouck Hurgronje, C. (1906) *The Achehnese* (2 vols), Leyden: Brill.

Soenarno, R. (1960) 'Malay nationalism, 1896–1941', *Journal of Southeast Asian History* vol. I.

References

Somervell, D.C. (1960) *A Study of History by Arnold J. Toynbee*, abridgement in 2 vols, London: Oxford University Press.

South (1987) 'Turkey, reality and progress', March (London).

Stavrianos, L.S. (1981) *Global Rift, The Third World Comes of Age*, New York: Marrow.

Sterling, Paul (1965) *Turkish Village*, New York: Wiley.

Sundaram, J.K., and Cheek, Shabery (1988) 'The politics of Malaysia's Islamic resurgence', *Third World Quarterly* April.

Tachau, Frank (1984) *Turkey: The Politics of Authority, Democracy, and Development*, New York: Praeger.

Talib, S. (1982) 'A Revolt in Malaysian Historiography' in Hairi and Dahlan (eds) *Peasantry and Modernisation*, Bangi, Selangor: Universiti Kebangsaan Malaysia.

Tekeli, I., and Ilkin, S. (1977) *1929 Dunya Buhraninda Turkiyenin Iktisadi Politika Arayislari*, Ankara: Ortadogu Teknik Universitesi.

Thillainathan, R. (1986) 'Private sector as an engine of growth – a review of performance and policies in Malaysia', *FMM Forum*, January, Kuala Lumpur.

Thornburg, Max W. *et al.* (1949) *Turkey, an Economic Appraisal*, New York: Twentieth Century Fund.

Tibi, Bassam (1988) *The Crisis of Modern Islam, A Preindustrial Culture in the Scientific-Technological Age*, Utah: University of Utah Press.

Toh Kin Woon (1989) 'Privatization in Malaysia, restructuring or efficiency?' *ASEAN Economic Bulletin* March.

Toprak, Binnaz (1981) *Islam and Political Development in Turkey*, Leiden: Brill.

Turkey (1988) *Main Economic Indicators*, Ankara: State Planning Organization, May.

Turner, Brian (1974) *Weber and Islam*, London: Routledge & Kegan Paul.

UNESCO (1963) *Ataturk*, Ankara: Turkish National Commission for UNESCO.

Vaitsos, C. (1976) 'The revision of the international patent system: legal considerations for a Third World position', *World Development* February.

Vasil, R.K. (1971) *Politics in a Plural Society: A Study of Non-communal Political Parties in West Malaysia*, Singapore: Oxford University Press.

Vatikiotis, P.J. (1987) *Islam and the State*, London: Croom Helm.

Vernon, R. (1985) *Exploring the Global Economy: Emerging Issues in Trade and Investment*, MD: University Press of America.

Volkan, V., and Itzkowitz, N. (1986) *The Immortal Ataturk, A Psychobiography*, Chicago: Chicago University Press.

Vorys, K. von (1975) *Democracy without Consensus, Communalism and Political Stability in Malaysia*, Princeton: Princeton University Press.

Wallerstein, I. (1974) *The Modern World System*, New York: Academic Press.

Walsted, Bertil (1977) *State Manufacturing Enterprises in a Mixed Economy, the Turkish Case*, Washington, D.C.: IBRD.

Weiker, W.F. (1981) *The Modernization of Turkey, From Ataturk to the Present Day*, New York: Holmes & Meier.

Wilder, William (1975) 'Islam, other factors and Malay backwardness' in D. Lim (ed.) *Readings in Malaysian Economic Development*, Kuala Lumpur: Oxford University Press.

World Bank (1980) *Turkey – Policies and Prospects for Growth*, Washington, D.C., March.

—— (1988) *World Development Report*, Washington, D.C.

World Commission on Environment and Development (1987) *Our Common Future*, New York: Oxford University Press.

Yunus, M. (1988) 'The poor as the engine of growth', *Economic Impact* no. 63.

Za'ba (1939) 'A history of Malay literature XIV: modern developments', *Journal of the Malay Branch of the Royal Asiatic Society* December.

Index